KEYWORDS FOR MODERN INDIA

Keywords for Modern India

Craig Jeffrey and John Harriss

OXFORD

UNIVERSITY PRESS

OXFORD
UNIVERSITY PRESS

Great Clarendon Street, Oxford, OX2 6DP,
United Kingdom

Oxford University Press is a department of the University of Oxford.
It furthers the University's objective of excellence in research, scholarship,
and education by publishing worldwide. Oxford is a registered trade mark of
Oxford University Press in the UK and in certain other countries

Published in the United States of America by Oxford University Press
198 Madison Avenue, New York, NY 10016, United States of America

British Library Cataloguing in Publication Data
Data available

Library of Congress Control Number: 2014931562

ISBN 978–0–19–966563–1 (hbk.)
ISBN 978–0–19–966564–8 (pbk.)

Printed and bound by
CPI Group (UK) Ltd, Croydon, CR0 4YY

CONTENTS

KEYWORDS FOR MODERN INDIA

A

B

C

D

E

F

G

H

I

J

M

N

O

R

S

INTRODUCTION

Could I embody and unbosom now
That which is most within me—could I wreak
My thoughts upon expression, and thus throw
Soul-heart-mind-passions-feelings-strong or weak-
All that I would have sought, and all I seek,
Bear, know, feel—and yet breathe—into *one* word,
And that one word were Lightning, I would speak;
But as it is, I live and die unheard,
With a most voiceless thought, sheathing it as a sword.
George Gordon, Lord Byron, *Child Harold's Pilgrimage*, Canto III, verse 97

Individual words are slippery and vague, and socially significant words—such as 'democracy' and 'rights'—especially so. Words like these are associated with a whole field of meanings. It is perhaps unsurprising that Byron felt it impossible to pour his life's feelings into a single word. Words are deeply political too, as is now well known in social science. Dominant institutions exploit the vagueness of words, deploying prominent terms—for example 'justice' and 'society'—to pursue their own ends. George W. Bush's use of the term 'freedom' to generate consent for his neoconservative foreign policy is a well-known example. At the same time, ordinary people are busy interpreting and reinterpreting words on the ground, such that key terms often take on alternative meanings in new contexts.

One response to such complexity might be to throw up one's hands, and proclaim the impossibility of making sense of the actual deployment of important words in the contemporary world and their changing meanings. Just as Byron refused to identify a word that would sum up his feelings, we might draw back from analysing the attempts of institutions and individuals to squash complicated ideas into a single term. Another response—a common one—is to try to fix in place the meanings of words through dictionaries and glossaries. In the social sciences in recent years there has been an explosion of large, glossy encyclopedias, dictionaries, and handbooks, many of them devoting considerable space to definitions of important terms. A third response, the one that we favour in this book, is to examine critically the various meanings of words as a means of learning. We show how a discussion of words' multiple and conflicting meanings and histories might open up a wider understanding of society, politics, and change. We do this with particular reference to India, the country in which the two of us have been primarily interested during our academic careers and where we both do research.

Underpinning this project is the belief that the capacity of words to encompass varied ideas, and the way in which they can mean quite different things to different people, is precisely what makes them interesting. In democratic countries—in all countries, indeed, to a greater or lesser extent—individual words become the ground for social debate. Struggles for power, aspirations, and changing values crystallize in the competition to make particular meanings stick. As Raymond Williams argues in his book *Keywords: A Vocabulary of Culture and Society*, 'some important social and historical processes occur *within* language' (1985 [1976]: 22). To investigate an individual word and its changing connotations through time and space is therefore to slice through existing debates in a very interesting way. A 'keyword' is a word that is *both* important *and* provides a window on processes of social and political change.

The idea of 'keywords' has by now become hardwired into academics' thinking. Academic journals commonly ask authors to identify a set of 'keywords' for papers—a move driven, in turn, by the needs of search engines. But the number of books dedicated to examining the idea of 'keywords' is rather limited. Those that have been written have tended to take their inspiration, as we have done, from Williams's *Keywords* (1985 [1976]). Williams's book discusses the meaning of what he thought to be the most important terms circulating in UK society in the 1970s. He included 131 words (twenty-one of them added in the second edition)—some, such as 'base' and 'superstructure', closely associated with academic debates, and others, 'sex' and 'jargon' for example, that are popular words. *Keywords* sparked imitators, including a *New Keywords* book published in 2005 (Bennett et al. 2005) and *Keywords for American Cultural Studies* (Burgett and Hendler 2007).

There are differences between such keyword publications and dictionaries or glossaries. Williams points out that a dictionary is very helpful for understanding, say, what is meant by the term 'shibboleth' or 'karst landscape'. But it is much less useful for discussing words like 'class' or 'culture', where there is obviously a wide range of definitions and meanings in play and their relative importance is highly contested. In such cases, looking for a definitive meaning 'is not only an impossible but an irrelevant procedure' (Williams 1985 [1976]: 17). An 'inquiry into a vocabulary: a shared body of words and meanings in our most general discussions'—which is how Williams (1985 [1976]: 15) describes his project—does not try to sweep contentious issues under the carpet, but seeks to illuminate the debate over what a word might mean, explaining why there is conflict over its definition and how meanings have changed over time. Similarly, unlike a dictionary, the outlining of keywords is always a consciously provisional project, one that actively invites debate, critique, and revision. Williams asked his publisher to leave blank pages at the end of his keywords book for readers to add their own views, revise definitions, and identify other keywords. Similarly, the authors of *Keywords for American Cultural Studies* have a lively website and blog where readers can comment on definitions: http://keywords.fordhamitac.org. The University of Pittsburgh's keywords project is also remarkable in this regard; see http://keywords.pitt.edu/contact_us.html.

In the *Oxford English Dictionary*, a 'keyword' is defined not only as a 'word or concept of great significance' but also as a word that 'acts as the key to a cipher or code'. Williams clearly understood keywords in the first sense, but his text is important in the second sense too. To read the book is to be taken to the beating heart of the UK in the 1950s and 1960s; a picture of the post-war Keynesian welfare state, burgeoning popular culture, and rapid consumerism takes shape before one's eyes more vividly than would have been the case had Williams penned a more conventional analysis.

Williams imagined his book in part as an exercise in what he termed 'historical semantics'. Reflecting historical change, specific words change their meanings over time and words may even come to mean the diametric opposite of what they meant before. At the same time, important words often retain some trace or imprint of their former sense—they are like palimpsests. There are also shifts in how words are normatively imagined: for example, 'democracy' once had negative connotations. Tracing the curious shifts and sometimes perplexing continuities in the meanings of keywords is like turning over a neatly patterned rug to see the tangle of threads on the reverse.

A word had to satisfy one of two criteria for inclusion in Williams's book. Either it had to be 'a strong, important and persuasive word' that was circulating in ordinary society, or it had to be a word that had emerged out of a specialized context but had come to describe wider areas of thought and experience. A further criterion not explicitly mentioned by Williams—but clearly at work in his selection procedure—was that the word had to be durable. Keywords do not disappear: they continue to inform public debate even as they travel through time, picked up and dusted off by new generations. For Williams there is therefore a difference between a 'keyword' which is debated over the *longue durée* and a 'catchword', which usually survives for several decades but then goes out of fashion. A word like 'culture' is a keyword, but a term such as 'social capital'—the stock of productive social connections in a society—is a catchword (see Putnam 1993; Harriss 2002). More ephemeral still are 'buzzwords', which appear briefly and then disappear from view. Of course, catchwords can turn into keywords and vice versa, and the decision about whether a word is a keyword, catchword, or buzzword is mired in controversy. *Keywords for Modern India* contains a few words that some readers will probably regard as catchwords rather than keywords—'empowerment' is one example. But we have tried on the whole to choose words that have been important for commentators on India and people in India for a long period of time. All the words have, too, we think, a self-evidently weighty, significant feel; they are not likely to 'go silly' any time soon.

Williams was centrally interested in the relationship between elite deployment of key-words and their vernacular use. Likewise, in this book we are interested in how ordinary people, as well as major organizations, use keywords. Here we face the difficulty that the vast majority of people in India do not speak English fluently. English is the first language of a minuscule section of the population. And yet English is one of India's main official languages. Under Article 343 of the Indian Constitution, English, together with Hindi, is an official language of the Union. It is often the language in which debates occur in the national parliament (*Lok Sabha*)—though less so now than in the past—and in which the deliberations of the Supreme Court are conducted. It is the language of trade and commerce and of the mass media: two of India's three largest selling newspapers are in English. Nor is English any more only a public language and one characterizing the elite. Increased travel, the expansion of global media, and—especially—the growth of education, including English-medium education, has rapidly expanded the importance and scope of English in India. Large numbers of people speak English as a second or third language. In addition, many of those who lack understanding of English nevertheless pepper their conversations with English terms. Notable examples are the use of the words 'time', 'problem', and 'adjust' in ordinary conversation. Some urbanites habitually speak a mix of English and an Indian language.

'Indian English', in so far as it is possible to identify such a single brand of English, is notably different from British Standard English (BSE). This is partly a matter of pronunciation; for example, English is spoken in a non-rhotic manner in the UK—the 'r' in 'firm' is not vocalized—but many English speakers in India pronounce English rhotically. There are also variations of meaning. For example, 'marriage' in Indian English covers the wedding as well as the act of marriage. And there are differences of vocabulary between BSE and Indian English. The Indian English 'prepone'—meaning to bring forward a meeting, perhaps, or the departure of an aircraft—does not exist in BSE (see Sailaja 2009).

We considered discussing Indian English terms in the book. For example, 'timepass', meaning passing time, is a word that intrigues us (see Jeffrey 2010), as does the Indian English term 'vote-bank' to describe a situation in which a community votes as a bloc. But we decided not to include such Indian English primarily for the simple reason of consistency, and also because we are mainly interested in words that resonate both in international academic circles and within India. Another dilemma was whether to include terms in Indian languages in a vocabulary of English words. Again for reasons of consistency we decided not to do so, although words such as '*dalaal*', which means 'broker', and '*bhadralok*'—literally 'big people', a term current in West Bengal—gave us considerable pause for thought.

We began our project with a list of 143 words that we thought plausible candidates for inclusion in a book of English language keywords for India. These words could be divided very roughly into two categories. First, there were words—like 'democracy' and 'economy'—that are crucial social science terms and public keywords across the world. A second set of keywords were ones more explicitly associated with India or South Asia and which again resonate within both academic and non-academic circles—words such as 'Bollywood', 'caste', 'Hindi', 'Hindutva', 'reservations', and 'Naxalite'. In this category, too, are 'Ambedkar', 'Nehru', and 'Gandhi' (unlike Raymond Williams we have included these few proper names, of men whose lives and ideas have inspired both social practice and continuing debate—in popular discussion, as well as among intellectuals). We then whittled down our long list of 143 to ninety-seven by reflecting on whether or not the word was 'forcing itself on our attention', to recall a phrase used by Williams. We also asked the following questions of each word: Does it have an interesting genealogy? Has it provided the grounds for key debates? And does it offer a window on recent and contemporary social, economic, and political change in India? The words that fell off our list were often ones that Williams had included in his book but which we felt, on reflection, were not absolutely compelling in an Indian context—words such as 'science', 'sociology', and 'personality'. The other group of words that fell off the list were those that had seemed important in terms of covering social change in India but which, on further consideration, could not be said to have interesting genealogies or be providing 'grounds for debate'; these were words that might properly be included in a glossary or encyclopedia but not in a book of keywords. In this category were words such as 'festival', 'industry', and 'Sikh'. Our final list of keywords in this book will doubtless appear arbitrary. Certainly, it reflects our own interests, which centre on questions of economic, social, and political transformation in India (see Corbridge et al. 2013). It reflects, too, our history of conducting social research in different parts of India: Jeffrey mainly in Uttar Pradesh and Harriss predominantly in Tamil Nadu and West Bengal.

Williams understood part of his function as an intellectual to be not only to expose the various ways in which words had been used but also to highlight new possibilities for a word's deployment in the social sphere. Words, and a proper understanding of their history and provenance, could actually encourage the emergence of a fuller democracy. We have written our book in this same spirit. We have favoured words that are actively used by organizations and individuals in India engaged in progressive social transformation. Thus, words like 'rights', 'politics', and 'equality' were at the very front of our minds when we embarked on this project, as were words like 'poverty', 'corruption', and 'violence'.

There is an old joke about a dictionary being a book with lots of characters but not much of a plot. We have found, exactly as Williams did, that we have dealt with clusters—'a particular set of what came to seem interrelated words and references' (1985 [1976]: 22). We identify links between different words—differences, similarities, and intersections. In a sense, we offer a dinner made up of complementary dishes rather than a selection of snacks. There is also a consistency of style, tone, and thought in *Keywords for Modern India*, which comes from our having collaborated together in the past, having similar political views, and both having considerable experience of field research in provincial India. We had an equal level of input into this jointly authored book. Finally, what we hope will spring from the text is the sense of how words are entangled in lives, contexts, and histories. Part of what makes a keywords project distinct from a dictionary is its concern with words that are currently in circulation: it is a 'vocabulary'—linked words in the process of being enunciated—rather than a fixed record of meaning.

What also gives the book its coherence is the picture that begins to emerge of contemporary India. As we go about discussing words like 'caste', 'gender', 'equality', and 'informal', we begin to get a sense of the scale and nature of change occurring across the Indian subcontinent. Some of these changes are economic. The economic reforms begun in the early 1990s have transformed social opportunities for a thin upper stratum of the population, but simultaneously heightened many inequalities and led to a revolution of rising aspirations that has had dramatic social effects. India has an emerging middle class and a tiny elite of extremely rich individuals. It also contains as many hungry, illiterate, and poor people as Sub-Saharan Africa, many of whom also suffer from the stigma of gender or caste oppression. Many people remain dependent on the land, and agriculture is often said to be in crisis.

Socially, the expansion of new media and global communications technology has radically altered the outlook of many Indians, even while many practices associated with 'traditional India' remain crucially important in the subcontinent today. Arranged marriages persist, even if they are now increasingly arranged partly via computer dating agencies or, especially, via mobile phones. Educational inequalities remain marked, even though increasing numbers of the poor get some basic schooling. Major diseases such as polio have been virtually eradicated but most people's access to health care is extremely limited.

In the political sphere, the book charts the qualified success of Indian democracy and competitive, plural party politics. Most people vote. New parties are springing up all the time to represent the marginalized. India has a vibrant civil society and people are fighting back against state malpractice and cronyism. Low castes and women have found their voice in politics. But against such points must be weighed the continued inability of poor people on the ground to find effective mechanisms for complaining about the poor functioning of the state. Clientelism and corruption rack the body politic. There is now even some disillusionment with 'politics' itself. All these arguments could of course be made in a standard textbook or research book on India. In our text they come out as an effect of our delving into the complexity of words like 'corruption', 'democracy', 'politics', and 'rights'. Perhaps this message is even more important precisely because it is not one we have tried to articulate clearly as an 'argument'.

One of the overarching themes is that of India divided. Like most clichés, the one about India as a society of opposites contains the seeds of several important truths: India is a place in which many people remain preoccupied with issues of food, basic security, and freedom from violence, even while Ferraris are now regularly seen on Delhi's streets. Another connecting theme is that of lived contradictions, for example in relation to people's expectations of education, visions of political transformation, and notions of gender empowerment. Yet another theme is that of ordinary people's agency on the ground, and particularly the capacity of citizens to rethink key terms themselves. We point to some of the ways in which words are being rethought in different Indian contexts: ordinary wordsmiths in everyday India are changing the country from below. Finally, what our book suggests substantively perhaps more than anything else is the impossibility of pinning down, once and for all, the meaning of words: the capacity for India and its complexity to constantly 'spill over the sides', complicating attempts at synthesis or settled definition.

We do not want to be prescriptive about how the book should be read and who might use it, except to note the diverse constituencies who might find it helpful. It could serve as an introduction to contemporary India, a type of handbook to be kept at the side of the student or scholar engaged in learning about this country. For more experienced scholars, *Keywords for Modern India* might catalyse collaborative reflection on specific words such that our—necessarily provisional—efforts be refined or opened up for debate. For those outside academia, the text might be a useful basis for learning about the similarities and differences between how words are used in, for example, the tea stalls and village homes of ordinary Indians and how scholars and those in major organizations discuss the same words.

More broadly, the project might show that words—like discussions of individual people or genealogies of objects—can serve as the starting point for fascinating conversations. Words can alter the course of history, and analysis of especially telling words—'keywords'—can be a wonderful heuristic tool. This book is a type of 'unbosoming', to use Byron's phrase, of keywords. It is an exercise in trying to identify not a single word that encompasses everything, but a collection of linked words that unlock understanding of one of the world's emerging powers.

Acknowledgements

A number of friends have helped us by reading all or some parts of our text, and have given us excellent advice, including very good ideas about keywords that we seemed to have missed out. We want to express our warm thanks, therefore, to Neera Chandhoke in Delhi, to Christopher Fuller of the London School of Economics, to Barbara Harriss-White and to Kaveri Qureshi in Oxford, Ronojoy Sen at the National University of Singapore, and to Steven Wilkinson at Yale. We especially want to thank Robin Jeffrey, historian extraordinary of Kerala and of Indian media, for his very careful reading of the whole text and for many good ideas; and our friend and fellow author in other projects, Stuart Corbridge. Stuart was to have joined us in writing this book too, but found in the end that his many duties as, now, Deputy Director of the London School of Economics made this impossible—save for providing us with the texts for five of our words. For this, and for much encouragement and advice, we want to express particular thanks to Stuart. And last, and most important, to our families, and to Jane and to Gundi most of all.

Adivasi

Literally, 'adivasi' means 'the original peoples of India', but more accurately it is a generic term for communities that are described, or seek to describe themselves, as the first populations of India. Adivasi is the term by which most of the indigenous 'tribal' people of India refer to themselves. Early censuses of British India referred to the aboriginal and semi-Hinduized aboriginal populations of India, of which there were more than eighty in Chota Nagpur and Santal Parganas in the late nineteenth century. Post-Independence, the official list of Scheduled Tribes for the same region, Jharkhand, runs to just thirty communities. Detribalization has been a common fate for 'aboriginal' communities that accumulate wealth or status. There is substantial continuity, however, in the modes of governance proposed for India's adivasi communities, both in central India and in the north-east of the country. The colonial state essentially took the view that India's 'primitive communities' had to be protected from unscrupulous Hindu landowners and merchants. They were to be ruled directly by the British in Scheduled Areas. The Chotanagpur Tenancy Act of 1908, which is intended to prevent the sale of tribal land to non-tribals, neatly expresses the view that adivasi men and women are incapable of holding their own against later 'Aryan invaders' (whether caste Hindu or Muslim).

India's Scheduled Tribes make up about 8 per cent of the country's population. Although many of the largest adivasi communities are to be found in central India—the Bhils, Gonds, Mundas, Oraons, and Santals—they make up just 12–15 per cent of that region's present population, while in the north-eastern states communities including the Mizos and the Nagas make up 20–30 per cent of the population. Far more than India's Scheduled Castes—the ex-untouchable communities who, along with the country's Scheduled Tribes, exist outside, or in some senses underneath, the Hindu caste system—India's adivasi communities have generally owned the land they work. The poor quality of tribal lands, however, which are mostly unirrigated uplands, has condemned many adivasis to acute income poverty. It has also necessitated a reliance on non-agricultural incomes, including in many cases from timber and non-timber forest products. The association of tribals with forests has led both to a romanticization of the Tribal Other—supposedly in touch with nature through their sacred groves and animistic gods and goddesses: relative gender equality being another feature of adivasi societies—and to a crass depiction of India's adivasis as ignorant 'junglees', often drunk on 'mahua' or other distilled products. This latter depiction has been strengthened over the years by the poor quality of government education in tribal areas. Many adivasi communities prefer to keep the state at a distance, and this distancing has been mirrored in some places by a breakdown in local state institutions. One of the attractions of the Maoist movement in tribal central India is precisely that it offers alternative forms of governance and public service delivery. Another, which is particularly to the fore in the mineral belt of central India, is that it contests the loss of tribal lands to mining companies and other corporations.

Policy debates on India's adivasi communities have embraced both isolationism and assimilationism. The discourse on isolationism was advanced most notably either side of Independence by Verrier Elwin. It informed Prime Minister Nehru's views that the wit and wisdom of tribal peoples had to be defended against mainstream (or more 'advanced') society. If, in Elwin's case, this led to charges that India's tribals were to be placed in a 'zoo' and sheltered from modern life, more recently some elements of the same discourse have been mobilized by tribal leaders themselves to valorize adivasi languages, cultural festivals, and popular heroes (for example, Birsa Munda in Jharkhand). Assimilationism likewise describes a spectrum of views and policies. Central to the state's dealings with its Scheduled Tribes has been a policy of compensatory discrimination. This has sought the progressive integration of tribal communities into 'mainstream India' by means of reserved places in higher education institutions, seats in legislative bodies, and jobs in government and public sector corporations. Legislation to this end was first passed in 1950 and was meant to last for ten years, by which time affirmative action was supposed to have done its job. The fact that similar legislation continues to exist tells its own story. India's adivasis continue to be among the very poorest in India, whether measured in terms of incomes, education levels, or health care outcomes. It also indicates the power of tribal India to act as a voting bloc that mainstream parties find hard to ignore. This is especially the case for the Congress party, which historically has won the most votes from tribal India. A tougher form of assimilation-ism was proposed in the 1940s by the great Indian sociologist G. S. Ghurye, in debate with Elwin. This holds that India's 'so-called tribals' are lapsed Hindus who need to be brought back into the fold.

The latter is the position taken by the Hindu nationalist *Sangh Parivar* (*see* Hindutva), which uses the term *vanvasi* (forest dwellers) in preference to a word—adivasi—that implies that the tribal people were the first inhabitants of India. This idea is in conflict with its claim that the Aryans, who brought Vedic civilization to the country, are the original inhabitants of the land. The Sangh has a number of organizations working amongst adivasis with the aims of 'bringing them back' into the Hindu fold, and of countering conversion to Christianity. In the 1990s, cadres of the *Rashtriya Swayamsevak Sangh* (the organization that is the core of the Sangh Parivar) moved into tribal areas of Gujarat, Jharkhand (then still part of Bihar), and Orissa, among other states. Sometimes violent struggles ensued with Christian tribals and local or foreign Christian missionaries. This violence is ongoing, and adds to the state/Naxalite conflicts that continue to disturb lives and livelihoods in much of tribal central India. Sixty-five years after Independence, the lives of many adivasis are becoming more precarious, not less.

• See also *commons, forests, reservations*

Ambedkar

Bhimrao Raoambedkar (1891–1956) was a twentieth-century political and popular leader in India, who remains a powerful icon for Dalits (low castes) and an inspirational figure for many Indians more widely. 'Babasaheb', as he is affectionately known, was born into a poor Mahar (ex-untouchable) family in modern-day Maharashtra. He was the first untouchable to study at Elphinstone High School in Bombay and later won a scholarship to study in the USA, gaining a Masters degree from Columbia University and also enrolling at the London School of Economics, where he took a PhD in Economics, and Gray's Inn, where he passed the Bar Exam.

From 1917, when he returned to India, and up to his death in 1956, Ambedkar was one of India's foremost public intellectuals. He displayed both a profound scholarly interest in issues of religion, morality, and justice and an equal eagerness to bring about social change. He was interested in trying to push forward transformations through non-violent constitutional means, and organized numerous political and social reform movements. These focused especially on questions of Dalit rights and the proposal for special reservations for Dalits in education, work, and politics—an issue on which he famously clashed with Gandhi. He also wrote many books on caste, social justice, and the challenges facing India.

Ambedkar was a renowned jurist. He served as India's first law minister and was Chairman of the Constitution Drafting Committee, charged by the Constituent Assembly to write India's new Constitution. Ambedkar was also a spiritual leader of sorts, and wrote a great deal about religion, especially Hinduism and Buddhism. Partly in protest against what he saw as the cruelties of Hinduism, he organized a formal public ceremony for himself and his supporters in Nagpur in 1956 in which he converted to Buddhism. Ambedkar's example has been important for millions of Dalits who have converted to Buddhism since that time.

What perhaps united Ambedkar's work across these multiple fronts—intellectual, political, legal, and religious—was his determination that Indians should free themselves of caste consciousness and associated notions of hierarchy, privilege, and social subordination. He wanted a type of 'social renaissance' to take place.

Ambedkar warned his supporters not to idolize him. But Dalit political movements and parties have repeatedly drawn heavily on the Ambedkar name and image. He has become, in the writer Ramachandra Guha's phrase, the 'darling of the dispossessed'. The most prominent among the parties celebrating Ambedkar's image has been the *Bahujan Samaj* Party (BSP) in the Indian state of Uttar Pradesh (UP), which had its origins in an earlier organization established by the Dalit intellectual Kanshi Ram in the mid-1970s: the All India Backward (SC, ST, OBC) and Minority Communities Employees' Federation (BAM-CEF). The BSP emerged on the political scene in the 1980s and has achieved several victories in the UP State Assembly elections in the 1990s and 2000s. Under the leadership of a Dalit woman, Mayawati—who has served as the Chief Minister of UP on several occasions—the BSP orchestrated a remarkable ideological programme of 'Ambedkarization', including the construction of vast numbers of statues of Ambedkar across the state, and the naming of parks, libraries, and schools in his honour. Most villages across UP state now boast at least one statue depicting Ambedkar. As these statues have mushroomed across the country—they now outnumber those of any other political leader in India in history—the very question of what 'Ambedkar' connotes has been brought into sharper focus. The statues take a variety of forms—many are made cheaply by low-caste craftsmen—but typically show Ambedkar in a three-piece suit and tie, and with a pen in his front pocket: features that are supposed to index his professionalism, civility, and success in higher education. He sometimes has an upraised arm, signalling outrage and protest, and he often carries a briefcase or has the Constitution clutched to his chest, underlining his role in nation-building.

Many on the political Left have criticized this Dalit-led ideological project for its tendency to place symbolic questions before the issues of poverty, exploitation, and everyday violence. But in societies with high levels of illiteracy physical symbols are extremely important. The insertion of Ambedkar into public space through statues, street names, and libraries highlights the wider inclusion of Dalits in society. Moreover, for vibrant local cultures, Ambedkar statue construction forms the basis of Dalit pride. Low castes across UP and in many other states use Ambedkar statues as the centrepiece in religious and social events. The annual festival of 'Ambedkar *Jayanti*' (Ambedkar's birthday), in particular, has become a major spectacle in many parts of provincial UP. Dalit leaders organize processions, poetry readings, plays, speeches, and other cultural events for local low castes.

'Ambedkar' is a highly charged political signifier, a lightning rod for 'awakened' Dalits as well as reactionary opponents. At the village and town level, higher castes have frequently attacked or vandalized Ambedkar statues as a means of reaffirming dominance. In Tamil Nadu in 2012, local government officials had to place Ambedkar statues in cages after they were repeatedly desecrated, and in the 2012 elections in Uttar Pradesh the authorities covered the figures of Ambedkar with blankets in an effort to prevent conflagrations.

Ambedkar topped a national poll of 'the greatest Indian after Gandhi' held early in 2012. This perhaps reflects the extent to which Ambedkar's achievements have been communicated outside the Dalit community, for example through television and in school textbooks. But several commentators have pointed out that 'Ambedkar' remains indelibly a caste leader. Dalits are much more likely than others to have read Ambedkar's work, and it is Dalits who organize festivals in his name. Many have called for an effort to mainstream Ambedkar so that his contribution to the founding of the modern nation is more clearly established. Ambedkar was not only a Dalit champion, he was also a committed advocate of an interventionist, modernizing state and equally ardent in his defence of the modern virtues of citizenship and secularism.

• See also *caste, Dalit, equality, Gandhi*

B

Bollywood

Quite when this word—the combination of the old name of the Indian city now called Mumbai, which was formerly Bombay, and that of Hollywood, the centre of the United States' film industry—came into use, and quite who was responsible for coining it, remain uncertain. But the term was certainly current in the 1970s, as the *Oxford English Dictionary (OED)* confirms—citing a usage in a novel by H. R. F. Keating, *Filmi, Filmi Inspector Ghote*, of 1976. The word was used then, as it has been used subsequently, to refer to the Bombay/Mumbai film industry—now the largest in the world in terms of the number of feature films produced each year; or to Hindi films in general; or just to popular films produced in India. It was a word at first regarded unfavourably in Bombay, because it was seen as reflecting insecurity about Indian cultural production, by implying that it is only able to claim stature by association with a Western icon—'needing a foreign crutch to lean upon' as one writer, Mihir Bose, puts it. But over time, and from the 1990s onwards, the term has acquired a positive valence, referring to a filmic style that is distinctively Indian, but which is popular over much of the world, including Pakistan. This includes, too, even the Anglo-Saxon world, which once—reflecting, no doubt, an instinctively racist attitude—disparaged Indian cinema. It is now a global space of cultural production and expression, and one in which members of India's diaspora in the West play a significant part. 'Bollywood' films bring together drama and comedy with music in a distinctive way. The films are not generally 'musicals' in the Western sense, in which music and songs carry the narrative forward. Rather, they often include large numbers of songs, even if they interrupt the storyline.

The deeper origins of the term lie in the coinage of 'Tollywood' in the 1930s, from the name of the part of Kolkata/Calcutta—Tollygunge—where the first film studios of that city were located. 'Tollywood' has been used more recently, however, to refer to the Telugu film industry, while 'Kollywood' has sometimes been used to refer to the burgeoning Tamil film industry of Chennai/Madras (because of the number of studios in the part of that city called Kodambakkam). The film industry flourishes not only in these centres, as well as in Bollywood, but in others too. There has long been a profitable industry, for further instance, in Kerala (in Malayalam, the language of that state), while Bengali films have been noted amongst film-lovers all over the world for many years.

Cinema has long been a vital part of Indian social and cultural life, projecting at different times different ways of being Indian. Film was a message bearer for nationalism; later for the modernizing aspirations of the Nehruvian state; and more recently for the idea of the global Indian. Film stars, meanwhile, have sometimes played major roles in politics—nowhere more strongly so than in the south, in Tamil Nadu and in Andhra Pradesh, where some film actors have come to take on major political roles. Bollywood has also been central to emerging youth cultures in India and to the cultural lives of the middle class.

• See also *culture, globalization, modern*

Bourgeois

A French word meaning 'citizen or freeman of a city or burgh, as distinct from a peasant on the one hand and a gentleman on the other', 'bourgeois' came into use in English early in the eighteenth century. Now the word is 'often taken as the type of the mercantile or shopkeeping middle class of any country'—though there is also the term 'petty bourgeois' (from the French *petite bourgeoisie*), which has been in use since the 1860s, and refers to 'the lower-middle or commercial classes'. Both 'bourgeois' and 'petty bourgeois' also have the connotation of 'a conventional person' and are used as 'vague terms of social contempt', as Raymond Williams puts it.

The growth in size and importance of the 'bourgeois' trading class in eighteenth- and nineteenth-century Europe had important consequences, Williams points out, for political theory, giving rise to a new concept of what, in English, is referred to as civil society (and in German, as by Hegel, as 'bourgeois [*bürgerlich*] society'). It is especially associated with Marxist writing, however, and from the later nineteenth century the noun 'bourgeoisie' has been used to refer to the capitalist class (or, disparagingly, to 'exploiters of the proletariat')—and it is in this sense that it has generally been used in regard to India. The Marxist historian (and polymath) D. D. Kosambi (1907–66), for example, wrote in a review of Nehru's *Discovery of India* in 1946 that the Indian bourgeoisie 'had come of age', and said of it that it was 'a class which may now be said to be firmly in the saddle'. This view is reflected by the Indian communist parties in their programme statements. The Communist Party of India, for example, says that 'The State in India is the organ of the class rule of the bourgeoisie headed by corporate big business and monopolies'; and the Communist Party of India (Marxist) that 'The present Indian state is the organ of the class rule of the bourgeoisie and landlords led by the big bourgeoisie.'

The expression 'the bourgeoisie' in writing on India generally refers to what is also described as 'the big bourgeoisie' or just 'big business', and authors are often talking specifically about a fairly small number of big (family) business houses that combine diverse sets of manufacturing, commercial, and financial activities. The most outstanding of these at the time that Kosambi was writing were those of the Birlas, a family from the Marwari community—historically a community of bankers—and of the Tatas, who are Parsis. The Birlas, in particular, played a significant role in India's struggle for freedom from colonial rule, and it is generally thought—not only by Indian communists—that the Congress leadership, regardless of the rhetoric of one fraction of it about establishing socialism in India, was in the end supportive of the interests of big business. Most of the older family business houses, like those of the Tatas and the Birlas, remain significant corporate groups, but there is also a new generation of big companies, set up by India's 'new capitalist class', of which the best known is Reliance, founded by Dhirubhai Ambani, who famously started out in life as a petrol pump attendant.

The use of the word 'bourgeois' in writing on India, therefore, rarely refers to a 'mercantile or shopkeeping middle class'. There is good reason for this since, as Raymond Williams notes, 'A *ruling* class, which is the socialist [Marxist] sense of bourgeois in the context of historical description of a developed capitalist society, is not easily or clearly represented by the essentially different middle class.' When Kosambi, for instance, used 'bourgeois' and 'middle class' interchangeably in his review in 1946, he introduced some confusion, for he was certainly not suggesting that merchants and shopkeepers constituted the class that was 'firmly in the saddle' in the new India that was then emerging. The 'mercantile or shop-keeping middle class' is more commonly referred to in writing about India as constituting, rather, the 'petty bourgeoisie' (people who, according to Marx's analysis, may both buy and sell labour power, or do neither—being the owners of small amounts of capital). It is widely considered, for instance, that support for the *Jana Sangh*, the precursor of the present-day Hindu nationalist *Bharatiya Janata* Party (*see* Hindutva), came principally from among the petty bourgeoisie of the smaller cities and towns of north and central India—meaning shopkeepers, traders, and moneylenders. There is a school of thought which holds that India, certainly in the 1950s and 1960s, presents an example of an 'intermediate regime', according to a concept proposed by the Polish economist Michał Kalecki (1899–1970). This is the controversial idea of a regime in which the petty bourgeoisie, in combination with the rich peasants, constitutes the ruling class. Even those who do not hold to this notion may agree that the petty bourgeoisie of the bazaars of Indian towns and cities has played an important political role since at least the eighteenth century.

• See also *class, middle class*

Bureaucracy

The word 'bureau' came into use in English in the eighteenth century to describe a chest of drawers that is also equipped with a writing board—though Williams tells us that the original meaning of 'bureau' was the baize used to cover desks. In the following century it also came to mean 'an office especially for the transaction of public business; a department of public administration . . . an agency for the coordination of related activities, the distribution of information, etc.'. And the word 'bureaucracy' had come into use by this time to refer to 'government by bureau' or 'government officials collectively', and also (reflecting the often negative evaluation of rigid public administration) 'officialism'. We may imagine that the connection between the item of furniture and the organization of public business was that bureaus were used extensively to equip offices. The bureau, as a site for writing and for keeping records or files, is an apt symbol as well as a practical instrument of a particular form of administration.

The form of administration that the bureau stands for is that classically analysed by the German sociologist Max Weber (1864–1920) as an essential element of what he described as rational-legal authority. Weber set out an ideal type of bureaucracy as an efficient form of administration bound by clear rules, which maintains records of its actions, and in which decision-making is not dependent on the personal whims of the officials employed within it. Bureaucracies should be bound by transparent, impersonal rules, applied universally; they should keep records (in the 'bureau') so as to be accountable; they should have clear lines of authority (it should be clear exactly where 'the buck stops'), which means that they should have a well-defined hierarchy of roles; and entry into them, and then promotion through the hierarchy, should depend on ability. Recruitment and career paths should be determined, in other words, meritocratically. Some recent research has shown that the developing countries that have such meritocratically recruited and run bureaucracies do tend to have better records of performance.

The Hindi words for bureaucracy—'naukarshaahi' and 'adhikaarivarg'—are less commonly heard in India than the term 'prashasan', which translates as 'administration'. It is also common to hear people on the ground referring to specific bureaucracies simply as 'sarkar'—a word that also refers to 'the state' in general. This elision of the bureaucracy with the state partly reflects people's awareness that bureaucrats are often linked via a nexus of corruption to politicians, political parties, and the machinery of state power more broadly.

India has a higher-level bureaucracy (the Indian Administrative Service (IAS), the lineal descendant of the Indian Civil Service (ICS) of the colonial era) that is quite fiercely meritocratic in terms of recruitment, and has many senior officials of exceptionally high calibre. It was the ICS, and since Independence it has been the IAS, that has supplied the District Magistrates, or the officials still described in some states as the Collector, who run India's administrative districts. Their powers in the colonial period over the collection of revenue, the administration of justice, and the maintenance of law and order were sweeping, and the role acquired a quite legendary status in some of the annals of empire. Their powers are still extensive, though rivalled these days by those of the District Superintendents of Police. Their roles now have much more to do with the management of development programmes, in which they are assisted by lower-level officials, among them the Block Development Officers, who are responsible for the coordination of programmes in the 'development blocks' into which districts are divided, and each of which includes several panchayats.

Senior bureaucrats from the IAS are generalists, though some do manage to develop particular expertise. Their career paths are much less clearly meritocratic than is their recruitment. And even their recruitment, as well as the career paths of the very large numbers of lower-level civil servants, is rarely entirely meritocratic, being subject to a great deal of personal and political discretion (to patronage, in other words). One of the critical problems of Indian bureaucracy, at all levels, is that officials are subject to 'transfers'. They may be moved frequently between positions according to the dictates, in the end, of politicians. Originally intended as a check upon inefficiency and corruption, the transfer system has become a major instrument of corruption in government. There is a more or less institutionalized—though of course quite unofficial—system of payments for securing, or avoiding, appointment to particular places and positions. Government teachers and health workers, for example, make payments to seniors in order to avoid being posted to remote places; or officials in irrigation departments may make payments in order to secure postings to areas in which they can expect to make a substantial income from side payments made to them by farmers. At even the highest levels in the civil service, officials may be moved between positions if they stand in the way of politicians' efforts to profit from their office. Frequent transfers detract from efficiency because even capable officials rarely have a chance to build their expertise in regard to a particular position. A further crucial problem is that at senior levels government is very often *under*staffed, so that sensitive functions depend very heavily on the skills of very few people. In international trade talks, for example, Indian delegations may include only a handful of competent officials, who are greatly outnumbered by their Chinese or Brazilian counterparts.

'Bureaucracy' can and should be a fair and effective way of managing public administration, but it is widely disparaged in India as elsewhere in the world. Bureaucracy is seen, often fairly, as blighted by 'officialism', and by 'red tape'. Officials in India are very commonly quite literally barricaded behind piles of files, each of them tied round with red tape—and only very slowly are the necessary records of government being computerized. There is an art to the management of files, which can be used to advance or to hold back the completion of an action. Official writing is commonly executed in line with the letter, but not with the intention, of government policy. Officers strive to meet the 'targets' that have been set for them, but without any concern for realizing the objectives those targets were supposed to satisfy. Thus, for example, agricultural officers distribute new seeds, but with no regard for whether they reach the people who can make best use of them. Bureaucratic action is very generally characterized by the indifference of officials to those whom they are supposed to serve, as well as being quite systematically biased against adivasis, Dalits, Muslims, and women.

Absenteeism is a huge problem in the bureaucracy. One research study in Rajasthan has shown that the diagnostic and other skills of doctors and nurses in the public health system are better than those of private providers. Yet people, even very poor people, overwhelmingly choose to go to private clinics where they also pay much more, because they can rarely be confident that the government health staff will be in their posts. Senior bureaucrats may connive with absenteeism because they benefit from side-payments made to them by health staff.

Reform of the bureaucracy so as to improve the responsiveness of government to citizens and to counter corruption remains an urgent and difficult task in contemporary India.

• See also *corruption, patronage, politics, state*

Capitalism

According to the *OED*, capitalism is 'an economic system in which private capital or wealth is used in the production or distribution of goods and prices are determined mainly in a free market'. This is surely a common understanding of a system that is assumed to have come into being first—at least in an industrial form—in the United Kingdom in the eighteenth century. Marxists, however, insist that capitalism is at heart a system in which wage labour is a commodity that is bought and sold like other commodities. Labour is formally free and not indentured in any form. They also maintain that capitalists are forced to compete with one another in ways that short-change the labouring classes, while producing constant technological change. Plato is credited with the phrase that 'necessity is the mother of invention'. But it is in the *Communist Manifesto* (1848) that a system of economic production is first described that *compels* the creation of new worlds. 'All that is solid melts into air', as Marx and Engels neatly put it. Standing still under the rule of capital is not an option—unless, that is, one wants to perish. Marx (1853) also famously inveighed against the brutality and unreason of Hinduism, the caste system, and Oriental Despotism in Hindustan. He welcomed British rule there to the extent that it allowed capitalism to take root, and with it the seeds of future 'social revolution'.

Later versions of Marxism have qualified this paean to modernity, just as they have also challenged the view that pre-capitalist forms of production and social organization must always give way to capitalism. By the early part of the twentieth century, it was commonly argued that an era of competitive industrial capitalism had given way to an era of monopoly capitalism. In the wealthiest countries some of the surplus generated by the new conglomerates paid for an emerging welfare state or was otherwise used to buy off an aristocracy of labour. The exploitation of labour and natural resources was then focused on the periphery of an emerging capitalist world system, and was made possible by new regimes of imperial subjugation.

Both these developments proved vital to Indian understandings of capitalism, at least until very recently. Early Indian nationalists spoke of a drain of wealth from India to the UK. They also bemoaned the way that Britain ran a balance of payments surplus with India to offset its losses with China. According to this analysis, which in key respects was adopted later on by the Communist Party of India, capitalism was held back in India by the interests of Empire. Instead of liberating Indians from casteism and 'feudalism', as Marx had earlier forecast, European capitalism was accused of reproducing itself on the back of superexploited labour in the Indian countryside and by virtue of the destruction of local trade and industry. It was the duty of the state at Independence, Nehru and others maintained, to build up a domestic bourgeoisie and local forms of industrial capitalism, whether in the private or public sectors. In the context of the Keynesian revolution in economic thought in the mid-twentieth century (which itself was galvanized by the apparent collapse of mainly market-based forms of capitalism during the Great Depression), and given the poverty of credit and stock markets in newly independent India, not to mention immediate concerns about foreign currency shortages, it is hardly surprising that in the 1950s India opted for a *dirigiste* model of industrial capitalist development. The Second and Third Five-Year Plans (1956–66: the period of the so-called Nehru–Mahalanobis model of growth and develop-ment) called for a de facto squeeze on investments in agriculture and the building up of large-scale enterprises in heavy engineering and chemicals, supported by improvements in transportation and power supply. Largely based in the public sector, these new develop-ments were planned to complement existing capacity in textiles and iron and steel.

What we might call 'capitalism with Indian characteristics' was made even more distinct-ive by virtue of the fact that India's enclaves of industrial capitalism sat amidst a vast sea of enterprises in the informal sector, most of which were not fully subsumed under the logics of capital. Much effort was expended by social theorists in the 1970s and 1980s on working out how unambiguously capitalist enterprises interacted—or 'articulated'—with enterprises that danced to another beat. Many farming enterprises, for example, were based on the self-exploitation of household labour, or even on indebted/bonded labour. They were nonethe-less linked to the broader capitalist economy in India by circuits of mercantile or usury capital. Very often, indeed, it was apparent—and still is apparent—that the reproduction of formal sector enterprises in India depends on the parallel reproduction of forms of unfree (or bonded) labour. It is a mistake to suppose that India has to be characterized as either capitalist or non-capitalist, just as it is a mistake to suppose that capitalism can't coexist with forms of socialized medicine. The reproduction of broadly capitalist relations of production and exchange is consistent with a huge spectrum of political forms (from democracy to dictatorship), as well as with diverse systems of ownership, governance, and management. Capitalism comes in many varieties.

Failure to recognize this fact has led to some confusion about India's recent economic reforms. In an economy in which nine out of ten people work in the informal sector it is hardly helpful to maintain that India is ditching socialism and embracing capitalism. Less unhelpful is the suggestion that capitalism in India is 'neo-liberalizing'—so long as the phrase is used carefully to describe certain forms of deregulation in formal sector labour markets and a general direction of travel in trade, fiscal, banking, and monetary policies.

• See also *bourgeois, class, development, neo-liberal*

Caste

In common parlance, caste suggests a system of stratification manifest in everyday aspects of lifestyle that is more institutionalized and slower to change than are other systems of hierarchy and which involves a greater degree of separation between strata than is typically characteristic of class-stratified societies. Thus, the assertion that a particular institution—a university, government bureaucracy, or hotel, for example—has its own 'caste system' conjures up an image of hierarchically ranked sets of people, functionally linked with one another but otherwise having little in common and, probably, eating and socializing independently.

This common-sense definition of caste—the assumption that caste equates with hierarchy and the underlying idea of caste as an especially 'deep' form of social difference—sits awkwardly with the contemporary Indian scene. There is no direct translation for 'caste' in India, where it seems to come from the Portuguese word *casta* meaning 'pure breed'. 'Caste' in India most closely approximates to two terms: *varna* and *jati*. Varna—which means literally 'colour' in Sanskrit—refers to the four subdivisions of the traditional Hindu hierarchy, first mentioned in Vedic literature written sometime between 1500 BC and 500 AD: Brahmins, who were traditionally priests; Kshatriyas (warriors); Vaisyas (merchants); and Sudras, who performed a broad range of other tasks. The Brahmins, Kshatriyas, and Vaisyas together comprise the 'twice born' or 'Forward' castes, the Sudras being commonly termed the 'Backward' castes (termed 'Other Backward Classes' or 'OBCs' in legal parlance). 'Dalits' lie outside the varna hierarchy altogether. Each varna is held to include very many jatis. Jati means 'species' or 'type', and refers to endogamous caste 'groups' historically associated with particular occupations and each with their own notion of how they are placed with respect to the varna hierarchy (although their position in the varna hierarchy may have changed through history). There are castes among Christians, Sikhs, and Muslims in India as well as Hindus. It is also important to note that there is a regional geography to caste within India. For example, there is a relatively high proportion of Sudras, and historically very few Brahmins and Kshatriyas, in the south of the country.

Not too long ago it was fashionable in some intellectual circles to imagine caste as a *colonial* invention: the British created caste, for example, by including caste on the census and inducting dominant castes into the lower reaches of the colonial administration. Caste was also a means to justify British rule because it entailed depicting Indian subjects as in some sense irrational. But caste ideas and elements of a caste system existed long before the British extended administrative control over India in the eighteenth century—colonial rule strengthened caste, but it did not manufacture it out of thin air.

In the first few decades after Independence there was a good deal of research on caste in India. Among the most prominent contributors to these debates was the French anthropologist Louis Dumont, who used an analysis of Hindu scriptures and existing village ethnographies to argue that notions of purity and pollution underpin the caste system, and that all castes are linked together via a complex system of ritual acts. In Dumont's writing, Brahmins were imagined as occupying a position at the top of this system. Other work examined caste more squarely as it was being practised in Indian villages. These studies showed that a landowning 'dominant caste'—usually from a higher caste but not very commonly Brahmins—was often found at the village level in India. These 'patrons' made payments (usually in kind, especially grain) to various less powerful castes ('clients') who were associated with hereditary trades—one jati might make pots, one might wash clothes, and one might carry water for the patron, and so on. The resulting set of social relationships among people of different jatis, underpinned by rules about the sharing of food, bodily contact, and marriage, came to be described by anthropologists as the '*jajmani*' system ('*jajman*' meaning 'patron' in Hindi).

This caste system broke down to a considerable extent during the second half of the twentieth century. Economic growth, India's policy of caste-based reservations, and the Government of India's attempts to empower low castes have had the cumulative effect of severing the link between caste and occupation; most castes do not perform the hereditary occupations with which they are putatively associated—Brahmins are not very often priests and Chamars are rarely leatherworkers, for example. Improved communications and urbanization, education, the expansion of the media, and the spread of notions of universal citizenship have altered what is considered acceptable in terms of the everyday practice of caste. Hierarchical notions of caste have become less evident (although they have not disappeared), and people regularly come into contact across caste lines. Moreover, in the sixty years since Independence, Dalits and other lower castes have increasingly challenged the notion that higher castes are their natural superiors, for example through their participation in social movements.

But as caste has declined somewhat as a 'system', it has been reinvented as an identity in the sphere of modern competitive politics. Political parties use caste in their search for votes, and the continued existence of caste-based reservations (selective benefits) offers a tool for politicians to manage the difficult business of competing in elections. The advantages that are perceived as attaching to reservations have, ironically, persuaded members of some erstwhile 'high' castes to claim a lower status for themselves—as has happened, for example, amongst Nambudiris in Kerala and Jats in Uttar Pradesh. Caste also influences politics at the everyday level, including union ballots, district board elections, even appointments to neighbourhood associations and student unions.

The partial decline of caste as a hierarchical system in villages and the rise of caste as an identity within politics led the Indian sociologist M. N. Srinivas to claim that a shift has occurred such that castes are now arranged 'horizontally'—separated from each other on the basis of their different identities—rather than 'vertically' along the lines of purity and pollution. But inequalities between higher and lower castes, and associated notions of hierarchy, persist. Dalits remain well behind upper castes and OBCs in terms of their access to education and secure salaried work. This is partly because of the manner in which caste and class overlap—low castes are, generally speaking, poorer than higher castes. It is also because of continued caste prejudices among those with the power to recruit to professional positions; there is considerable evidence of caste discrimination in interviews for jobs in information technology (IT) and other lucrative sectors of the economy—in these situations being higher caste often acts as a form of 'cultural capital'.

Marriage is another sphere in which caste hierarchy remains important. There has been no widespread move away from a system of caste-based arranged marriages in India, and advertisements for brides and grooms in newspapers and on websites are often organized by jati or varna. Moreover, caste in marriage has a hierarchical element: parents of higher castes are usually less concerned about a son or daughter marrying another higher-caste jati than about them marrying a Dalit. Such judgements are rarely made openly, but operate instead on the unconscious levels of presupposition and taste—caste is a type of reflex located at some deep level in the psyche. The continued importance of caste hierarchy is also evident in recent writing on untouchability in India. A survey of 565 villages across eleven states of India found that in over half the villages sampled Dalits were still denied entry into non-Dalit houses, and the Dalit Human Rights Commission has chronicled the continuing problem of caste-based violence in both rural and urban India, often a result of caste prejudice.

The debate about caste in contemporary India is therefore no longer about village 'caste systems' or about providing some type of definitive description of the rules of purity and pollution. Rather, the debate is about how caste continues to matter as an identity and aspect of everyday practice.

• See also *class, Dalit, equality, faction, Hinduism, panchayat, reservations, tradition*

Charity

Charity is a word of profoundly ambivalent meaning. As Raymond Williams points out, it had come to mean Christian love between man and God, and between man and his neighbours, by about the twelfth century, and the sense of 'benevolence to neighbours' and specifically of 'gifts to the needy' became established not long afterwards. The latter meaning—of 'help to the needy', which is how charity is most commonly understood today—was probably already dominant by the sixteenth century, and the idea of a charity, an institution, was established in the following century. But the word took on a negative sense at about the same time, reflected in the phrase 'cold as charity', which expresses the feelings of many of those who are the needy recipients of 'help'—as Williams puts it, they may experience 'the freezing of love'. The ways in which charity is given may offend the dignity and self-respect of those who are the intended beneficiaries, and so it may be rejected and incur resistance. Charity may also be subject to qualification, being restricted to 'the deserving poor' rather than showing general 'benevolence to neighbours'. Thus it is that sometimes governments have defended welfare spending as 'not a charity but a right'.

The concept of charity, in these common senses, evokes the idea of 'a gift'—referring to the 'transference of property in a thing by one person to another, voluntarily and without any valuable consideration' (*OED*). Gift-giving, which is of great importance in Indian ethical traditions, is culturally meaningful, and generates moral relations—such as relations of solidarity (as when gift exchange is reciprocal), or dependence (as may be the case if the recipient of a gift is unable to reciprocate), legitimacy, or reputation—among persons or groups of people. Conceptions of kingship in India included the expectation that kings should 'give' to the community over which they rule, with the effect of ensuring their legitimacy. On the other hand, giving gifts to state officials was often thought perfectly acceptable, though it has come increasingly to be seen as bribery, and therefore corrupt. Gift-giving and charitable activities are closely linked, therefore, to the matters of moral authority and political legitimacy. Historians such as Douglas Haynes have shown how merchants engaged in major acts of giving—building temples, or rest-houses for pilgrims, constructing wells, or sponsoring festivals. They themselves regarded these actions as acts of propitiation or of service to deities, through which they would acquire merit; and for merchants, channelling their wealth into activities like these that were highly valued in their communities was a way of establishing their own eminence and of building the reputation of being trustworthy. Their giving was more about building and maintaining reputation than it was about the idea of humanitarian service to others.

Charity in the modern English sense, or philanthropy (meaning 'love of mankind' or 'effort to promote the happiness and well-being of others'), became an established idea in India in the colonial period. Indian merchants and other wealthy people began to emulate their peers in England by establishing or contributing to schools, colleges, hospitals, and other kinds of public works and causes. In part this was an investment in their good relations with the colonial rulers. Their philanthropy, like their earlier forms of gift-giving—which they often still continued—played a significant part in the reproduction of their status and social dominance.

The colonial state, the nationalist movement, and the postcolonial state alike may be seen to have engaged in charitable work, as part of the way in which they sought to establish their legitimacy and moral authority—and in all cases these actions, well intended though they may have been, involved claims of moral or cultural superiority. In the colonial period, such charitable work played an important part in the 'civilizing mission' of the colonial state, intended to bring the benefits of Enlightenment rationality to 'the natives' of India—though it also played a part in the ways in which the state aimed to pacify and to discipline the subject population. The social policies of the postcolonial state, which have generally been targeted at particular groups of people deemed to be in need of special assistance, may be seen as having offered charity rather than satisfying the rights of social citizenship. Somewhat ironically, too, the values and attitudes of those involved in social service as part of the nationalist movement, or in the social service organization established by the Nehruvian state in the 1950s, the *Bharat Sevak Samaj*, or more recently in the many community development non-governmental organizations (NGOs) that have appeared in India, share in many of the same ideas as those of the 'civilizing mission' of the colonial rulers. The beneficiaries, or intended beneficiaries, of these social service organizations were to be helped to become 'citizens', generally by adopting or certainly by acknowledging the superiority of the upper-caste values of those who provided services to them. Teaching others basic rules of hygiene, for instance, or helping them to improve sanitation in their living spaces, may help to change their lives for the better, but it is also about disciplining them. The ambivalence that Williams detects in the meanings of 'charity' in English is evident in charitable work in India too.

• See also *citizenship, patronage*

Citizenship

The meaning of the word 'citizen' in English was, to begin with, simply that of 'an inhabitant of a city', but it soon came to connote as well the idea of one 'possessing civic rights and privileges', specifically 'a burgess or freeman of the city'. By this time, too—from the fourteenth century in England, but especially from the sixteenth century onwards—the word also had the meaning of 'a member of a state, an enfranchised inhabitant of a country, as opposed to an alien' (definitions from *OED*). This today is probably the most general understanding of the idea of 'citizenship'. Though fundamentally important, as it certainly is for the many refugees, migrants, and displaced persons in the world today, this idea of citizenship in terms of the status of membership in a particular state may be thought of as being only a 'thin' notion. A key question is: what else—what rights and privileges—are implied by holding the status of membership in a particular country?

The idea of the citizen in England and elsewhere in Europe came to be associated with those who possessed some property and who held a bourgeois class position, and citizens were distinguished from members of the nobility and the gentry. Later still, in the nineteenth century, citizenship was associated with the idea of civil society, implying the possession of a whole range of civil and political rights, along with the obligation to perform certain duties, too—what might be described as a 'thick' notion of citizenship. The extension of such rights of national citizenship to the working class, it is argued, brought about the incorporation of that class into capitalism, and what the British writer T. H. Marshall describes as 'class abatement' was accomplished through the establishment, as well, of welfare institutions.

The rights and privileges of the people of India were inevitably restricted so long as they were subject to the coercion of British imperial rule. They were 'subjects', not 'citizens'. The British rulers did seek, however, to secure the legitimacy of their rule by various means, and there were those amongst them who sought to extend liberal principles to the government of India. A small, propertied and educated minority of Indians were gradually granted some of the civil and political rights associated with full citizenship, and through their own political activity they sought to extend them, eventually through the struggle for freedom from imperial rule.

The members of the Indian National Congress, through their deliberations in the 1920s and 1930s, and then—with some other independent members of the Constituent Assembly—in debates over the design of the Constitution of independent India, developed a grand conception of what citizenship in their country should mean. They sought to weld the members of an extremely diverse society, marked by deep inequalities, into a national–civic community. Citizenship was to be inclusive. All those who were entitled, principally by right of birth, to the status of being 'citizens of India' were to have equal civic and political rights (those laid down as Fundamental Rights in Part III of the Constitution), and the initial idea, eventually watered down in the Constitution, was that all should have at least the basic range of economic and social rights necessary for their well-being. After all, the whole purpose of independence from imperial rule was to make it possible, Nehru argued, for all Indians to develop themselves according to their abilities, unconstrained by want. At the same time, the

Constitution aimed to take account of the cultural rights of minorities, and of the particular needs of those Indians who had been historically disadvantaged and were regarded as suffering from 'backwardness'. Citizenship rights were to be modestly differentiated, within the larger national–civic identity, having regard for these needs (*see* reservations). There was in this, according to the scholar Niraja Gopal Jayal, 'a radical notion of citizenship [that] held out the promise of transforming a deeply hierarchical society into a civic community of equals'.

It is generally held that this promise has not been fulfilled. The political philosopher Partha Chatterjee argues that only a minority of the people of India (all of whom are citizens in the 'thin' sense of the term) are able to enjoy fully the rights and privileges of citizenship, and that only they are able to participate in civil society. The majority are prevented from doing so because of their material circumstances, and because of the ways in which their relations with the state, and with each other through those relations, have evolved. They are often treated by the state, Chatterjee says, as labelled 'populations', with certain very specific entitlements—which often have the effect of marking them out as less than full citizens of the country. The absence of the word 'citizenship' or any Indian language equivalent term in everyday discussions in India would seem to bear out Chatterjee's point, although notions of 'rights' ('*haq*' in Hindi) are being discussed with increasing frequency.

And in India what T. H. Marshall spoke of as 'class abatement' has been brought about by the ways in which citizenship has come to be mediated through different group identities. There are tensions between individual rights of citizenship and rights that are mediated by membership in particular social groups—tensions that were rather papered over in the formulation of the Constitution. Over time, through the life of independent India, citizenship has become increasingly fragmented as claims to particular privileges on grounds of 'backwardness', generally defined in terms of caste status, have proliferated, and as intolerance of difference, particularly differences of religion, has grown. In these respects the challenges confronted in India are in common with much of the rest of the world. It is said that ethnic division is the principal problem facing citizenship today.

The particular promises of the struggle for independence in regard to economic and social rights, already attenuated by their relegation in the Constitution to the status of injunctions about policy (non-justiciable 'Directive Principles' rather than 'Fundamental Rights'), have been further disappointed by the practices of social policy. Even now, when basic education has finally become a matter of right, when rural people have been endowed with certain legal rights to employment, and there is a commitment on the part of government to make provision for food security, economic and social rights are compromised by restrictions arising from attempts to target social benefits (for instance to those deemed to be 'Below the Poverty Line'; *see* poverty), and by the commitments of government to private provision of basic social services. The word 'citizen' is indeed increasingly linked with the idea of the 'consumer'—the 'consumer-citizen'. Jayal's conclusion that 'there remains little that is recognizably civic about Indian citizenship' is pessimistic, but one which is widely supported by Indian scholars.

Some writers have begun to identify 'alternative citizenships' or 'insurgent citizenships' in India. People may have a keen sense of their rights and responsibilities with respect to each other, and therefore be engaged in developing forms of 'citizenship', but they do not understand these rights and responsibilities with reference to the nation state.

• See also *civil society, constitution, fundamentalism, Hindutva, reservations, secularism*

City

India has often been thought of—by nationalist leaders and later policymakers as well as by travel writers—as a land of villages. There is good reason for this, given that even by 2011, according to the census of India, the share of the population classified as 'rural' had dipped only marginally below 70 per cent (it was still 68.8 per cent of the total). India has urbanized much less dramatically than many of the other former colonies. These considerations, however, may lead to underestimation of the significance of the city in Indian society and civilization. There have been urban centres in the Indian subcontinent since the construction in the Indus Valley of Mohenjodaro and Harappa in the third or fourth millennium BC. Some anthropologists have argued that it was in the towns and cities that the caste system was most fully developed, while others think that Indian society was centred more on the courts of kings, around which urban settlements developed, than it was around the pre-eminence of Brahmins.

British officials and scholars, perhaps because they associated urbanization with industrialization, may not have fully recognized the significance of pre-industrial urbanism in India—cities such as Ahmedabad, Surat, and Cochin that were important commercial centres, or those like Benares or Madurai that were great religious cities, as well as political and administrative centres, amongst which Delhi was only the most notable. The layout and social organization of these cities, in neighbourhoods of work and residence, segregated by caste, sect, and religion, was quite distinct from that of the cities that the British created. With few exceptions—such as Jaipur in present-day Rajasthan, which was laid out for its princely ruler in 1727 in spacious rectilinear streets—Indian cities were not planned. But large parts of some of the old cities were demolished by the British to make way for planned urban spaces. This gave rise to a pronounced duality, with a closely packed and perhaps once-walled old city, commonly beside a fort or a palace, and then laid out beyond it a severely designed military cantonment, as well as the more generously organized 'civil lines', with a British club and perhaps a racecourse. The great colonial cities, however, and the capitals of the three major presidencies of British India—Calcutta (now Kolkata), Bombay (now Mumbai), and Madras (now Chennai)—had their own distinctive character, deriving in the first place from their initial establishment as bases for trade. They were organized around the two axes of Fort and Government House on the one hand, and wharves and docks on the other. They were clearly divided, too, between 'Black Town' and 'White Town'—as the different urban areas occupied by Indians and Europeans were once designated in Madras.

The major cities of India are, therefore, 'creatures of colonialism, or ripostes to it', as Sunil Khilnani has put it. The British created, he says, 'a masquerade of the modern city, designed to flaunt the superior rationality and power of the Raj, but deficient in productive capacities'. The Marxist intellectual Boudhayan Chattopadhyay once put it more pithily when he suggested that whereas British cities are the creation of a production system, those of India are rather 'the excreta of a consumption system'—sites for the consumption of wealth derived from exploitation of rural people. Neither this statement, nor Khilnani's, is entirely accurate, of course, for there were new industrial cities, such as Kanpur and Coimbatore, as well as Bombay, where the cotton textile industry became established in the later nineteenth century. The 'masquerade of the modern city' reached its heights in the architectural splendours of New Delhi. The city designed by the architects Sir Edwin Lutyens (1869–1944) and Sir Herbert Baker (1862–1946) was meant to advertise the staying power of the Raj. First proposed in 1911, it was largely completed by 1935—ironically, just twelve years before the British were driven from India. Lutyens was also keen to ensure that India's capital was writ large with the straight lines of 'western Reason', much as Pierre Charles L'Enfant had achieved in Washington DC. The greatest riposte, meanwhile, to the colonial city was probably Ahmedabad, the principal city of present-day Gujarat, which had long been both an important political and commercial centre, and was largely ignored by the British. Ahmedabad modernized on its own terms, becoming known as 'the Manchester of India' (reflecting the success of its many textile mills).

After Independence the city came to be seen as the engine of modernity. Nehru took a close personal interest in the design by the celebrated French architect Le Corbusier of Chandigarh, which was to become the capital of Punjab. The city that he created was resolutely modern in its conception, and stripped of all historical associations. For Nehru it was 'symbolic of the freedom of India, unfettered by traditions of the past, an expression of the nation's faith in its future'. Yet the city was laid out in such a way as to reinforce a strict social hierarchy.

In the twenty-first century, the importance of the cities as cradles of 'the new generation of Indian enterprise' has been widely proclaimed, and both the English word 'city' and Indian language equivalent terms, such as '*shahr*' in Hindi, are metonyms for modernity. The major metropolitan cities (city regions, with populations in 2011 of more than 5 million)—the 'metros'—Delhi, Mumbai, Kolkata, Chennai, Bangalore (now Bengalaru), Hyderabad, Ahmedabad, Pune, and Surat, are generally thought of as the principal sites of the 'new India' and as homes to the 'new middle class' of young professionals and entrepreneurs. No city in India, however, is more symbolic of the dynamic 'new India' than Gurgaon, the satellite city south of Delhi, which was no more than a village until the 1990s. Described as 'the millennial city', it has experienced phenomenal growth, but both architecturally and socially it is marked by deep divisions and inequality. Gradually, smaller cities and even the erstwhile '*mofussil*' (provincial) towns have taken on something of this character too. Each of the metros has plans for becoming a 'global city', with Singapore often taken as a model. Bangalore and Hyderabad have vied for recognition as the 'cyber capital'—the dominant centre of the IT industry—of India. Over the first decade of the twenty-first century, their development has made them scarcely recognizable to those who knew them before. The flip side is the further marginalization of the poor, even as work in the cities—especially in construction and the provision of private security services—has come to have ever greater importance in the ways in which very many poor people survive.

• See also *globalization, middle class, modern*

Civil Society

Civil society is a slippery term. In seventeenth- and eighteenth-century Britain, it referred to a social order shaped by government and counterposed to an anarchic state of nature. But in the nineteenth century Georg Hegel argued for a vision of civil society distinct from government. Hegel also linked civil society to a particular form of sociality: in civil society, people meet as autonomous individuals, blind to differences of background and status. During the last third of the twentieth century, commentators seized on this Hegelian vision and attributed to civil society a range of causative powers. Civil society, in this sense, can nurture democracy in formerly authoritarian states, trigger social harmony in the wake of sectarian strife, prevent communal and ethnic violence, and even promote economic growth through its positive effects on levels of trust and cooperation in society.

At the same time, many influential commentators argued that developing countries could not reap these benefits because they lacked a broad-based civil society. Partha Chatterjee made a version of this argument for India. In Chatterjee's view, it is only the very rich in urban metropolitan areas in India who have developed modern associations analogous to civil society, and it is only in elite circles that one encounters the English phrase 'civil society'. The poor and lower middle class occupy instead a sphere of 'political society', in which they form into specific groups on an ad hoc basis to bid for state resources. Political society is comprised of temporary mobilizations and usually underpinned by particularistic solidarities based, for example, on caste and religion. Political society is often violent and para-legal in nature, and operates through vertical networks of patronage and clientelism.

Chatterjee's tendency to imagine the rich as guardians of civil society is problematic, however. There is considerable evidence of the uncivil and antisocial nature of elite political action in India, as recent reports of land-grabbing and slum clearance make clear. More importantly, the poor often do participate in civil-society-type organizations in India, such as grassroots environmental protest, Dalit resistance, and mobilization in defence of rights, even if they do not often understand their action with reference to the term 'civil society' or any local language equivalent.

People also often inhabit some type of 'civil society' and political society at the same time. Student leaders on provincial Indian campuses frequently campaign in organized groups against corruption, while also launching violent mobilizations to obtain resources for their particular caste group. Likewise, the poor in many parts of India strike secret deals with local brokers to get access to state services, while also campaigning for greater transparency. Such apparent double dealing reflects conflicts between people's short-term interests and long-term goals and between pragmatism and principle.

There are also many forms of politics in India that have some of the characteristics of civil society in its Hegelian guise but not others. For example, there are caste associations that campaign for the rights of fellow caste members and provide scholarships, schooling, health care, and employment advice to poorer members of their caste. These associations exhibit many of the characteristics of civil society but are founded on a communal identity rather than impartial solidarities. A similar point might be made about Hindutva organizations like the Rashtriya Swayamsevak Sangh (RSS). There are also many examples of local activists conducting civil-society-type work—helping poor people get access to state services, motivating poor populations, critiquing corruption, for example—who are nonetheless not part of named associations. It is also unclear whether legality and non-violence should always be imagined as prerequisites of civil society: para-legal organizations that sometimes employ strong-arm tactics—such as illegal student unions in colleges—might be included in the ambit of actually existing 'civil society' in India if they are also deliberative, inclusive, and function as a check on the abuse of state power. It may be necessary to broaden notions of civil society in an Indian context to take account of non-institutionalized political forms and those based on particularistic identities and, possibly, to take account too of political actions involving some level of violence and illegality. The stakes in these debates over labelling are not only academic. 'Civil society' is a term loaded with positive associations, and the claim to be part of civil society can be important in the efforts of individuals and organizations to bid for resources.

The meaning of civil society in India is changing in other ways, too. An increasing number of civil-society-type organizations in India emerge out of public/private partnerships or more complicated amalgams of grassroots organizations, government bodies, and larger NGOs, in part reflecting the particular institutional effects of economic reforms across the country. The state has often withdrawn from its commitment to providing health, educational, and other services to its population, and increasingly invites or allows the private sector to take up the slack. For example, government schools in India are in practice run by a collectivity of social actors, including government teachers, instructors appointed by the state to assist with teaching through development programmes, and oversight committees partly comprised of local citizens.

Likewise, the scale of civil society organizations and networks is changing radically. New technologies—most notably mobile phones and the internet—offer a means of knitting together interests across space in ways unimaginable even two decades ago. Partly reflecting these trends, international bodies have become much more active in intervening in the civic life of India, creating new opportunities but also new dangers for local NGOs and activists. For example, the International Dalit Solidarity Network, a civil society group putatively representing the interests of Dalits in India and abroad, has been accused of serving only elite sections of Dalit society and ignoring issues such as land rights that are at the forefront of Dalits' minds on the ground. In a more positive vein, Arjun Appadurai has argued that transnational organizations can improve poor people's access to key services, thus constituting a type of global civil society.

• See also *Dalit, democracy, politics, state*

Class

Raymond Williams devotes nine pages to 'class', the longest entry in his *Keywords*, and he starts his discussion by saying that it is 'an obviously difficult word, both in its range of meanings and in its complexity in that particular meaning where it describes a social division'. Deriving from a Latin root—a word referring to a group of Roman citizens distinguished on the basis of property—the word entered the English language in the sixteenth century, and fairly soon took on the general meaning of a group or division (or 'a set of things having properties or attributes in common'). It was applied to people as well, but other words such as 'order', 'rank', 'estate', and 'degree' all remained more common descriptors of social divisions into the nineteenth century. These terms, however, carry the strong connotation that the distinctions to which they refer are determined by birth, whereas class 'as a word that would supersede [such] older names for social divisions relates to increasing consciousness that social position is made rather than merely inherited' (Williams). This consciousness developed in the period of the reordering of English society in the context of the industrial revolution between about 1770 and 1840. Distinctions such as 'lower class', 'middle class', 'upper class', and 'working class' all came into use in this period and were common terms by the mid-nineteenth century. They then came to have particular meanings in Marx's analysis of capitalism—though Marx himself actually wrote rather little about the concept of 'class'—and later, in sociology from the early twentieth century, through the work of Max Weber (1864–1920). A critical difference in the meanings of class in reference to social divisions is that of whether it is used only descriptively, or—as it is in Marx's work—to refer rather to a social process.

The sociological concept of class, whether derived from Marx or from Weber, refers to the significance of economic endowments—whether material means of production or possession of particular skills ('human capital'), cultural traits (sometimes referred to as 'symbolic capital'), or social connections (sometimes described as 'social capital') that influence a person's power in the markets for labour or for money—for the differences in the sets of opportunities and constraints that confront all human beings as they 'make out' through their lives. Different groups of people broadly share particular combinations of opportunity and constraint according to their positions in the structures of production and distribution through which societies are reproduced; and their relationships are substantially determined by these differences in class position. This is the class structure, or what Marx refers to as 'class-in-itself'. It is another question as to whether the groups of people defined by the class structure actually think of themselves in these terms and are aware of and act upon their commonalities. This is the dimension of *class consciousness*, or of 'class-for-itself' as Marx defines it. It is possible then to examine the historical social processes of *class formation*—

those that bring about collective organization among people who broadly share class positions—and of *class struggle*, when classes pursue their interests in opposition to those of others. A Marxian interpretation of history finds in these processes the essential dynamics of societal change over time, while in the Weberian view class is only one dimension of power relationships (the others being 'status' or honour, and 'party') and it is envisaged that change comes about as a result of complex interactions among the different dimensions of power.

The historian Christopher Bayly has shown that by the 1840s in India there was a radical intelligentsia, amongst whom there developed a 'sociological imagination' (he uses the term of the American sociologist C. Wright Mills). These radicals—many of them students of a remarkable Eurasian radical, Henry Derozio (1809–31), who taught at the Hindu College in Calcutta, and who was commemorated in a stamp issued by the Indian Postal Service in 2009—knew little, Bayly says, of the European Marxist tradition that was emerging at the time. They rather discovered for themselves 'class and positional social subordination' through their observations of the effects of landlordism and rack-renting in the Indian countryside, and of the fate of coolie labour exported from India as the international economy developed in the mid-nineteenth century. The radicals developed a critical sociology of their own, recognizing that India was divided by class as well as by caste, and presaging 'the emergence of a powerful and enduring Indian left, at odds with the very social order from which its members had emerged'.

The colonial government of India, meanwhile, was also greatly concerned to classify the population over which it ruled, but it sought to do so—most clearly in the decennial census, first attempted in 1871—through the categories of caste, in particular, and also occupation. The word 'class' was used principally in the label 'backward classes', applied from the mid-nineteenth century onwards to adivasis and low-caste people in general, and then in the term 'depressed classes', which came into use in the 1920s to distinguish 'untouchables' from others on the list of 'backward classes'. This use largely ceased with the Government of India Act of 1935, which introduced the idea of drawing up a 'schedule' of social groups that should benefit from affirmative action, and gave birth to the categories of Scheduled Castes and Scheduled Tribes. Later, after Independence, the Government of India started to extend the principle of affirmative action to other groups, described as 'Other Backward Classes' (OBCs) (*see* reservations). In these cases 'class' is used with reference to a category of people presumed to have the same social status.

The Marxian, relational concept of class was brought into analysis and reflection upon Indian society early in the twentieth century, principally by communists, such as E. M. S. Namboodiripad (1909–98) who was for a long time an influential communist leader in Kerala. The mainstream of Indian sociology, however, focused on caste, arguing that this is the way most Indians themselves regard the principal divisions in their society. For some time scholars opposed a 'class view' of Indian society to the 'caste view'. Thus the few sociologists influenced by Marxian ideas were concerned with analysis of class formation in Indian rural society, and with distinguishing between 'rich', 'middle', and 'poor' peasants, while most researchers were interested much more in caste relations. The possibility that class relations might be experienced in terms of caste, for example when employers such as larger landowners come mainly from one caste group, and labourers largely from another, lower-caste group, was hardly considered.

In practice, caste solidarities can contribute to the development of class consciousness and class mobilization, where there is a near identity between caste and class in particular contexts, or cut across them where workers, whether in the rural economy or in cities, are drawn as they often are from different groups. The possibilities of working class political mobilization are also cut across by the important distinction between the small share of the Indian labour force that is in formal employment, enjoying the benefit of various protections under labour law, and extensively organized in trades unions, and the great majority of informally employed workers, who do not enjoy protection and who, when they are unionized, mobilize rather against the state, in agitating for welfare benefits, than against their employers. The extent to which the working class in India has been mobilized politically as a 'class-for-itself' (in Marxian terms) has been severely constrained, outside a few centres such as Mumbai and Kolkata, at some times, and few people refer to the language of 'class'. It is nevertheless evident that many people on the ground do have a sense of themselves as belonging to a particular economic 'stratum' within society, as most clearly expressed in the idea of being 'poor' ('*garib*' in Hindi).

India's upper or dominant classes, too, are divided, as the capitalist class, or 'big bourgeoisie', and the commercial cultivators or landlords and rich peasants have competed over access to resources from the state. Now an increasing share of the population of India is considered to be middle class, and shows signs of greater consciousness of common class interest, and of having the ability to pursue it politically, certainly than the working classes of the country. Many people in India, including prosperous sections of the rural population and middling sorts in urban areas, are using the term 'middle class' to refer to their position.

• See also *bourgeois, capitalism, communism, labour, land, peasant, socialism*

Colonialism

Deriving from a Latin word, by the sixteenth century the word 'colony' in English had come to have the meaning of 'a body of people who settle in a new locality, forming a community subject to or connected with their parent state' (*OED*). The United States of America, of course, has its origins in the thirteen such colonies of settlement that eventually fought to break away from their subjection to their 'parent state'. But the term 'colony' also came to be used more broadly to refer to those territories—literally 'overseas'—over which European maritime powers exercised rule. India was never a 'colony' in the sense of a settlement—and indeed remarkably few British people ever actually settled there on a permanent basis. The numbers of Britons in India, in relation to the numbers of Indians, were always remarkably small, even by comparison with those of the citizens of other European powers in some of their Asian colonies. By the later nineteenth century, 'colonialism' was used to refer to 'the colonial system or principle', or in other words it referred to the ways in which Britain and other imperial powers exercised their rule and for what purposes. As the *OED* goes on to note, the term has come often to be used 'in the derogatory sense of an alleged policy of exploitation of backward or weak peoples by a large power'. This is certainly very often how it is used and understood in India.

Modern India has been influenced in many ways by colonialism, and it remains a major focus of enquiry and debate among scholars. The economic nationalists, including Dadabhai Naoroji (1825–1917), who is considered to have been one of the founders of the Indian National Congress, argued forcefully well before the end of the nineteenth century that British colonial rule had impoverished India for the benefit of Britain. In the language of later theorists, colonialism had *underdeveloped* India, and for all the systematic efforts of a good many economists and economic historians—starting, in some sense, with Marx in the 1850s—to prove the benefits of colonial rule, there remain very powerful arguments in support of the nationalist view. It is important, however, also to recognize the role of many powerful Indians in the economic structures of colonialism, and that there were Indian capitalists who benefited very significantly from them—though this is not to support the colonialists' fiction that their rule over India was for the good of Indians. On the other hand, there is also an important argument which holds that British colonial rule created modern economic institutions in India which have together supplied the framework for the country's recent successful economic growth.

There is a complementary debate about the social impact of colonialism. Did it bring about fundamental change in Indian society—the 'first social revolution' to have taken place in India as Marx anticipated? Or rather was there continuity between the precolonial, colonial, and postcolonial periods? Did colonialism actually consolidate and entrench existing structures of power and domination? There is evidence and argument on both sides. There is no doubt that colonial rule often did depend on local powerholders, and so consolidated their positions, but the view expressed by the historian Eric Stokes, that 'The modernizing impulse [of the colonial government in the mid-nineteenth century] was not the less real or significant because society in the Guntur district [for example] still appeared to be quite untouched by the transfer of power to British hands', is one that is widely accepted. And while it is not accurate to think of democracy and ideas of universal citizenship as being the 'gift' of the colonial power to India, it is important to recognize the influence of colonial institutions in their establishment in independent India.

More recent historical scholarship on India, forming a significant part of the current of postcolonial studies which examine and respond to the cultural legacies of colonialism, has focused on the colonial construction of knowledge about India, and on the uses of that knowledge in colonial governmentality. Scholarship on India actually anticipated much of the influential argument of Edward Said about what he called 'Orientalism'—about how Europeans constructed, or understood, the Orient, and how they used this knowledge as an instrument of rule. The British, as the historian Nicholas Dirks puts it, defined to their own satisfaction what they thought to be Indian rules and customs, and Indians then had to conform to these ideas. Colonial government worked through a 'rule of difference': Indians were held to be in some fundamental ways different from Europeans, and for this reason had remained outside the path of progress that had been achieved in the West. Colonial rule was then sought to be legitimated as being the means whereby India was to become 'modern'. The work of Dirks, and earlier of his teacher Bernard Cohn, has produced convincing evidence and argument about the ways in which colonial rule helped to create what was thought of as 'tradition'. It led, for example, to the idea that 'Hinduism' is a distinct and coherent 'religion', and to its construction as 'a systematic . . . all-embracing religious identity', when it seems clear that there were in fact a number of very distinct religious traditions in Hindu India. And while Dirks most certainly does not argue that British rule invented caste, he offers a powerful case in support of the view that the ways in which the British used their understandings of caste in government substantially created 'the caste system' as it appeared as a focus for study by anthropologists in the middle and later twentieth century. He argues, for example, that 'The idea that varna—the classification of all castes into four hierarchical orders with the Brahmin on top—could conceivably organize the social identities and relations of all Indians . . . was only developed under the peculiar circumstances of British rule.' According to this school of thought, therefore, colonialism did bring about a great deal of social and political change, but it did not modernize India in the way that both some scholars and some colonial officials anticipated.

In sum, colonialism in India may be seen as a form of rule in which the exercise of power depended substantially upon constructions of difference, both between colonial rulers and the ruled, and among the latter. It brought about a great deal of change, but not invariably in such a way as to bring what Westerners construed as modernity to India. Colonialism was in many ways a deeply conservative force.

• See also *caste, history, modern, tradition*

Commons

Raymond Williams says of the word 'common' that it has 'an extraordinary range of meaning in English'. Underlying many of its uses, however, is the sense of 'generality'; and one of its specific meanings is that of something 'belonging to the community at large [or "in general"], or to a [particular] community . . .' (*OED*). One of the key understandings of the related word 'commons' in English is that of natural resources—and cultural resources, too, which have become increasingly significant—to which all the members of a society, or the members of a particular group of people or community, have rights of access. This use of the word, which is distinct from the meaning 'common people', or the third estate in the English and some other political systems (as in the House of Commons, the lower house of parliament), is of particular significance in regard to land use and government in India.

The original idea of 'the commons' was probably that of an area of land, usually pasture or forest land, to which the members of a community had rights of access and use (by virtue of their membership in the community). Similarly, there might be common rights to fishing, or to water, or to other resources. Such resources have come to be labelled 'common property

resources' or 'common pool resources' (CPRs), as distinct from 'open access resources'—
those to which anyone and everyone has access. CPRs are seen as being the property of
particular communal groups. Such resources may, however, be subject to what is described
in a seminal article as 'the tragedy of the commons'—that is, to be subject to overuse and
consequently to degradation. Thus, many fisheries in different parts of the world have been
depleted by overfishing; or grazing lands are found to be over-exploited, to have ceased to be
of value, and perhaps to have been subject to desertification. One way of addressing 'the
tragedy of the commons' is by privatizing—so that individuals have an incentive to maintain
the resource; another is for the state to regulate their use (as has happened historically with
regard to India's forests). In either case the commons are made subject to enclosure, in the
case of land-based resources often marked physically by fencing. It has been recognized,
however, that there are also many instances of successful, sustainable management of CPRs
by communities, and it is argued that, for instance, community management of forests can
work much better than having them managed by state agencies alone. India now has some
systems of participatory community management of forests in place, and, in some cases at
least, these are reported as being effective.

The idea of 'the tragedy of the commons' is deeply rooted in classical theories of political
economy that influenced the colonial government of India. An important distinction—going
back, certainly, to the ideas of the philosopher John Locke—was made between waste, or
wasteland, and value-producing, productive land, and common land was generally equated
with the former. For Locke, and for later political economists, common land use was seen as
unproductive, and individual appropriation of land believed to be desirable, so that it might
be improved. These arguments justified the enclosure of common land in England, and the
same arguments were used to justify colonialism in the Americas—these judgements being
based on the criterion of 'the best possible use of the land'. In the colonies, 'common' uses of
land were seen as being part of what defined the 'savage', and privatization or enclosure as
part of the passage from the state of nature to civilization. In India an equation was made
between the peoples of the forest lands and the ways in which they used the forests, for slash-
and-burn, shifting cultivation, for pasture, hunting, and the collection of fruits and nuts. The
people were described as 'tribes', and regarded as being in a state of nature; their forms of
land use were regarded as wasteful. The Indian Forest Act of 1865 began the process of
restricting their uses of the forests, overruling their customary rights, in order to manage the
forests more productively. The state has in effect sought to make the areas that it defines as
'forest' subject to a form of enclosure, and to bring forest people into 'civilization'.

Latterly, the forests of eastern and central India have been subject to further 'enclosures' in
the interests of major infrastructural projects, and of Indian and foreign mining companies
and steel manufacturers. Resistance to their dispossession on the part of tribal people plays a
part in fuelling the Naxalite/Maoist insurgency in these areas of the country, to which the
state has responded in some measure by the passage of a Forest Rights Act in 2006, which
provides for greater protection for those who have historically been forest-dwellers.

There is also a formal category of wasteland, referring to land classified as uncultivated or
uncultivable in the village land records, or in other words land that does not contribute to

government revenues arising from cultivation. These areas are part of the village commons, which may also include, for instance, trees and small areas of forest, fisheries, pasture, and water sources. In some cases the revenues from these resources were (and perhaps still are) the sources of common village funds, used for public purposes in the local community. Research has shown that such common property resources may make a significant contribution to the employment and income especially of poorer people, but also that they are declining everywhere and are often being subjected to different forms of enclosure.

• See also *environment, forests*

Communism

The meaning of communism in India has been a matter of contention more or less since the foundation of the Communist Party of India (CPI) in the 1920s (exactly when and where is debated). In its early years one of its founders, M. N. Roy, was critical of Lenin and then of Stalin for their unwillingness to grant the possibility that the communist parties of the colonial countries could have an independent role in anti-colonial revolutions. The Soviet leadership, influenced by the stage theory of history that holds that a bourgeois revolution must precede that of the working class, took the view that communists in the colonial countries should support bourgeois nationalists. Roy, however, thought there was a possibility of establishing communism before the working class was much developed, and Indian communists at first stayed outside the Congress—seen as a bourgeois party. They decided, however, on a change of tactics in the 1930s, when a number of communists joined hands with socialists in the Congress Socialist Party (CSP), with the objective of moving the Congress movement to the left. The CSP enjoyed considerable influence in the Congress towards the end of the 1930s.

The CPI supported the British war effort in the Second World War after the Nazi attack on the Soviet Union, believing that the struggle against fascism must take precedence over the fight for independence—and it was in this context that the party entered the political mainstream (becoming a legal entity in 1942). Thereafter, however, the party was riven by tensions between those amongst the leadership who thought that there could be a route to communism through participation in the parliamentary system, and others who wanted to adopt the line of armed struggle. There were bitter struggles within the party. For a time in the later 1940s the revolutionary line was pursued, and communists played a leading role in the struggle against the Indian state in the Telengana region of what subsequently became the state of Andhra Pradesh—a struggle that was eventually crushed by the Indian army.

After 1951 the CPI reverted to the parliamentary line, and became the second most important party in the country, though a long way behind the Indian National Congress in the 1950s. Yet the tensions within the party over the appropriate line for it to pursue did not go away, and—in the aftermath of the Sino-Soviet split—the party divided in 1964. Those who broke away to form the Communist Party of India (Marxist) (CPI(M)) stood out against support for the ('bourgeois nationalist') Congress while remaining within the parliamentary system. There was then a further split when a group broke away from the CPI(M) to pursue an armed insurrection against the state.

This group, known as the Naxalites, formed the Communist Party of India (Marxist–Leninist) in 1969. The lineal descendants of those militants—many of whom were killed by security forces—now lead a Maoist insurrection that affects, it is said by the Government of India, around a third of the districts in the country.

Indian communism has always been constrained by the general lack of a mass base, especially from among the rural working class, outside a few pockets. The notable exceptions to this general rule are the states of Kerala and West Bengal. The CPI won elections to the state assembly in Kerala in 1957—the first time that a communist party had won power through the ballot box anywhere in the world—and in this state in particular the CPI, and later the CPI(M), have been supported by mass movements of peasants, workers, and women, and have delivered higher levels of social welfare (or 'human development') than in any other major Indian state. The record of the CPI(M), as the core party in left front governments that ruled the state of West Bengal continuously from 1977 through to 2011, is more controversial, though here too the party has a positive record in regard to alleviating rural poverty.

Though the communist parties have never won much support nationally, outside their bastions in Kerala, West Bengal, and in the small north-eastern state of Tripura, they have at times played a critically important role as opposition parties, as they did in 2004–5, when they helped to ensure the passage of the National Rural Employment Guarantee Act. The CPI(M), for some time the more powerful of the leading parliamentary communist parties, remains staunchly anti-imperialist and is strongly critical of India's recent tilt in its foreign policy towards the United States.

• See also *class, constitution, equality, labour, politics, socialism*

Community

Raymond Williams argues that the range of meanings of this commonly used English word gives it considerable complexity. It became established in the fourteenth to seventeenth centuries with several uses that refer to actual social groups, and others that refer to a particular quality of relationships. One of the former uses, from the fifteenth century, is that of 'the body of people having common or equal rights or rank, as distinguished from the privileged classes; the commons; the commonalty'. *OED* describes this as now being obsolete, and yet it still reflects one of the contemporary senses of 'community', meaning a group of people that is fairly homogeneous, with an equality of rights and where status distinctions are held not to be significant. It conveys, too, ideas about the quality of social relationships, implying the existence of a sense of social obligation and mutual dependence, and of social solidarity.

From the seventeenth century onwards, Williams explains, a distinction started to be made between community and society, which became particularly important in the nineteenth century, in the context of urbanization and industrialization. It was thought that these social forces must often draw people away from more immediate close-knit relationships based in small localities into bigger, impersonal societies in the rapidly expanding cities. The title of one sociological classic, 'the loneliness of the crowd', suggests the distinction between living among large numbers of others in an atomized and individualistic society, and life in a community in which people know each other well, share many relationships, and are mutually dependent, and where there is a sense of social solidarity. 'Community' is a term often used to refer to experiments in alternative living, which set out to recreate what is believed to have been lost in modern societies. Whether or not the distinction between community and society accurately reflects reality—and there is empirical evidence to support this, but other evidence that falsifies it—the conception itself has become a very powerful idea. One influential idea of nationalism holds that 'the nation' is an 'imagined community'. The members of a nation cannot possibly know each other in the way that is supposed to be the case in a small, 'face-to-face' community, but nationalism is founded on the idea of such intimacy in the relationships between people.

The idea of community, with its connotations of mutuality and social solidarity, has been very important in India. The notion of 'the village community'—sometimes rendered in Hindi as the '*biradiri*' (literally 'brotherhood')—was significant in Gandhi's thought, and his conception of an independent India was that it should be a nation based on such solidarities, administered by their local councils, the panchayats. These ideas entered only very partially into the way the Indian state has been organized, but they have continued to influence some official perceptions and the ideas of some activists in civil society. Gandhi had also encouraged educated young people to go to work in the villages, for their own and the villagers' 'improvement', and this experience was one of the influences behind the Community Development Programme established by the Government of India in the 1950s. An important assumption made in the design of the programme was that 'village communities' across the country are fairly homogeneous, and that their members are ready to act collectively in the interests of all. In practice this assumption was often proven unjustified, as village elites took over the resources made available through the programme for their own private benefit. Still, the idea that Indian society is characterized by a strong sense of community, and that this is one of the more important ways in which the country, and other postcolonial Asian countries too, are distinguished from the West, remains important among some intellectuals. Partha Chatterjee, for example, once argued that 'in the new political societies of the East communities are some of the most active agents of political practice'.

There is another sense of the word 'community' that is of particular political significance in India (though it is not quite the sense that Chatterjee had in mind). This is the idea of 'the adherents of a religion considered in their totality', which was in use in English in the eighteenth century, and again has its equivalent in Hindi, where people sometimes refer to co-religionists as members of their 'biradiri'. In some cases people in India refer, rather euphemistically, to 'the members of a certain community' or 'members of our biradiri', which remains unnamed but is clearly, in the particular context, referring to either 'Hindus' or 'Muslims', or sometimes 'Christians', or perhaps the members of a particular caste group. This is the idea of community that informs the concept of communalism, which the *OED* tells us is 'originally and chiefly South Asian'. It means 'strong allegiance to one's own ethnic or religious group, rather than to a society or nation as a whole; religious factionalism, ethnocentrism. Also: the structuring of society or politics on the basis of this.' It was used in the latter sense in an article in the London *Times* in 1923, in the course of a discussion of the implications of separate electorates for Hindus and Muslims. It is used quite frequently in India today with reference to what is more generally described as 'ethnic conflict' or violence. Communalism, it is held, is conducive to conflict between social groups, though it is important to recognize that some instances of 'communal conflict', at least, have been the outcome of manipulations by influential people, and sometimes by criminals. The political scientist Paul Brass, on the basis of the study over many years of communal relations and of riots in the north Indian city of Meerut, has concluded that in such Indian cities there may be an 'institutionalised riot system', or in other words leaders and groups of people who have the potential quickly to turn a small incident into a violent confrontation.

• See also *Muslim, nation, panchayat, village*

Congress

'Congress' is the common shorthand for the name of India's leading political party, the Indian National Congress (INC). The party started out, in 1885, as an association originally set up at the instigation of, among others, a British former civil servant, Allan Octavian Hume, to lobby with the colonial government for the interests of mainly upper-caste and upper middle-class Indians, who were mostly lawyers and editors. The name comes from the fact that the association was brought together each year in a 'congress'—where the language spoken was usually English. Early in the twentieth century it became the first organized group seeking independence from colonial rule. It was Gandhi, however, who more than anyone else built the Congress into a mass movement, through the organizational work that he carried out at the beginning of the 1920s, opening it up to mass membership and encouraging the use of Indian languages—partly through the establishment of local and provincial Congress committees. Mass movement though it became, the top leadership of the Congress remained in the hands of a mainly high-caste, English-speaking professional elite, and the fears that were expressed by some non-Brahmins as early as 1889, when they published a paper proclaiming 'We do not want the National Congress because it does not represent the interests of the people', may well be thought to have been justified. By the 1930s, however, the local leadership of the Congress was increasingly taken over by larger landed proprietors, with the result that the socially progressive fraction of the top leadership, around Nehru, when in government in the 1950s, found itself unable to implement the more radical policies to which it had been committed, such as redistributive land reform. After Independence, the party became a political machine in which the links between locality and centre were welded by patronage.

The Congress and its national leaders enjoyed great authority in the early years of Independence, after 1947, and the party was absolutely dominant in national politics—until 1967 winning the great majority of seats in national and state-level elections, albeit with never more than 48 per cent of the popular vote nationally. In this period India had what was called by political scientists a 'dominant party system'. The country was not subject to one-party rule and 'dominance [by the Congress] coexisted with competition—but without a trace of alternation [of parties]'. Subsequently, however, the party was split in 1969 by Indira Gandhi, in the course of a struggle for power with older leaders, and since that time both its organization and internal democracy have broken down. The Congress became in effect a dynastic party, depending heavily on the charisma of the Nehru family. Indira Gandhi (prime minister from 1966 to 1977 and again from 1980 until her assassination in 1984) was Nehru's daughter. She was succeeded by her son Rajiv, who was prime minister from 1984 to 1989, and led the party until his own death at the hands of an assassin in 1991. Thereafter, although the party was led in government by P. V. Narasimha Rao between 1991 and 1996, party members increasingly looked for leadership to Rajiv's widow, Mrs Sonia Gandhi, and then to her son (and Nehru's great-grandson) Rahul Gandhi.

The Congress has been regarded, certainly by its members, as India's 'natural party of government', the only truly national party, standing somewhat to the left of centre, and commanding wide support across different social groups and classes—though often securing electoral victories because of particularly strong support from amongst Dalits and Muslims. It has been seen as the bastion of Indian secularism, though this reputation was badly dented by the actions of both Mrs Gandhi and then of Rajiv, who manipulated communal senti-ments in pursuit of electoral strength. Since the 1980s, the party has never succeeded in winning back the level of support that it enjoyed before, and it has had to manage coalitions with other parties in order to secure ruling majorities at the centre. Its reputation of being to the left of centre is challenged, too, because of its shift towards economic liberalism, and there has been very little difference in economic policy between the Congress and the principal opposition party, the Bharatiya Janata Party, since 1991. The Congress-led government that came to office in 2009 became mired in corruption scandals, and whatever remained of the authority that the party had held nationally, because of its historic role, was finally lost.

• See also *Gandhi, Nehru, politics*

(The) Constitution

The character of the independent state of India was established in the Constitution prom-ulgated on 26 November 1949. It was the outcome of prolonged debate among a mainly high-caste and English-educated elite, and drawn largely from the ranks of the Congress party, who were the members of the Constituent Assembly that met between December 1946 and 1949. As the Preamble to the Constitution now states, India is constituted as 'a SOVEREIGN SOCIALIST SECULAR DEMOCRATIC REPUBLIC', and, although the words 'secular' and 'socialist' were added by an amendment only in 1976, this phrase accurately reflects the intentions of a majority of those who drew up the Constitution. Their goals were to maintain the unity and integrity of the country (in the interests of which they were concerned to agree upon a form of secularism and upon a language policy, in a country with so many different languages, and to lay down principles for ways in which Indian federalism should work); to promote democracy; and to bring about social and economic reform directed at the establishment of an equitable society—'socialism', broadly understood—though with special treatment (affirmative action—*see* Dalit, reservations) for those who were considered to have been unjustly disadvantaged historically. The pillars of the constitutional design are democracy, federalism, secularism, and socialism.

The Constitution is, the writer Sunil Khilnani has said, 'interminably long', and it lays out in great detail the ways in which the different departments of government are to operate, and what their relations should be. It defines the responsibilities of central government and of state governments. The core of it, however, is in Part II, which defines Indian citizenship, Part III, which lays out 'Fundamental Rights'—essentially what are generally described as civil and political rights—and in Part IV, which sets out the 'Directive Principles of State Policy'. The latter, which unlike the Fundamental Rights are not justiciable, are statements of intent, concerned with economic and social rights. Part III is concerned with establishing rights that provide for universal citizenship, including equality before the law, 'prohibition of discrimination on grounds of religion, race, caste, sex or place of birth', and the abolition of the practices of untouchability; and rights to freedom, and to freedom of religion, while also protecting the cultural and educational rights of minorities. The Directive Principles in Part IV are said by one authority, Granville Austin, to be 'the conscience of the Constitution'. They commit the Indian state to promoting 'the welfare of the people'; to providing for rights to work and to education, and 'to public assistance in certain cases'; to achieving 'living wage etc., for workers'; to the 'promotion of educational and economic interests of Scheduled Castes, Scheduled Tribes [*see* adivasi, Dalit] and other weaker sections'; and they refer to the 'Duty of the State to raise the level of nutrition and the standard of living and to improve public health'.

The Constitution therefore sets out an almost impossibly ambitious set of objectives for the state, and there are, fairly clearly, tensions between the commitments that it makes to social and economic reform, and certain of the Fundamental Rights. Affirmative action in regard to admissions to educational institutions for certain sections of the population, for instance, was challenged through the courts at an early stage on the grounds that it represented 'discrimination on grounds of caste'. This particular instance of the more general tension in the Constitution between individual and group rights caused the government to enact the First Amendment, which provides that nothing in Part III should prevent the enactment of special laws for the educational and social advancement of backward classes. There are tensions between different articles regarding religious freedom and over what secularism should mean. Then, property rights that are guaranteed by the Constitution conflict with its broadly socialist objectives—this became a matter of contention when the government of the day sought to carry out land reforms. Dealing with such conflicts has led governments to seek to amend the Constitution—Nehru as prime minister, for example, was often impatient in his wish to change the Constitution in order to achieve reform—and these attempts have led, in turn, to conflict between the legislature and the judiciary.

For all these difficulties, and the wide (and possibly widening) gap that has obtained between the reforming intentions that are set out in the Constitution and the reality of what successive governments have achieved, it is generally considered that it has provided a foundation for political stability and the establishment of an open society. It has been an instrument of social change that has contributed to weakening the hold of caste values in Indian society. Universal citizenship is still constrained in practice, and, as some scholars maintain, the rights and freedoms that the Constitution lays out may only be meaningful for a relatively small fraction of society. Yet there is also reason to think that the values that are encapsulated in the Constitution have become a point of reference among very many people, even at the bottom of society, and that India's political culture bears its indelible marks.

The status of the Constitution in India's political culture is very different from that of the Constitution of the United States in that country. It is significant that, whereas the Constitution of India has by now been subject to more than a hundred amendments, the United States Constitution over its much longer life has been subject to only twenty-seven, and ten of these were passed in 1791 as the Bill of Rights. Governments of India have always been ready to change the Constitution according to perceptions of need and interest, or in other words to treat it as a 'living' document. And while there are Indian jurists who seek in their judgments to interpret the intention of those who drew up the Constitution, the idea of the 'Founders', and of their intentions, is much stronger in the United States. There is an influential body of opinion in the United States which holds to the principle that is now described as 'originalism'—the idea that judgments should be based on the original meaning or intent of the Constitution. Any such sentiment is much less pronounced in India.

• See also *citizenship, democracy, federalism, justice, reservations, secularism, socialism*

Consumerism

A first and perhaps primary meaning of consumerism is 'the protection or promotion of the interests of consumers', but it can also refer to 'the preoccupation of society with the acquisition of consumer goods' (*OED*), where 'consumer goods' refers mainly to non-essential, often branded, products such as televisions, refrigerators, and cars. The first definition is older, coming into use in the first two decades of the twentieth century in the West. The second definition only came into widespread use in the 1950s, with the USA's global economic hegemony resulting in the increased flow across the world of brands such as Levi jeans and Coca-Cola.

In 1986, the Government of India passed a Consumer Protection Act that gave consumers a right to safety, right to information, right to choose, right to be heard, right to redressal, and right to consumer education. This led to the establishment of consumer tribunals in different parts of India and fairly widespread use of public interest legislation to defend consumers' rights. But it is consumerism in its second sense—a 'preoccupation with the acquisition of consumer goods'—and the linked process of globalization that has been a much greater concern in recent years. Up until the mid-1980s in India, even wealthy urban households tended to rely on state-run television. The purchase of something as simple as a small motor scooter required weeks of negotiation and form-filling, and consumerism in the local market was often limited to the purchase of a small assortment of household products. But this situation changed in the mid-1980s, when Rajiv Gandhi began to move away from India's post-Independence policy of protectionism and import-substitution industrialization towards encouraging private-sector growth (see development). In 1991, the Indian Government made a more decisive move to open up Indian consumer markets to foreign brands. The past two decades have been a story of growing, indeed in some people's views 'rampant', consumerism in India. Economic growth and the emergence of a financially powerful elite in metropolitan India have partly powered this trend. An Indian 'new middle class' has emerged which defines itself in large part by reference to its purchasing power and consumer choices. At the same time, corporate efforts at expanding distribution networks and producing smaller packaging have opened up the enormous rural market in India. Soap, TVs, fans, wristwatches, shaving blades, toothbrushes, and mobile phone credit are among the most significant non-food items being sold, in terms of value. Simultaneously, a decline in subsistence agriculture in some areas has resulted in increased consumption of store-bought food. The rapid rise of privatized health and education markets are also forms of consumerism.

The social and material implications of these transformations are profound. Consumerism has created new forms of social stratification and a new medium for the expression of caste and class inequalities. Consumerism has also transformed intimate aspects of the human experience in India including sex, via the spread of contraceptive devices, and marriage, especially through the practice of dowry. Likewise, the physical landscape of India has changed substantially through the erection of signboards advertising brands, the construction of shopping malls, and the rapid effective 'urbanization' of villages, many of which have come to resemble small towns.

For some economists, the spending power of Indian citizens is a major sign of strength and acted as a bulwark against economic recession in the period between 2007 and 2010. But for many others in India, consumerism is a dirty word. There is a political critique from among those representing Hindu nationalist parties or organizations, especially the Bharatiya Janata Party (BJP) (see Hindutva). In their view, consumerism is a form of cultural imperialism, corrosive of India's traditional (Hindu) cultures. Gandhians also pick up on the idea of cultural imperialism but with the emphasis on a disjuncture between a foreign consumer ethic and India's tradition of equity, frugality, and self-provisioning (swadeshi). Others focus more centrally on the environmental damage done to India by increased consumption, either with reference to the problem of waste or through focusing on the poor environmental records of major corporations producing branded products.

Champions of consumerism, such as ex-Procter and Gamble executive Gurcharan Das, say these arguments miss the point. According to Das, consumerism is absolutely essential for Indian development, and citizens cannot pick and choose which aspects of consumerism to allow into the country: 'you cannot have computer chips without potato chips', Das once pointed out. Likewise, Das claims that India's culture is resilient and polyglot—it can survive the overlay of new ideas. Advertisers and corporations have busily tried to communicate the same message, often incorporating into their campaigns a nostalgic appeal to tradition, Hinduism, Gandhi, or India's natural environment—even critiques of consumerism have been commoditized.

• See also *development, media, middle class, neo-liberal*

Corruption

Corruption (*bhrashtechar* in Hindi) is defined in many social science textbooks as 'the abuse of public office for private gain'. In India it refers to a much broader range of practices and ideas, including the nefarious practices of citizens and business. It is also a term that constantly wriggles free of simple definition because what people regard as 'acceptable practice'—and therefore what they regard as 'corruption'—changes as you move around India, according to the person you ask, and through time. Thus, for example, a person bribing a guard to get a better berth on a train might be considered corrupt by one individual and not by another, and the person who regarded it as corrupt might think so today but not ten years later.

It is no surprise that corruption is widely discussed in India. The abuse of public office for private gain is endemic in the country. It manifests itself when huge scams come to light, for example when it emerged that state officials had appropriated money in the marketing of bandwidth for second-generation mobile phones—the notorious '2G scam'. Corruption is also evident at the everyday level, where government bureaucrats demand or expect payment for providing services that they should offer free of charge; where government officials or private contractors embezzle the money earmarked for development projects; or where a police officer excuses a motorist from paying a large traffic fine in return for being given a small tip—known euphemistically as 'money for water and tea'. In these examples, a portion of the money collected 'on the ground' is passed up through government hierarchies—for example, from police constables to police inspectors to superintendents of police—and on up to politicians, who use the funds in part to pay off supporters and finance elections (*see* criminal). A normal 'income' becomes unofficially attached to each post in this hierarchy, and superiors will expect inferior officers to pass on a fixed-in-advance portion at regular intervals. In this system, it is very difficult to remain 'straight', and a popular joke in India concerns the degree to which even the vigilance officers appointed to stem corruption have themselves become corrupt.

People debate everyday corruption vociferously in India. Everyday systems of corruption systematically disadvantage marginalized sections of society, partly for the simple reason that the poor lack money and partly because transactions within this system are never straightforwardly about money but also about respect and reputation. A poor, low-caste man with no 'connections' in a government office will pay more, say, for a driving licence than will a rich man with a friend in high office (although this may not always be the case and the rich may sometimes be tapped for more money, for example in the case of a traffic offence). Corruption is therefore partly a system through which the powerful mark, reproduce, and extend their social advantage.

Corruption carries heavy moral overtones. By labelling an action 'corrupt'—using the English word or an Indian language equivalent—people stake out what they find acceptable and unacceptable about the everyday practice of state representatives and others. Citizens may regard it as appropriate for a police officer to assist a relative in getting a post cleaning the police station, but they may criticize as 'corrupt' a fellow officer who makes money by hiring out a police vehicle for weddings. Because corruption can refer to many different things at the same time—from embezzling funds meant for school scholarships to taking a tip to allow someone to cremate a relative's body on a favoured spot by the river—the word serves as a type of discursive thread connecting disparate public concerns together. By going out on the street against 'corruption', citizens can simultaneously express their anger at the obstructive clerk in the local electricity office, the teacher who demands a bribe before he will give a class, and the high-level officers making money out of large scams.

Some social scientists have argued that the anger internationally over Indian corruption is simply the function of Western ideas being inappropriately imposed on a place where things happen differently. But people in India across the social spectrum increasingly regard corruption as morally wrong. The Anna Hazare movement active in India in 2011 and 2012 has been especially important in channelling this public anger, and in so doing politicizing corruption. Hazare has called on the Indian Government to introduce a *Lokpal*—a type of public ombudsman committee made up of reputed notables with the legal power to investigate charges of corruption against government. But beyond these large movements, and probably more important than them, there have been numerous smaller-scale efforts at ensuring that corruption becomes a matter of pressing political debate. This includes village-level and regional movements, legal battles involving people's use of public interest legislation, NGO- and government-led efforts at reform (some of them involving Western academics), and piecemeal efforts by individuals to bring 'corrupt' officials to book—especially common since the passing of the Right to Information Act in 2005, which allows citizens to request information on almost any aspect of government functioning. These various efforts have been partially successful in terms of reducing corruption, and they have been more successful in changing the public mood, providing an outlet both for India's new middle class, frustrated by state inefficiencies, and for the poor, who regularly lose out as a result of corruption.

Whether corruption will continue to be at the forefront of political debates in the future is unclear. There are some areas where corruption seems to be on the wane, for example in elections, where vote rigging and the capture of electoral booths is much less common than it was in the 1960s, and also in recruitment to some government jobs. But in equal measure the growth of the Indian economy and the increase in government spending on development projects have created new niches for brokerage and corruption, and increased the overall quantity of money being made. The common mismatch in contemporary India between people's ambitions and opportunities has led to a new pragmatism in some sections of society and new vocabularies of corruption. Many young people in India have started to make a distinction between 'corruption', the ordinary system of kickbacks and bribes, and 'fraud', where an official takes a bribe and still does not act, or comes up with some outrageous new practice that is not part of the moral system of corruption. This point reminds us that corruption can also be about honesty: keeping to the rules of a shadow system of practice may in certain situations be a 'lesser evil' and not as bad as 'fraud'.

• See also *caste, criminal, democracy, patronage*

Cricket

Cricket has its origins in England, and was played in India before the end of the eighteenth century. It was not until about the middle of the nineteenth century, however, that Indians themselves began to play it. Interest was partly stimulated by some of the Indian princes, who fought out struggles for status through their patronage of the game, bringing together teams that crossed lines of caste and class; cricket also became well established in the colonial cities, where it was one symbol of modernity. Since that time, the game has assumed great significance in India. An influential Indian intellectual, Ashis Nandy, has said that 'Cricket is a religion in South Asia'—a remark that reflects, in part, the way the game became a vehicle for nationalism. Playing cricket well was a way in which Indians could prove themselves and their masculinity in relation to the colonial power—even if this involved a tension between whether this meant, in a sense, 'becoming British', or rather asserting 'Indianness'.

Later, after Independence, when Indians seem often to have felt their country to be of marginal significance internationally, cricket became the most important way they could aspire to become world leaders—as indeed they have. Indian teams have at times been the best in the world, and the country is now emphatically the centre of world cricket. Indian cricketers are national heroes in a way that is true nowhere else in the world, even in the other South Asian countries, with the possible exception of Sri Lanka—and the game is a particularly important arena in which the relations between Indians and Pakistanis, as well as those between their nation states, are worked out. For these reasons, among others, as Ashis Nandy has also said, 'Cricket is an Indian game accidentally discovered by the English.'

If at first the game involved players from across castes and classes, it became for a time in the twentieth century rather an elite sport. Latterly, however, it has come to have a mass following, in rural as well as in urban India, and the images of the leading players are seen everywhere, especially in advertising. The commercialization of cricket in India has transformed the sport internationally—towards shorter and more immediately exciting forms—reflecting the country's changing economic values and the elevation of competition, efficiency, and productivity, as well as showing up the blight of corruption. The Indian Premier League (IPL), which began in 2008 with some of the world's best players representing city-based franchises owned by India's rich and famous, is the latest example of the extreme commercialization of cricket. By 2010, a consultancy firm pegged the value of the IPL at US$4.13 billion. The commercialization of cricket has come at a price, however, with the IPL being a magnet for controversy, the latest being a betting scandal in 2013. The historian and writer on cricket, Ramachandra Guha, has described the IPL as 'representative of the worst sides of Indian capitalism and society'.

• See also *consumerism, media, middle class, nation*

Criminal

The term 'criminal' has a particular colonial history in India. British colonialists identified specific tribal populations—such as the Kallars in Tamil Nadu, Maghyar Doms in Bihar, and the Kunjurs in Bundelkund—as potentially dangerous threats to the social order. Through a series of pieces of legislation covered under the heading of the Criminal Tribes Act (1871), the British imagined crime to be the hereditary occupation of these groups. Underpinned by the science of anthropometry, the British set about recording the habits of the so-called criminal tribes. The label of criminality became an important mechanism through which colonialists managed populations in areas of India that were difficult to administer.

It is hard to grasp the full import of what it meant to be labelled 'criminal'. Members of the criminal tribes could be searched and arrested without warrant and had to report weekly to police stations. They were also subject to strong-arm efforts at pacification and 'civilization'. By 1947, there were 13 million people belonging to 127 communities that were marked as criminal, and they were not freed of this label until 1952. Anthropologists have charted the colonial and postcolonial suffering of those thus identified, highlighting how they sometimes absorbed and sometimes fought back against the stigma of criminality. Members of the former criminal tribes have often suffered from long-term poverty and exclusion from education and secure salaried work.

'Crime' in the *OED* refers to 'an action or omission that constitutes an offence and is punishable by law'. There seem to be two different visions of criminality embedded in this definition that might need to be teased apart in the Indian context. First, criminality may be defined solely in relation to legality—crime is simply the contravention of the law. Second, criminality may be a larger cultural category referring to action that constitutes a moral 'offence'.

Several prominent commentators have suggested that the very idea of 'law' in India is misplaced, and therefore that those who defy the law may not be 'criminals' in the second, moral sense of this word. According to this view, Indian citizens evaluate conduct not on the basis of abstract rules, but through reference to the context in which an action takes place. Driving through a red traffic light may be 'criminal' in the narrow legalistic sense, but is widely held as acceptable if the conditions are right—if there is no traffic coming the other way. Some commentators likewise argue that in India what determines whether an act is 'criminal' is not its relationship to the law but the degree to which it accords with moral ideas of community. A government official who makes a lot of money through corruption but spends this money on his wider family and on local temple construction may not be regarded as 'criminal', even though his conduct contravenes legal norms.

Another argument associated with Partha Chatterjee is that action that is 'criminal' in the sense of illegal may actually be constitutive of how democracy works in India. Poor people lack the money, time, and know-how to form into legal civil society organizations or pursue their objectives through lengthy legal channels. Instead, they make ad hoc efforts to persuade government to act in their interests, often through illegal methods, such as violence, bribes, or blackmail. Chatterjee argues that this murky world of everyday deal-making is part and parcel of how politics works: criminality and democracy may go hand in hand.

Notwithstanding these arguments, there are good reasons to suspect that the poor and lower middle classes in India have absorbed liberal democratic legal norms and that people's perceptions of criminality in its legal sense and criminality in the moral sense are often quite closely aligned. Indian citizens typically value the law, seek legal redress after a crime, and cherish the fact that they live in a place where the law offers some protection. Popular use of public interest legislation and the Right to Information Act (2005) demonstrates this point, as does the number of movements that appeal to Indian legal norms in an effort to achieve their demands. Likewise, most of the poor in India regard the illegal activities of powerful members of society as morally indefensible. They regard venal public officials and exploitative landlords as 'criminals'.

One of the most pressing subjects of public concern is that of the criminalization of politics in India and the wider issue of elite criminality. More than a fifth of the members of the Indian Lok Sabha face criminal charges, including murder, and as of February 2012, 139 out of 404 legislators in the Uttar Pradesh Assembly were awaiting trial. It should be noted, however, that it is not too difficult to get people charged with a crime, and that it is for this reason that there are not stronger rules about the eligibility for office of those with criminal charges standing against them. Still, many even senior politicians use crime as a means to accumulate personal incomes that they then use to fund election campaigns. Even where politicians have no direct involvement in crime, they are frequently part of dense networks of social relationships that include professional criminals. The commonplace notion of a criminal as in some sense marginal to society does not fit with the contemporary Indian scene.

• See also **civil society, community, corruption, justice, politics**

Culture

It was fascination with the word 'culture' that partly spurred Raymond Williams to write his original book, *Keywords*. Williams argued that culture as it was discussed in the sixteenth and seventeenth centuries in Britain referred to the act of tending or nurturing. In the eighteenth and nineteenth centuries this sense of cultivation was applied to human development: culture became associated with the growth and further progress of the human race. Williams charts two further shifts: first, a move in Europe in the late nineteenth and twentieth centuries to apply the term 'culture' to the specific customs, beliefs, and practices of people in a region, as in 'the culture of Italy' and, second, the move to associate 'culture' with various forms of art, including painting, literature, and high intellectual achievement. Williams is at pains to point out that these different meanings of culture—as the general process of (human) cultivation, the specific characteristics of a region, and high intellectual achievement—coexist; they did not neatly replace one another.

There are therefore multiple contradictions built into the term 'culture'—between the symbolic (culture as representation) and material (culture as manifest in sculpture, for example); between culture as high art and culture as everyday, ordinary life; and between culture as a 'noun of process', as Williams puts it, and culture as accumulated achievement. It is for all these reasons that culture is such a complicated word, and it is still more complex when viewed through the lens of a country as diverse and rapidly shifting as India.

Colonialism in India can be read as a conversation between two different definitions of culture. During the colonial period in India, anthropologists set out to map, catalogue, and describe the distinct 'cultures' of India, which they usually imagined as 'ancient' and 'exotic'. They did so secure in the knowledge that Indian practices were 'curios', markedly different from European culture. The particular normative value attached to Indian cultures varied, however, as Edward Said famously pointed out in his book, *Orientalism*. Colonialists sometimes romanticized Eastern cultures, which then came to serve as a critical commentary on the excesses and artificiality of Western high culture. More commonly, the British disparaged Indian cultures as a means to justify their rule and bolster their belief in the superior value of European intellectual achievement; India had 'culture'—a set of values, practices, and beliefs that were of anthropological interest—whereas the colonizing power (Britain) had 'culture' in the sense of fully realized human development (cultivation) and in the 'elite' sense of a set of valuable intellectual and artistic products that were the material realizations of that development.

During the postcolonial period, and especially in the 1960s and 1970s, anthropological approaches to India changed. Instead of imagining cultures frozen in time, scholars increasingly wrote about Indian social life as a product of history. Commentators also critiqued the idea that India is made up of a patchwork of different cultures with various distinctive 'traits'. There is nothing as simple as 'Indian culture', nor is it very often helpful to write of 'Gujarati culture' or 'Rajasthani culture'. The contemporary anthropological approach is instead to emphasize the fluid, fractured, and ambivalent nature of culture and to stress histories of contact and cross-fertilization—internationally and within India. At the extreme, the term culture is hardly used at all, so concerned are anthropologists not to generalize. A more moderate position is to recognize the impossibility of describing in any general way the customs, beliefs, and practices of an area or population but to recognize that in certain situations people's practices 'thicken' and take on regular features through time. In such situations it may be possible to speak of a culture of a set of students (college cultures), specific urban space (café cultures), or government bureaucracy (cultures of the state), for example. The best studies examine culture, in Williams's sense, as a 'noun of process' and tack between consideration of the symbolic and material dimensions of cultural practice. Even in these cases, however, anthropologists tend to be cautious, hedging any assertion to have identified a distinctive culture with references to the ambivalences and variations within populations. The irreducible complexities and idiosyncrasies of everyday life in India are indeed a strong emerging theme in contemporary anthropology, travel writing, film, and the arts.

At the very moment at which culture has become unfashionable in the seminar rooms of Indian universities, however, people in India are using the idea of 'culture' to define their own goals and to pursue political ends. Hindu nationalist forces in India have worked hard, especially since the 1980s, to develop a politically motivated theory of culture founded on the notion of India as a place fundamentally Hindu in its customs and in some sense threatened by outside forces (Islam and/or the West). This sense of a culture under siege then provides the grounds for a Hindu nationalist project manifest, for example, in the reconstruction of temples and rewriting of school curricula to reflect a glorified Hindu past. At the same time, at smaller scales, regional movements have made great play of their distinctive 'cultures', as have farmers' movements and people seeking compensatory discrimination from the state on the basis of their caste or indigenous status. At a still smaller scale, people often refer to their 'caste culture' as a basis for rationalizing endogamous marriage. It is also common for people to refer to the specific 'culture' of their village, town, or city. In these everyday discourses, people may use the English term 'culture' or else various local language equivalents, such as *sanskriti* in Hindi.

The notion of high culture—culture in something like its first sense—is also significant in India. In the common absence of opportunities for people to express a sense of social distinction through exercising their purchasing power, claims to embody 'high culture' provide a useful additional means of marking social mobility. 'Culture' is a type of 'capital' separating the relatively rich from the relatively poor. India's middle classes, for example, trade in part on their superior educational qualifications, consumerism, and taste—all dimensions of what the sociologist Pierre Bourdieu termed 'cultural capital'—and various cultural intermediaries have emerged to cater for urban and rural populations keen to acquire 'culture' and 'civilization', including educational entrepreneurs, beauty specialists, and the legion of lifestyle and spiritual gurus.

It is difficult to generalize about the precise content and meaning of high culture in contemporary India. Formal education is often key, and in many parts of rural and urban India schooling and culture are synonymous. Likewise, people often equate culture with city life, such that the urban and the urbane are intimately intertwined. Assertions of one's cultured status may incorporate elements of the cultural paraphernalia of the West; wearing jeans may be a means for young people to mark their 'culture', for example. But it is also clear that 'high culture' in India is imagined differently in different parts of the country, and in some places and at certain times education, the urban, and Western may not be straightforwardly equated with cultural superiority. Certainly normative understandings of what constitutes high culture have moved very far beyond the notion popular in early twentieth-century Britain of European art as cultural beacon.

• See also *development, middle class, modern*

Dalit

'*Dalit*' means literally 'broken' or 'oppressed' in Sanskrit, and usually refers to former untouchables in India's caste system, who were associated with occupations that caste Hindus regarded as polluting, such as leatherwork, drumming, and the removal of human waste. Dalits constitute about a sixth of India's population (roughly 180 million). The term is commonly said to have originated with Jyoti Rao Phule (1827–90), a low-caste activist in western India in the late nineteenth century. Dalit is an umbrella term, and in many areas jati (caste) identity is more important than the notion of being Dalit. Moreover, 'Dalit' has particular associations with political struggle. Activists and politicians among the ex-untouchables are often more likely to use the phrase than are others. In some areas, ex-untouchables refer to themselves as 'SC' ('Scheduled Caste')—a legal term created by the British in the 1930s. Dalits tend to regard the label '*Harijan*' ('children of god'), a phrase coined by Mahatma Gandhi, as patronizing, but this is not always the case, and some ex-untouchables still identify with this term.

Dalits have benefited from government reservations. Just over 17 per cent of government jobs are reserved for SCs in India today, and they also receive positive discrimination in educational institutions. A thin upper stratum of Dalits have joined India's new middle class. But Dalits remain economically and socially disadvantaged in contemporary India—caste and class overlap to a very significant extent. They are more likely to be illiterate, more likely than others to be employed in informal, poorly paid work, and more likely to die young from preventable illnesses than most other sections of the Indian population—with the exception of Scheduled Tribes (adivasis) and possibly also Muslims and some migrant communities. Dalit women are considerably worse off than men, and some Dalit jatis are in a much poorer position than are others.

Continued caste discrimination compounds Dalit subordination. Very large numbers of Dalits continue to be excluded from worshipping in temples and some are forced to stand in front of people from higher castes. 'Dalit atrocities'—murder, rape, and other forms of violence—remain rife, in spite of decades of legislation and the enactment of a Scheduled Castes and Scheduled Tribes Prevention of Atrocities Act (POA) in 1989. Discrimination also occurs in modern settings, such as cinemas, private corporations, and in the sphere of contemporary marriage. It is telling that some provincial universities continue to have separate hostels for Dalit castes.

Dalit is a term with a particular political resonance. Dalit mobilization can be traced to nineteenth-century South India and became more pronounced in many southern states from the 1970s onwards, for example in the form of the Dalit Panthers, active in the 1970s in

Mumbai, and the Dalit Panther *Iyakkam* in Tamil Nadu in the 1990s and 2000s. Dalit assertion has also spread to the North, as manifest in the emergence of the Bahujan Samaj Party (BSP) in Uttar Pradesh (UP). The BSP has held power five times in UP since 1995 and made explicit attempts to raise Dalits' standing in society, through implementing the POA, inducting Dalits into the bureaucracy, and constructing statues and other monuments in honour of Dalit heroes. These political dynamics have had notable effects on low castes' livelihoods, particularly for specific jatis among Dalits well represented within the BSP. But more important than any economic transformation has been the recent politicization of caste that has followed on from the rise of the BSP. Dalits have acquired a new political confidence, and an increasing number of ex-untouchables have come to imagine themselves as 'Dalit' and deploy this term in describing their relationship to the state. And yet political parties have not transformed Dalits' life prospects. This is partly because parties claiming to represent 'Dalits' in the South and North tend to cater only for specific jatis among ex-untouchables, and partly because Dalit parties have diluted their radical agenda once in power: for example, the BSP has formed alliances with higher castes.

Dalit politics is associated with the paradox—one not lost on many Dalit activists—that at the very moment at which campaigners are trying to move beyond caste as a mode of categorizing populations, they are using their caste status as a basis for staking claims vis-à-vis the state. This has led some commentators, notably Partha Chatterjee, to argue that low castes in India do not tend to recognize an abstract form of citizenship but express their sense of rights only through reference to notions of caste and community. But other ethnographies of low caste political action suggest that Dalits understand both the language of universal rights and the moral claims they might make as members of an oppressed caste.

Dalit is also a term that has globalized. There is considerable debate about the degree to which Dalit disadvantage is analogous to the suffering experienced by blacks under apartheid in South Africa. Another issue concerns whether international NGOs claiming to represent Dalit interests are guilty of projecting their own preoccupations onto a subordinated population whose real concerns—access to basic goods, and labour exploitation, for example—may not fit with the priorities of their foreign supporters. The questions of who precisely has the right to speak on behalf of Dalits and whether it is possible to frame a 'Dalit agenda' remain live. It may also be important to bear in mind that Dalits, unlike, say, African-Americans, are divided by language and by internal caste differences, and lack concentrations of population comparable with those of African-Americans in Chicago or Washington. There are very big obstacles to the creation of all-India solidarity.

• See also *caste, class, politics, reservations*

Democracy

Democracy is defined in the *OED* as 'control of an organization or group by the majority of its members' or, more broadly, 'the practice or principles of social equality'. Raymond Williams argues that democracy was associated in late medieval Britain with rule by the multitude. 'Democracy', as defined for example by Thomas Aquinas, was simply popular power: 'all had the right to rule and did actually rule'. In the US in the late eighteenth century a new distinction was made between what Bentham termed 'direct democracy'—rule by the people—and 'representative democracy': rule by elected officials, usually accompanied by the presumption of political equality between citizens. Whereas the former term amounted to 'democracy' during the sixteenth, seventeenth, and eighteenth centuries, the latter idea of representative democracy became widely current in the nineteenth and twentieth centuries. Williams nevertheless points out that the two principles of direct democracy and representative democracy continue to be promulgated in different parts of the world and may be in conflict, as where those in power place restrictions on free speech to preserve 'people's rule' or where those in representative democracies place restrictions on mass mobilization on the grounds that democracy has already been established by other means.

India—the world's largest democracy—provides a fascinating example of the success, albeit partial, of democracy in its representative, liberal sense. Reflecting a commitment to the adult franchise developed during the nationalist movement and the development of a system of representative government by the British colonial power, the Indian Constitution established India as a sovereign democratic republic. The Constitution defined the 'Fundamental Rights' of all citizens, including equality before the law, freedom of speech and association, personal liberty, and protection against exploitation.

That many of the democratic guarantees enshrined in the Constitution survived remains a major achievement of postcolonial India. India's success as a democracy can be measured in the continued vibrancy of elections, which remain free and fair for the most part; widespread participation in elections and electioneering; the existence of a robust civil service, at least at the upper levels; and the strengthening of many democratic institutions, such as the Supreme Court and Election Commission. It is also evident in people's widespread acceptance of the value of democracy and the positive connotations of the word 'democracy' (in English)—or Indian language equivalent terms such as '*loktantr*' in Hindi—in everyday conversation.

Weighed against such arguments must be the observation that the Indian Government has routinely rigged elections in Kashmir and has occasionally been guilty of human rights abuses. The increasing deployment of paramilitary units to discipline civilian populations, arrogation of powers by India's Supreme Court, the continued power of political dynasties, criminalization of politics, rampant corruption at all levels of the state, and the lack more generally of intra-party democracy in India—all speak to a democratic deficit in India.

But the achievements of India's democracy are nevertheless notable. Democracy in India has arguably prevented widespread human rights abuses and large-scale famine. Elections occur regularly, democratic institutions are strong, people are usually free to protest, and civil rights are guaranteed. The media are lively and social movements are tolerated by the state. The masses feel more involved in politics and are articulating their own understanding of what democracy means. Broad-based rights movements have become a prominent feature of the political landscape. Read alongside studies of democracy's fragility in Latin America and the political experiences of its neighbours Pakistan and Sri Lanka, India's achievements are notable.

Yet India remains an unlikely and puzzling democracy. It is commonly held that a culture of equality, strong economic growth, and a vibrant civil society are required for representative democracy to flourish. India, in the first few decades after Independence, had a low economic growth rate. It was a highly unequal society and lacked a vibrant civil society. Pratap Bhanu Mehta explains this paradox with reference to the political sociology of colonial rule. The British placed power in the hands of a small coterie of rich leaders at the centre, while buying off local bigwigs. In this system, elected 'native' boards, comprised mainly of powerful sections of society, were responsible for multiple aspects of governance. Local elites, for example rich peasants in the countryside, became key intermediaries in patronage networks that effectively suppressed popular dissent. Relatively untroubled by threats to its power, the Congress was able to concentrate on consolidating formal democracy. Mehta argues that Indian elites in the postcolonial era have used this patronage system to strengthen democratic institutions. Large sections of Indian society, however, lack direct access to protective, judicial, and developmental arms of the state and must instead operate through patrons and brokers.

India may therefore be considered formally democratic but highly unequal at the local level. An extreme response to this observation would be to revive the debate about whether democracy is, in fact, the most desirable form of government for a developing country. Williams, after all, pointed out that until the nineteenth century democracy was 'a strongly unfavourable term'. Another response, which is actually being rehearsed by Naxalites in central India, would be to revive the debate about the relative strengths of direct democracy—people's rule—and representative democracy. Yet another response might be to rethink politics itself. One might point to the efforts by a new *Aam Aadmi* Party ('ordinary person's party'), formed in India recently, to banish illegality, discrimination, and corruption from the business of formal politics.

The disjuncture between democracy and inequality also creates a definitional problem, one that is reflected in popular debates within India about whether the country is in fact becoming more democratic. As Williams points out, and as suggested by the second *OED* definition, 'democratic' as an adjective has the sense of 'unconscious of social distinctions' or, more broadly, of 'practices of social equality'. India may be becoming more democratic at the level of formal institutional politics while at the same time becoming less democratic in the sense of the ubiquity and intensity of social distinctions and inequalities, such as those based on a person's sex. Similar points have been made by those who distinguish between formal democracy and substantive democracy, where the latter term applies to aspects of social, economic, and political life that are not straightforwardly concerned with elections and political power narrowly defined—do people have access to police protection, for example, or are they able to raise their voice at the local level? Again, India may be formally democratic, but not substantively so.

• See also *corruption, patronage, politics*

Development

The root of the word 'development' is in an Old French term meaning 'to unfold' or 'to unroll'. By the eighteenth century, development had come to have such meanings as 'evolution', or 'bringing out from a latent or elementary condition', and in the nineteenth that of 'bringing out the latent capabilities (of anything)' (*OED*). The latter sense is reflected in the way the word is used in photography, when the process of developing a film brings out the image that is latent in the chemicals with which it is coated. The word also came to be used to refer to the act of developing an estate, mine, or other property—action which is intended to bring out the potential that is latent within the property. These are the senses of the word that are reflected, as well, in what Raymond Williams refers to as 'the most interesting modern usage... [that relating] to certain ideas of the nature of economic change'. By the mid-nineteenth century, the idea was being expressed that societies pass through definite stages, with the later manifestations of their historical development 'being potentially present in the earliest elements', and a clear link was established with the idea of progress. In the later twentieth century, in the aftermath of the Depression of the 1930s and of the Second World War, economic development became a major focus of public policy, especially in regard to former colonial territories. A whole body of theory began to be built up, concerned with explaining how and why the process of economic development takes place, and with determining how best it can be encouraged. 'Development' then became a field of contestation, in which different ideas about what constitutes a good society came into conflict with each other. Another line of debate was over whether the former colonies should be thought of as being simply undeveloped, or as having been actively underdeveloped as a result of their exploitation by colonial capitalism. And then over whether the support given to international development by rich countries didn't show that it was really about continuing the dependence of the poor countries on them, and on their big capitalist corporations.

The idea that India had been subjected to active underdevelopment as a result of colonial rule was central to the thinking of those known as 'economic nationalists'. As they saw it, India had been impoverished by the drain of its wealth to Britain, by the taxation of agriculture in the form of land revenue, and as a result of the ways whereby the colonial power had destroyed Indian industries—what came to be referred to as 'deindustrialization'. Jawaharlal Nehru, India's first prime minister, reflected these ideas when he argued before the Constituent Assembly that 'The first task of this Assembly is to free India through a new constitution, to feed the starving people, and to clothe the naked masses, and to give every Indian the fullest opportunity to develop himself according to his capacity.' The legitimacy of the newly independent state then came to depend very substantially upon its project of bringing about economic development, through industrialization, which was to be achieved by means of planning. At this time—in the mid-twentieth century—the necessity of economic planning was almost universally supported, not least because of the apparent success of the Soviet Union in bringing about the very rapid industrialization of what had been considered to be a 'backward' economy. India has had a whole series of five-year plans since the first, which was initiated in 1951. The Twelfth Five-Year Plan is being implemented in 2012–17; and the Planning Commission, chaired by the prime minister, though it is less powerful than it was in the 1950s, remains at the heart of economic policymaking.

Nehru's statement before the Constituent Assembly suggests an idea of human development—that of 'every Indian [being given] the fullest opportunity to develop himself according to his capacity'—which corresponds closely with the view of the Nobel prize-winning economist, Amartya Sen, that development should be understood in terms of expanding the real freedoms of people to lead lives that they have reason to value. But in practice Indian governments have always given absolute priority to the goal of achieving high rates of economic *growth*, and social goals—such as the fulfilment of the constitutional commitment to realizing basic education for all within ten years—have had to give way to this prior objective. It has always been argued by policymakers that achieving economic growth is essential if social goals such as, especially, the elimination of mass poverty, are to be achieved. While there is no doubting the truth of this, there is still a great deal of room for disagreement—as there has been among Indians—about *how* economic growth should be brought about, and over an appropriate balance between objectives of growth and of the distribution of wealth and opportunity through society.

The period of India's first three five-year plans saw the achievement of high rates of growth in the industrial economy, and its transformation, with the establishment of a heavy industrial base. But by the end of this period it was also recognized that India was still characterized by very high levels of acute poverty. Economic planning itself entered into crisis, partly because the state was no longer able to maintain investment. Economic growth continued thereafter, but at lower levels, and India continued to be regarded as more or less the archetype of a poor developing country.

This has changed since the 1980s, and over the closing two decades of the twentieth century and the first of the twenty-first, India has generally sustained high rates of economic growth; the country is no longer seen as a developing economy, but rather as an 'emerging market economy' that is already one of the largest economies in the world. The explanation of the change that has come about is much debated among economists, but there is little room for doubt that the 'economic reforms' that began to be implemented in earnest from 1991 have played an important part. The reforms have seen the application of neo-liberal ideas in India's economic policymaking, with the intention of establishing a liberalized market economy. They connote trade liberalization, deregulation, and, in principle, privatization—though in practice the privatization of state-owned enterprises has often been resisted. In general, indeed, economic reform has not gone nearly as far as its protagonists have desired. At the same time, critics point to the failure of economic growth in India to create productive jobs. India, they say, has experienced 'jobless growth'; and because of this the stated aim of the Eleventh Five-Year Plan (of 2002–7), of realizing 'inclusive growth', has not been achieved. Goals of human development—of improving the quality of people's lives, as Nehru suggested was the purpose of India's freedom from colonial rule—have not been achieved. People on the ground are increasingly voicing concerns, too, over the negative effects of economic development on the environment.

A popular saying in North India is that there is no 'development' ('*vikaas*' in Hindi) without 'ruin' ('*binaas*'). It seems to critics that growth, in and for itself, has become ever more the obsession of politicians and policymakers, who have sacrificed the broader objective and understanding of what development should mean.

• See also *capitalism, labour, neo-liberal, poverty*

Diaspora

Derived from a Greek word meaning 'dispersion', the word diaspora came into use in English in the nineteenth century, inspired by Biblical sources, to refer to 'the whole body of Jews living dispersed among the Gentiles after Captivity'. It came to be applied, too, to the dispersion of both Armenians and Greeks. In all these cases—now sometimes thought of as 'the traditional diasporas'—people were understood as having maintained, over generations, a strong (albeit largely mythical) sense of their having a 'homeland' from which they had been displaced and to which they would, at some time, return. In the later twentieth century the term began to be applied to other transnational dispersions. A journal entitled *Diaspora* was first published in 1991, and was described by its editors as being 'dedicated to the multi-disciplinary study of... the traditional diasporas and those trans-national dispersions which in the past three decades have chosen to identify themselves as "diasporas"'. Generally now 'diaspora' has come to be used with reference to any group of people that defines itself as living in displacement but with a sense of having a homeland elsewhere. The diasporic condition has come to be seen as being quintessentially one of late-modernity.

It was only in the 1980s that the idea of an Indian diaspora became current. In 1989 the novelist and anthropologist Amitav Ghosh wrote of 'The modern Indian diaspora—the huge migration from the subcontinent that began in the mid nineteenth century', and described it as 'one of the most important demographic dislocations of modern times'. Now, according to the Ministry of Overseas Indian Affairs, set up by the Government of India in 2004, there are around 25 million 'overseas Indians', spread across more than 200 countries, though with particularly large concentrations in the United States (between 2 and 3 million people), Saudi Arabia (1.78 million), the United Arab Emirates (1.75 million), the United Kingdom (1.5 million), and Canada (about 1 million), as well as in earlier sites for migration such as Malaysia (1.9 million), Sri Lanka (1.6 million), South Africa (1.2 million), Mauritius, Fiji, and the Caribbean. Though the Ministry describes these movements of people as constituting a diaspora second in significance only to that of the Chinese, it also says that it is 'difficult to speak of one great Indian diaspora [for] the overseas Indian community is the result of different waves of migration over hundreds of years'. There are great differences, for example, between the movements of indentured labourers in the nineteenth century to countries such as Sri Lanka and Mauritius, and the migration of highly educated Indians to North America in recent decades.

Amitav Ghosh, in his influential essay of 1989, went on to argue that the Indian diaspora 'now represents an important force in world culture', referring to several English language authors from the diaspora—Naipaul and Rushdie in particular—who, in his view, count among the finest of all contemporary writers, and he discussed ways in which they have become an important force within India. Ghosh pointed out 'the curious nature of India's cultural relations with her diaspora'. Nehru and the other authors of the Constitution insisted that overseas Indians were not to be counted as citizens of India. Their rights and duties of citizenship should be those of the countries in which they were settled. Diasporic Indians have not, historically, been bound to India by any institutions, or by India's economic and strategic interests, nor even by language—for Indians have proven adept at acquiring the languages of the places in which they have settled. Their relationship with India has essentially been one of the imagination. As James Clifford put it in commenting on Amitav Ghosh's essay, the Indian diaspora is 'not so much oriented to roots in a specific place and a desire for return as around an ability to recreate culture in diverse locations'. Latterly there has developed, for instance, a distinctly 'British Indian' culture, reflected in literature and in film, in works such as those, for example, of the film-maker Gurinder Chadha—*Bhaji on the Beach*, or the more widely celebrated *Bend it Like Beckham*. These are instances of what is sometimes referred to in terms of cultural 'hybridity'.

The diasporic experience for Indians, as for others, has changed quite radically even since Ghosh wrote in the late 1980s, very largely because of advances in information and communications technologies—the development of the internet, and the much greater ease and the low cost of keeping in touch across continents by phone—as well as because of the relatively low prices of international air travel. These have made it possible for families to maintain much stronger transnational links than was usually the case before. There are, for instance, families with farms both in Punjab and in British Columbia, or with businesses in Gujarat and in the English Midlands, family members in both cases moving fairly freely between their two places. There are religious teachers, too—gurus—who work both in India and in North America or the UK, and who encourage a kind of modern religiosity that may well be more attractive to Indians living outside India than it is to residents of India. But another important way in which the diasporic experience has changed is that connections across and within the diaspora may be more important than links with India; and there are places such as Southall Broadway, in West London, which have become sites of diasporic nostalgia that may be as significant as India itself—a place in which, in this case, to experience 'real' Punjabiness.

Remittances from diasporic Indians play a very important part in India's balance of payments. Diasporic Indians are sometimes very actively involved in Indian politics too. The movement for Khalistan—for the independence of Punjab—in the 1980s may have been driven as much from the UK, and especially from British Columbia, as it was from within Punjab. Some members of the wealthy and often immensely successful Indian diaspora in the United States are staunch supporters of the Bharatiya Janata Party (BJP)—and it was under the BJP-led National Democratic Alliance (NDA) that moves were first made to give such affluent overseas Indians ('NRIs'—non-resident Indians—as they are commonly known), if not dual citizenship, then at least easier rights of access to India. It was under the NDA that an annual convention for the Overseas Indian Community was established (in 2003). Called the *Pravasi Bharatiya Divas*, the convention takes place each year on 9 January, the day when Gandhi, an 'overseas Indian' in his time, at last returned to India from South Africa. NRIs are strongly encouraged to invest in India, and some are very active in the financing of NGO work. Economic interests have driven the Government of India, pragmatically and even cynically, to shift its stance on the citizenship claims of some overseas Indians—though certainly not of all. Poor refugees from Pakistan living in Rajasthan, for example, are not treated in the same way as the 'NRIs'.

• See also *citizenship, culture, globalization, modern*

E

Education

Education refers most commonly to a system of instruction taking place in schools or universities. In India it has long been a major goal of the state and citizens, and Article 45 of the Indian Constitution directed the new postcolonial government to provide free and compulsory education to all children under 14 within ten years.

Indeed, education is a key focus of desire for citizens of all backgrounds and classes in contemporary India. Primary school enrolment in India increased from 46 per cent in 1987 to 83 per cent in 2006 and, according to UNESCO, the youth literacy rate in India in 2010 was 74 per cent for girls and 88 per cent for boys.

But there remain huge inequalities in people's experiences of education in India according to gender, caste, region, and religion that reflect the failure of the state to provide good-quality, low-cost schooling for Indian citizens and the wider absence of a well-functioning welfare state. Only 59 per cent of boys and 49 per cent of girls attend secondary school in India, and just 18 per cent of youth attend higher education. National Sample Survey data from 1999–2000 showed that 70 per cent of Dalit girls and women in rural India were illiterate. The poor have to balance a desire to educate their children against other urgent calls on their meagre financial resources. Illness, an expensive wedding, or need for food often forces the poor to withdraw their children from school in order to economize or obtain a child's help in the home. This is an especially pressing problem for girls.

Even where the poor and lower middle classes have managed to send their children to school, they often find that the education they receive in educational institutions is of a very low standard and out of kilter with the local economy. In spite of recent efforts by the National Council of Educational Research and Training (NCERT) to improve curricula in India, school syllabi are often outdated. There is little in the way of new approaches to learning, continuous assessment, careers advice, or life skills training. Moreover, corruption is rife in the government school system. Teachers often bribe the authorities to be posted in favoured areas, leaving rural and remote schools without adequate staff. In addition, teacher absenteeism is a major problem in many parts of the country. These problems also beset the higher education sector. Aside from a tiny upper stratum of elite institutions, universities and colleges often contain substandard educational facilities. Curricular review, in-service training for teachers, and active learning are rare, which means that some young people continue to follow syllabi developed during the colonial era. Most states have gone through the motions of revising the curriculum, but the implementation of change in teaching practice remains very patchy. Government failure has also encouraged the rampant privatization of the school and higher education sectors, where corruption and poor service provision is also evident. This has led to a widespread sense that schools and colleges provide 'qualifications' but not 'education'. The inadequacies of the Indian education system threaten the country's chances of benefiting from its expected 'demographic dividend'— the advantage that it has for some years been deriving from the burgeoning numbers of those who are, or who should be, in the labour force, in relation to the numbers of those who are their younger and older dependants.

The difficulties faced by the poor and lower middle class in obtaining decent schooling for their children, combined with their fervent belief in their right to education, have precipitated lively mobilization in India for broad-based educational investment and reform, especially through well-publicized Right to Education campaigns. These campaigns culmin- ated in a new Right to Education Act which came into force in 2010 and provides children with the legal right to education up to age 14 as well as special provisions for children from disadvantaged backgrounds. The Act is a positive move, but the state has consistently reneged on promises to increase spending on education to 6 per cent of GDP, and a meagre 0.37 per cent of GDP is spent on higher education. Education has also been politicized through efforts by the Hindu Nationalist Government in the late 1990s and early 2000s to rewrite school and university curricula to reflect Hindutva ideologies.

One implication of this educational malaise in India has been to provoke renewed reflection on precisely what value inheres in 'education' (which often translates as '*shiksha*' in Hindi, or as '*parhai*' which also refers more specifically to reading). It is of course a key tenet of thinking on international development that education will lead to a better life. Amartya Sen has formalized this idea, pointing to the intrinsic value of education and its instrumental importance. He argues that education leads to a range of social benefits such as a job, confidence, and political power. But even when young people in India have acquired qualifications, they often cannot obtain secure work. There are not enough jobs to meet the growing demand from high school matriculates and college graduates. Moreover, schools and colleges may inculcate notions of failure and, in some places, reinforce feelings of gender, caste, or religious marginalization. Education may, in the circumstances, come to operate as a 'contradictory resource'—at least for the poor and lower middle classes— providing people with basic skills but also drawing them more tightly into systems of inequality.

• See also *development, poverty, rights, youth*

Empowerment

Though this word, meaning 'the action of empowering; the state of being empowered' came into use in English, the *OED* tells us, in the nineteenth century, the verb from which it comes has older roots. 'To empower' means 'to invest legally or formally with power or authority; to authorize, license'; or 'to impart or bestow power to an end or purpose; to enable, permit'; or, used reflexively, 'to gain or assume power over'. These uses go back to the seventeenth century.

Latterly, however, the idea of 'empowerment' has come to take on a rather different, particular meaning: that most generally of 'people gaining control over their own lives'. In India it has been used especially in regard to women, and to people who have been marginalized historically, such as Dalits and adivasis (or tribal people). It began to be used in this way by feminists in the 1960s and 1970s. One Indian feminist, early in the 1990s, spoke of 'empowerment' as meaning 'altering relations of power...which constrain women's options and autonomy and adversely affect health and well being'. The important Indian journal, the *Economic and Political Weekly*, shows increasing frequency of use of the word from the 1990s, most commonly in relation to women. It is now current not only in the academic and policy literature, but also in everyday language. Rina Agarwala reports a young, lower-caste woman who is a migrant construction worker in Kolkata using the word 'empower', in English—though she does not speak English—while explaining the benefit she experienced by becoming a union member. The identity card she received from the union gave her a much greater sense of security than she had known before.

'Empowerment' became a buzzword in the discourse of international development only in the 1990s, when it became established as a development strategy following the UN-sponsored population conference held in Cairo in 1994. A search on the website of the World Bank brings up over 12,000 references to 'empowerment'—of the poor, specifically, or of women, or in references to 'community empowerment'. The great majority of these references have occurred in documents dating back no more than ten years (before 2012). More or less the standard definition proposed by the World Bank states that 'Empowerment refers broadly to the expansion of freedom of choice and action to shape one's life', and even more precisely to 'the expansion of the assets and capabilities of poor people to participate in, negotiate with, influence, control and hold accountable institutions that affect their lives'.

These statements reflect ideas of the Indian Nobel prize-winning economist and philosopher, Amartya Sen—though Sen himself has not generally used the term 'empowerment'. The language, however, of 'expansion of freedom of choice and action to shape one's life' and of 'expansion of capabilities' reflects his conception of the means and ends of development. Ultimately the objective of development, for Sen, is that people are able to lead lives that they have reason to value. For them to be able to do this, they must enjoy freedoms of choice and of action, exactly as the advocates of programmes of empowerment suggest, subject only to the constraint that others should enjoy the same freedoms.

The ways in which the idea is used in contemporary development practice, however, in India and elsewhere, have been criticized as being part of the discourse of neo-liberalism. Critics are wary of the emphasis that is given to choice; they see the idea of empowerment as being linked with liberal arguments that suggest people should be 'looking after themselves' rather than relying on state provision; and they argue that in practice the programmes that are supposed to deliver greater empowerment rarely do much to redistribute material assets in a way that enables more people to lead fuller lives. In the main these programmes, when they focus on women, propose the establishment of women's self-help groups, or other microfinance schemes, which are expected to enhance women's autonomy and to help them to create assets for themselves; when they are concerned with communities, or with 'the poor' generally, they may also involve microfinance for the creation of assets, and the establishment of local organizations that are expected to build a capacity for collective action. Generally, ensuring access to education, to employment in public works (since a government Act of 2005 in the Mahatma Gandhi National Rural Employment Guarantee Scheme), and the reservation of positions in local government institutions (*panchayati raj*) for women, for Dalits, and for adivasis, are expected to be 'empowering'. But whether these and other interventions by government do have this effect is much debated.

• See also *development, feminism, microfinance*

Enterprise

Enterprise often refers to a project or business, frequently one that is novel or daring in some way. The emergence of new enterprises, especially in IT and allied services, has been one of the drivers of India's economic growth since the early 1990s. The IT firm Infosys, established by a group of young engineers, including the now noted public intellectual Nandan Nilekani, is among the most prominent examples of successful Indian business development, but there are now numerous IT start-ups across India, especially in the larger cities in the South.

Enterprise is also a term that circulates frequently within the Indian Government and many NGOs. During the Nehruvian period the state tended to focus on promoting large industries. But since the 1970s, and especially after 1991, development practitioners have placed increasing emphasis on small enterprise as a means of countering poverty. The Honey Bee Network of 'grassroots entrepreneurs' has been a highly successful venue for the exchange of entrepreneurial ideas. The clothing and furnishing company Fabindia has been similarly successful, and now employs over 40,000 craft-based rural artisans across the country. Perhaps most notable of all, the Self-Employed Women's Association of India, established in 1972, has provided support for hundreds of thousands of small-scale Indian businesswomen, typically engaged in low-technology craft activities. Dalit enterprise has become more common, sometimes founded on efforts by the state to source services and materials from Dalit-run firms. More broadly, the enormous proliferation of microfinance self-help groups has promoted collective small enterprise among women in India and also served in some cases to challenge gender norms. A nascent 'social enterprise' sector, in which companies prioritize human and environmental well-being over profit in the promotion of small business concerns, is also beginning to make its mark, for example in the sphere of off-grid solar electricity provision.

Partly reflecting the success of these initiatives, the idea has proliferated that Indians have some type of innate capacity for enterprise—'enterprise' and Indian identity have come to be intrinsically linked. Much of this writing has focused on the notion of '*jugaad*', a Hindi word which means 'improvising shrewdly with available resources'. Jugaad is captured in the image of a wooden bullock cart that has been fitted with a modern engine. As the argument goes, Indians have long been able to survive, and indeed some have built large companies, through exploiting their instinctive capacity for jugaad-type enterprise. Policymakers recently established a National Innovation Council in India, which is partly devoted to encouraging jugaad. In its PowerPoint presentation entitled 'Ideas', and prominent on the Council's website, it is stated that 'informal improvisation ["jugaad"] needs to be scaled up to a system of frugal engineering geared towards Indian needs'. There is also now an organization devoted to 'jugaad urbanism', which explores how the rise in India's enterprising spirit can be an inspiration and a catalyst for architects, designers, and urban planners around the world. Jugaad has even been presented as an environmental philosophy, celebrating the creative reuse of materials, for example in the manufacture of clothing and appropriate technologies. References to Indian's capacity for 'frugal innovation' were also sprinkled through India's Twelfth Five-Year plan published in 2011.

Some argue that India should not be aiming for 'jugaad solutions', but rather seeking to foster businesses that are 'proper'. More importantly, the notion of the enterprising self encapsulated in the idea of 'jugaad' can be seen as part of a neo-liberal ethos that effectively allows the state off the hook: if people can do 'jugaad', they do not need a great deal of support from the state. Large sections of Indian society remain excluded from opportunities to develop successful small businesses precisely because of their inability to access state services. There is growing evidence of the Indian Government's inability to invest effectively in the infrastructural facilities, training, and research and development that would foster genuine broad-based enterprise development in the country. The recent reports of the National Commission for Enterprise in the Unorganized Sector (NCEUS) draw on large-scale surveys in India's large informal sector to argue that the vast majority of enterprises in India consist of a single person or a small group of people working long hours in poor, insecure, sometimes treacherous conditions. During the first decade of this century, the productivity of this vast informal sector went up but there was stagnation in employment levels—dynamics that suggest that the self-employed worked increasingly long hours to survive. The NCEUS has also pointed to other problems: declining real wages, people's lack of access to new technology, an absence of skills training, and a lack of cheap credit.

• See also *consumerism, development, microfinance, neo-liberal, poverty*

Environment

In the *OED*, environment is defined in two ways. First, it refers to 'the surroundings or conditions in which a person, animal, or plant lives or operates'. Second, environment refers to 'the natural world, as a whole or in a particular geographical area, especially as affected by human activity'. In popular and scholarly discussion, the term 'environment' is often preferred to the word 'landscape', which carries with it the association of a distanced perspective, suggesting 'scenery' and the 'bird's-eye view'. 'Environment' is also often preferred to the term 'nature', which refers either to a realm untouched by human activity or to the entire living world, including humans.

Much of the popular commentary and scholarly work on the environment in India is concerned with political and economic questions and it often presents a story of decline, contrasting a relatively egalitarian, stable, and harmonious environmental past with inequality, uncertainty, and degradation in the present. Ramachandra Guha's work has been especially influential, showing how British colonial policy and postcolonial development planning served on the whole to reduce poor people's access to their local environment and local resources. These are themes that have influenced the work of the Delhi-based Centre for Science and Environment (CSE), founded by the late Anil Agarwal, which has the mission of researching, lobbying for, and 'communicating the urgency of development that is both sustainable and equitable'. The eco-feminist Vandana Shiva, who holds a doctorate in the philosophy of science, has written more stridently of the 'plunder' of Indian environmental resources, pitting a feminine Indian environment against masculine external threats.

These critiques have considerable force in the current conjuncture. The entry of large foreign corporations into manufacturing and resource extraction in India has often led to environmental degradation, and—as in the case of the Bhopal gas leak in 1986—environmental catastrophe. In addition, large corporates have often appropriated land from the poor and reshaped rural and urban environments in pursuit of their own goals.

But the popular narrative of an Indian environment under threat can in certain circumstances distract from the extent to which subaltern populations are able to respond actively to environmental problems. The poor have been at the forefront of several large mobilizations oriented around the idea of protecting the environment, for example from logging contractors or those intent on building large dams. Difficult questions concerning rights often surface in these struggles. For example, farmers have campaigned against foreign multinationals threatening to patent knowledge of agricultural practices that they regard as part of their own intellectual property. Environmental debates also often relate closely to questions of land and territory. There have been heated disputes between different states in India concerning access to river water, and at a finer scale no less intense battles over access to water, forests, and agricultural land between different villages, castes, households, and gendered individuals.

Recent concerns over the impact of climate change on the Indian environment and people's livelihoods are changing the terms of debate. Climate change also raises thorny questions about the Indian Government's duties with respect to environmental protection vis-à-vis those of other nation states. Some sections of the Indian population contest the notion that they should be responsible for reducing carbon emissions, given that India is still a developing country and has much lower per capita emissions than the United States. More broadly, discussions of climate change globalize people's understanding of the environment since they entail reflecting upon how practices in one country affect the environment in other places. Environment is no longer such a straightforwardly national, regional, or local idea. This may be reflected in a shift from an understanding of the 'environment' as one's immediate surroundings—as expressed in the Indian language term *'jungal'*—to more abstract notions of 'environment', encapsulated in use of the English word 'environment' or the analogous Hindi terms *'paryavaran'* or *'parivesh'*.

The term environment often refers to those aspects of people's surroundings that have utilitarian value. But the environment in India is also a significant cultural category. Rural Indians often have an intimate relationship with the environment, developing their own sense of identity from their daily interactions with natural resources, the soil, and agriculture. Cultivation of the land and cultivation of the self are intrinsically linked. Likewise, the environment is of religious importance, especially in relatively remote areas and among tribal populations, but also among mainstream Hindus, for whom mountains, rivers, and trees form key points on pilgrimages.

From the perspective of many contemporary commentators, the word environment, used in either of the *OED*'s senses, is also problematic because it tends to place humans at the centre of natural systems: people are 'surrounded' by an 'environment'. Recent environmental debates in India raise questions about the appropriateness of such an anthropocentric approach. Some conservationists have questioned the degree to which the state should grant local populations the right to hunt in protected areas. From a different standpoint, people living on the edge of a National Park have sometimes argued against a vision of environmental sustainability that places the needs of tigers above their own rights as forest users. The debate over genetically modified organisms (GMOs) raises the still more complex ethico-religious (as well as economic and political) question of what precisely a 'natural' environment should look like and the appropriate bounds of human intervention with respect to the natural world.

• See also **culture, development, forests, land, poverty**

Equality

The core meaning of 'equality' is that of 'the condition of being equal in quantity, amount, value, intensity, etc.'. The word has been in use in English, both in this sense and, with reference to society, in that of 'the condition of having equal dignity, rank, or privileges with others', since the fifteenth century (*OED*). Thereafter, Williams argues, the meaning of the word in regard to society shifted to an assertion of a more general condition—as in a statement such as 'all men are created equal'. This is the idea that was given so much emphasis in both the American and French Revolutions of the later eighteenth century, reflected in the reform of what had been statutory inequalities between people and in the idea of equality before the law. A century later, and even more in the early twentieth century, the idea of 'equality of opportunity' came into use. Defined formally by *OED* as meaning 'the equal chance and right to seek success in one's chosen sphere regardless of social factors such as class, race, religion and sex', Williams puts it more pithily as 'equal opportunity to become unequal'. The ideas of 'equality' and of 'equality of opportunity' are reflected in two branches of social thought. The first looks to a process of equalization, based on the premise that all men are naturally equal as human beings; the second to 'a process of removal of inherent privileges, from the premise that all men should *start* equal, though the effect may be that they become unequal in achievement or condition' (Williams). The idea and value of equality have been much contested. The first, the radical egalitarian view, is criticized on the grounds that the attempt to establish social equality must threaten individual freedoms, and it is for this reason that public policy in most societies has come to be grounded rather on the idea of equality of opportunity. Rather than striving for equality of condition among the members of society, the focus has generally come to be on such ideas as the 'empowerment of excluded groups'.

It has been argued, most influentially by the French scholar Louis Dumont, that Indian society has been founded, historically, on the idea of hierarchy rather than on a conception of equality between individual human beings. The idea of 'hierarchy' is of a 'ladder of command', as in an army, or in the ranks of the priesthood of the Church, where it also has the clear sense of 'different degrees of dignity'. Formally, the word is defined by *OED* as referring to 'a body of persons or things ranked in grades, orders, or classes, one above another'. Dumont used the expression '*homo hierarchicus*' (or 'hierarchical man') in the title of his most important book on the Indian caste system, contrasting this idea deliberately with the idea of '*homo aequalis*'. What he argues is that, at least since the Enlightenment, ideas of the individual and of equality between individuals, as human beings, have characterized European thought and culture, but that they are generally lacking in Indian culture and society, except at the margins. In India, he suggests, 'all men' are definitely *not* equal. Society is organized hierarchically, by varna and jati, which are identities that people acquire by birth and that are associated with different activities, all of which are necessary for society to function. They are differentiated by their 'different degrees' of purity—a religious idea that, broadly, refers to the distance of a person and his actions from god. These different degrees of purity establish a social hierarchy in which the Brahmin (the priest) is at the top and the untouchable is at the bottom. What people are, as human beings, is supposed to be given by their status in the caste order.

This theory is controversial, and other scholars advance evidence in support of the view that there is a very clear idea of the individual in Indian society, and even ideas of equality between people, as reflected in the positive moral associations that usually attach to the Hindi term '*samanata*' ('equality') in India. But there is broad agreement that a sense of hierarchical distinction permeates Indian society. The Dutch sociologist Jan Breman writes, on the basis of half a century of ethnographic observation in part of rural India, that 'the idea of natural inequality continues to be the cornerstone of the social fabric'. In these circumstances, what drives a lot of political action is the quest for distinction. The ambition that motivates many politicians is that of securing a 'higher' position for 'me and my people' rather than bringing about wider reform and social change. There has been remarkably little concern about equality/inequality in what we may call the 'strong' sense, and attention has been focused much more on equality of opportunity. Historically disadvantaged and socially excluded groups—Dalits and adivasis, and members of the Other Backward Classes—are to be empowered through affirmative action (*see* reservations), while poverty also attracts a great deal of attention in public policy. It remains to be seen whether this will change now that, in the context of economic liberalism and globalization, India is becoming very much more unequal in terms of the distribution of assets and income. It is now calculated that India's forty-six 'dollar billionaires' account for around 10 per cent of GDP—or at one point in the recent past for more than 20 per cent of GDP. In these circumstances inequality may become more significant politically than it has been hitherto.

• See also *caste, empowerment*

Faction

The idea of a 'faction' began to become current in English in the sixteenth century, when the word had the meanings of 'a class, or set of persons', and also of 'a party in the state or in any community or association'. The latter usage was, *OED* tells us, 'Always with opprobrious sense, conveying the imputation of selfish or mischievous ends or turbulent or unscrupulous methods.' By the nineteenth century the word was 'In Ireland applied to certain mutually hostile associations among the peasantry, consisting usually of the members of a particular family (which gives its name to the faction), and of their relatives and friends.' It was in this sense that British officials used the term in India as well. R. Carstairs, who served in Bengal in the later nineteenth century, and who wrote about his experiences in *The Little World of an Indian District Officer* (published in 1912), says of one of his official tours that '…in every village there were generally factions raging. Active minds were busy…devising plans for dishing the other side, detaching members from it, and generally putting their own side ahead.' He writes, too, that 'It was a common official complaint that there was no public spirit in the land…any public body that could be set up in the villages would be captured by, and become a prey to this fell demon [of factionalism].' The idea that Indian society is characterized by factiousness was well established by the end of the century.

Then, later, in the twentieth century, with the development of the study of Indian society by social scientists, the idea was confirmed. The French anthropologist Louis Dumont, for instance, argues in his important study of Indian society, *Homo Hierarchicus*, that 'Very commonly the Indian village is divided into "factions". People have long recognized the importance of quarrels, rivalries and legal wranglings in the Indian village.' Such rival groups were thought most commonly to form around the leadership of a member or members of the locally dominant caste, with their followers including clients recruited from their dependants among the subordinate caste communities. The exchanges between leaders and followers were asymmetric, no doubt, but they were the means whereby both were able to pursue their own interests. Leaders were helped to win power or honour, followers to secure their livelihoods.

It seemed to many observers in the 1950s and 1960s that, in the words of another anthropologist, Ralph Nicholas, 'The dominant mode of political conflict in Indian villages is between factions', and that village people were not generally mobilized politically on lines of caste or class or political ideology. Factional politics seemed, therefore, to be a transitional or even 'traditional' form of politics, based on patron–client relations, as opposed to 'modern' politics based on class, party, or ideology. A number of scholars thought that the failure of India's higher-caste and upper-class political elites to develop a political language that was meaningful to the mass of the people meant that political mobilization depended essentially upon a chain of factional networks, linked by clientelism, between the village and the district and the state. The Congress party, notably, was described in these terms, as a pyramid of such patron–client relations between factional networks. It appeared to the political scientist Paul Brass to be unlikely that party loyalties or ideology would play much of a role in local politics in India for a long time.

Later, such ideas as these came to be seen as reflecting an Orientalist mindset, founded on the colonial construction that there is a fundamental difference between East and West. Critics such as the historian David Hardiman suggested that observers were so influenced by the idea that Indian politics is all about faction that they failed to recognize the significance of horizontal solidarities, whether of class or caste, in explaining, for instance, the way the nationalist movement had worked in different parts of India. And developments in Indian politics over the last thirty years or so, which have seen the rise of various political parties based on caste or regional identities, show that faction is no longer, if it ever was, necessarily the dominant mode of political organization in India.

• See also *caste, patronage, peasant, politics, village*

Family

The 'family', which takes many different forms, is the 'elementary' (or foundational) unit of social life in almost all societies, and the arena in which, for most people, the drama of life primarily unfolds. The word itself, in English, is polysemic—with a wide range of meanings—from that of 'the retinue of a nobleman' to the idea of a group of objects of some kind that are connected together or have features in common that distinguish them from other such groups or assemblages. Perhaps the most important meanings, however, are those of (i) 'the body of persons who live in one house or under one head, including parents, children, servants, etc.' (what might also be referred to as a 'household'); and (ii) 'the group of persons, consisting of parents and their children, whether actually living together or not; in a wider sense, the unity formed by those who are nearly connected by blood or affinity'. When 'family' is understood in this way—as it is, very commonly, in India—then the definition of its boundaries becomes problematic: what, for instance, distinguishes a 'family'—'*parivaara*' in Hindi—from a 'clan' or a 'lineage' ('*biradiri*' or '*gotra*')? And, indeed, another understanding of the meaning of the word is of 'those descended or claiming descent from a common ancestor: a house, kindred, or lineage' (all of these definitions from *OED*). The translation and explication of terms in different Indian languages relating to kinship remains a challenge for anthropologists; whether the different terms that are held to be equivalent to 'family' mean quite the same thing for Indians as the English word does for native speakers is still a matter of debate.

Over most of India, families are patrilineal (descent is reckoned down the male line) and they are usually virilocal (a bride moves to her husband's house and joins his family of birth). Amongst most Hindus it is held, in law, that the family is a 'joint family'—a unit consisting of a common ancestor and all his lineal male descendants up to three or more generations, together with the wife or wives (and widows), and unmarried daughters of the common ancestor and the lineal male descendants. The joint family is a commensal group (its members share food); its members worship together; and they share property, under the management of a senior male member. It is usually thought of also as a co-residential group, though in practice it may be that brothers live and work in different places but still share property. Families of this kind—in which, perhaps, one brother remains in the village to manage the family lands, while others take up other occupations outside, but all continue to share property and income—have been described by anthropologists as 'share families'.

The idea of the joint family and the principle of 'jointness' are widely shared amongst Hindus, and reinforced in their epics and in folk tales as well as in law, but the practice of family life is often very different. Historically, it seems that family organization has differed between classes. It is likely that the incidence of joint families was generally higher amongst wealthier, higher-caste people, and probably therefore—given the higher proportions of people from such backgrounds in urban centres—higher in towns and cities than in villages. It has commonly been supposed that with economic and social development, and the progressive 'modernization' of Indian society, the numbers of joint families will decline and that the 'nuclear family' (composed of a married couple and their children), which is thought to be the characteristic family form of the West, will become the norm in India as well. Empirical research, however, challenges this presumption. It is clear neither that the incidence of joint families is declining, nor that the values that are associated with the joint family are weakening.

There are now large numbers of people who are part of the Indian diaspora, and among them there are many 'transnational families'. Modern means of communication and of relatively cheap international travel make it easier than it used to be for Indians who have migrated to other parts of the world to maintain strong and meaningful family relationships. And it is not only among such diasporic Indians that what are held to be 'Indian family values' are seen fundamentally to define what it means to be 'Indian'. Some of the most successful Indian movies of the past twenty years—such as *Dilwale Duniya Le Jayenge* (Aditya Chopra, 1995)—take as their theme the tension between the idea of marriage as a relationship that is freely chosen between individuals who are able to fulfil themselves and their desires, and family values that stress the principle of the joint family, the idea of marriage as an alliance between families rather than between two individuals, and the rights of parents to dispose of their children in marriage. Differences between their respective family systems have long marked out the distinction between Indian society and the 'West'. Even now, among highly educated, sophisticated young people who are employed in well-paid middle-class jobs, for example in the IT industry, it is very often the case that they defer to 'Indian family values'. Many young women may recognize injustice in the ways in which they are subordinated in family relationships, but still accept parental—mainly paternal—authority.

In the context of a society in which, until very recently, there has been little or no public provision of social welfare, family ties have been the most important form of insurance available to people. The strength and the significance for people of family and kinship networks can partly be explained in this way. 'Family-centredness' helps to account, however, for the way in which Indian society is segmented, and—clearly—may give rise to nepotism, when those in positions of some power give preference to their relatives. This happens, not least, in politics. The Congress party has been led through most of the life of independent India by a member of 'the family'—that of Jawaharlal Nehru.

The joint family has been, historically, the basic unit of Indian business. Though India has long had joint-stock companies, and now has some highly successful modern corporations, even some of the very biggest and most successful of Indian companies, still, are family businesses. Family relationships may be the basis for trust, which is essential in successful business enterprises. But then giving preference to family members in recruitment to senior positions can mean that businesses come to be poorly managed, and tensions between family members can create difficulties that lead eventually to the breaking up of once successful companies. Academic specialists in the management of family businesses in India often advocate the establishment of separate boards, one for the company—in which professional outsiders may be involved—and one for the management of the family. Tensions remain, in different spheres of life in India, over the positive and the negative aspects of strong family ties.

• See also *caste, marriage, middle class, modern*

Federalism

The general meaning of federalism, according to *OED*, is 'that form of government in which two or more states constitute a political unity while remaining more or less independent with regard to their internal affairs'; and the word has been current certainly since the eighteenth century. The first great experiment in establishing a federal form of government was in the United States of America in the later eighteenth century, when the thirteen original colonies, each with its own government, came together to form a union. Then 'centralizers'—those who sought to establish a more highly centralized state—came into conflict with 'provincialists', who wanted more powers to remain with the individual states. This tension has characterized other experiences of federalism as well.

Federalism, together with democracy, secularism, and socialism (in some form), may be seen as one of the founding principles of independent India. The Indian experience is somewhat different from that of other countries, partly because the provinces of India, thanks to the last constitutional acts of the British government of India, were already members of a federal union during the period of the framing of the Constitution. As Dr Ambedkar said in the course of the debates of the Constituent Assembly (that drew up the Constitution): 'The Federation was not the result of an agreement by the States to join in a Federation', and 'the Federation not being the result of an agreement no state has the right to secede from it'. In this context the task of deciding on the form of federalism was made easier by the fact that there was a strong party, the Congress, with nationwide authority, while there were at that time no strong provincial parties at all. And the experience of Partition in 1947 had provided all too powerful a demonstration of the dangers of separatism.

Subsequently, however, in response to popular demands in some parts of the country, and starting first in what became the state of Andhra Pradesh, it was decided, following the recommendations of the States Reorganization Commission of 1955, that they should indeed be reorganized on linguistic lines. The Indian federal system does contain the seeds of Balkanization, and there continue to be demands in different parts of the country—most especially in the Telengana region of Andhra[1]—for the recognition of separate statehood within the Union of India. The country has not, however, succumbed to fragmentation as was anticipated by some observers in the 1950s and 1960s.

As it turned out, the Constituent Assembly produced, in the words of the constitutional historian Granville Austin, 'a new kind of federalism to meet India's peculiar needs'. It was, he argues, a 'cooperative federalism', with a strong central government, yet without the provincial or state governments being reduced to merely administrative agencies for central policies. As Ambedkar put it, the Constitution was to be 'Federal inasmuch as it establishes what may be called a Dual Polity (which) . . . will consist of the Union at the Centre and the States at the periphery each endowed with sovereign powers to be exercised in the field assigned to them respectively by the Constitution'. The various powers of central and state governments are laid out in the Seventh Schedule of the Constitution. The Union's responsibilities include defence and security, foreign affairs, the currency, and national services such as the railways; the states' powers include responsibility for public order and policing, public health and sanitation, agriculture, water, and land; and there is a 'concurrent list' of shared responsibilities, including those for education, for social welfare, and for economic and social planning. Emergency powers (under Article 360 of the Constitution) lie with the centre, however, and the central government has, on more than 100 occasions—though much less so latterly—used the constitutional mechanism of President's Rule to take over the government of different states for varying periods. The state of Jharkhand was brought under President's Rule in January 2013 (until July of that year).

Indian federalism is widely thought of as being a form in which government is actually highly centralized. As was said by one authority at the time of the promulgation of the Constitution, it was as though the paramount powers of the British government had been taken over by the Union. The states have always depended heavily upon the centre for their funds, and successive Finance Commissions, appointed every five years—the fourteenth such Commission is due to report in 2014—have been entrusted, under Article 280 of the Constitution, with the task of making recommendations to government regarding the distribution of the proceeds of taxation both between the Union and the states, and between the states. There has been an expectation that these Commissions should ensure that marked inequality between states not be allowed to develop. In fact, however, inequality between states in terms of the level of net state domestic product per capita has steadily increased, and

---

[1] The separate state of Telengana came into existence in June 2014.

especially so in the context of India's economic liberalization, when the states have increasingly competed with each other for investment, both public and private. Some scholars now speak of a process of 'provincial Darwinism', as the economically more successful states such as Gujarat or Tamil Nadu increase their lead over poorer states such as Bihar or Orissa. Alongside these trends there have developed powerful regional political parties, with their bases in particular states, which have come to hold the balance of power in the coalition governments that have ruled the Union over the twenty-five years until 2014 (when the Bharatiya Janata Party gained an absolute majority in the general election). The powers of the states are also shown up in the problems that India has experienced in managing electricity on a national basis. There is no national grid, and different states have arrived at very different ways of running their power sectors, which has helped to make coordination extremely difficult. On the other hand, the central government has been bypassing the states in some programmes, using the mechanism of what are called Central Sector Schemes to channel funds directly to local levels in its efforts to alleviate poverty. This might be seen as compensating for some of the powers that the centre has lost, for example with the removal of industrial licensing. It remains true, however, that, as Austin said, 'The state governments may often be instruments of Union [national] policy, but without their help the Union could not give effect to its programme.'

• See also **constitution, nation, state**

Feminism

The *OED* defines feminism as 'the advocacy of women's rights on the ground of the equality of the sexes'. In practice, feminism is both an intellectual position and political practice. Intellectually, feminists typically seek to highlight the social construction of sex and gender roles and engage with questions of identity, experience, and social practice. Politically, their focus is often on the economic, social, and political rights of women in relation to those of men.

The term 'feminism' has been traced to the writings of the French philosopher Charles Fourier in 1837, but it was not until the 1870s that it was widely used in Western Europe. It became still more prominent in the first decades of the twentieth century, for example through the campaign for the women's vote—what became known later as 'first wave feminism'. Commentators typically argued that 'second wave feminism' started sometime in the 1960s in the West and was associated with a new focus on questions of unity and sisterhood.

Early nineteenth-century reformers in India, influenced in part by Western ideas, sometimes championed women's causes, especially women's education. But it was not until the mid-nineteenth century that reformers were sponsoring girls' schools, and only in the late nineteenth century did women themselves become involved in political mobilization in India. During this period and the first three decades of the twentieth century, women's mobilization concentrated on escaping the practice of '*purdah*' (veiling) and tackling patriarchal customs. Women met mainly in sex-segregated organizations, such as the

Women's Indian Association, established in Madras in 1917, and the All-India Women's Conference, set up in 1927. Women tended to reject the English label of feminism because they thought it anti-nationalist—it implied that women's rights came before the establishment of the nation—and because it was perceived as anti-men.

These feminist struggles contributed to the introduction of new laws abolishing social restrictions on women in independent India and new bureaucratic structures to improve women's position, and, partly as a result, a considerable amount changed for women in the decades following Indian Independence. For example, the female literacy rate rose from 9 per cent in 1951 to 65 per cent in 2011, and women began to challenge received ideas about women's capacity to participate in the public arenas of work and politics.

But the battle of India's first wave feminists against 'custom' largely failed in practice. Women in India continue to face the double burden of balancing work and family maintenance to a greater degree than do men. They are paid less, more likely to be in casual, insecure employment, and have lower educational levels and nutritional status than do men. Amartya Sen has pointed out that the differential care of boys and girls, combined increasingly with practices of sex-selective abortion, mean that the sex ratio is badly skewed in many parts of India—over 50 million women in the country are 'missing'. Women continue to lack bargaining power within households and they rarely have rights over land. They are exposed to violence to a far greater degree than men, including rape. Feminists have pointed out that these problems affect women differently in different parts of India and vary, too, according to their caste, religion, and age.

Some scholars have identified India's 'second wave' feminism—by which they typically mean feminism since the 1960s in India—as being marked by considerable diversity. The topics discussed in women's groups and networks in India include, for example, police violence, rights pertaining to government development schemes, marriage and maintenance, minimum wages, dowry, women's role in government, rape, and property and inheritance. If there is a common thread connecting these discussions, it is a commitment to showing how women's social disadvantage is crucially bound up with the state's failure to address gender inequalities effectively, and the related issues of corruption and clientelism. Yet the Indian state has made some efforts to improve women's political position, and the impact of positive discrimination in local government on women's power has been an especially hotly debated question in women's activist circles. The seventy-third and seventy-fourth amendments of the Indian Constitution reserved 33 per cent of seats in village and town councils for women, and emerging evidence suggests that this may have had a positive impact on women's power and the manner in which government resources are disbursed in some regions.

As in an earlier era, Indian women addressing gender issues in recent times have sometimes adopted critical positions relative to Western feminists. But they have done so more by stressing their distinctive position and concerns as women vis-à-vis their Western counterparts than through claiming to be anti-feminist. For example, Indian feminists have recently critiqued the notion that women's interests are homogeneous across various communities worldwide, showing how the challenges facing Indian women reflect Indian conditions.

It is also increasingly obvious that feminism in India is itself comprised of multiple competing feminisms—and there are intense debates over what precisely the term means and who can claim to be feminist. One example of such a debate is that between eco-feminist, Vandana Shiva, who has critiqued modern science as inherently 'Western' and 'patriarchal' and Meera Nanda, who has argued that scientific rationality can generate a critical stance towards patriarchal practices and discourses. Another debate concerns the extent to which feminists in India are becoming 'NGO-ized' or 'neo-liberalized' and, by implication, somehow less radical. At the same time, scholars have started to write of a 'third wave' of feminism in India to reflect the point that feminism is being expressed in a wide variety of new ways, often outside formal politics and organizations. This includes, for example, women's increased focus on lesbian, bisexual, gay, and transgender rights; greater use of the internet (especially social media); and greater consideration of masculinity and issues of disability and gender.

• See also *gender, masculinity, politics, rape*

Forests

Something approaching one-quarter of the Indian land mass is reportedly under forest cover—which is not at all the same thing as saying that dense forests cover 25 per cent of present-day India. The degradation of India's forest stock has been a significant political issue for most of the past forty years. This remains so notwithstanding some improvements in the management of India's temperate and tropical forests since the 1990s. Loss of effective forest cover has been blamed on increased demand for timber and non-timber forest products, as well as on governance arrangements that have provided few incentives for forest-dependent populations to manage local forests in sustainable ways. More recently, loss of forest cover has been associated in the public imagination with changes in local and national climate regimes, as well as with human-induced climate change more generally. The proper pricing of forest products (and carbon), and of ecological services, is an issue that exercises government planners and economists.

In the mid-nineteenth century, extensive forest cover in India encouraged a view that the supply of timber was more or less limitless. The colonial power(s) represented forests as distant, unproductive, and even evil (or enchanted) domains. They were home to wild animals and communities of aboriginals and other untutored 'junglees', or 'primitives'. The conversion of forests to agricultural land was broadly to be encouraged, and with it the slow introduction of India's adivasis to civilization, the apogee of which, of course, was the town or the city, or simple urbanism (*see* commons).

Demand for timber—particularly sal (*shorea robusta*) and teak (*tectona grandis*)—increased dramatically with the development of a railway system in India, and began to prompt a first set of murmurings about what later would be called environmental sustainability. The British established an Imperial Forest Department in 1864 and enacted the first Indian Forest Act a year later. It is really with the Forest Act of 1878, however, that the

British began to assert their authority over India's 'wastelands'. From this time, too, came a forest governance system that would define forest management in India for more than a hundred years. Under this system, Reserved Forests were established under the sole authority of the Forest Department (FD). FD officers trained in the principles of scientific forestry were now responsible for key planting, coppicing, and harvesting decisions. Timber was made a priority, rather than the non-timber forest needs of local communities. Indeed, local populations found themselves excluded from forests in which previously they had collected edible products, drugs, and small timber (or bamboo), and in which they grazed their animals. There were also Protected Forests, which granted more usufruct rights to local populations than Reserved Forests, but it was only the much smaller and soon overused Village Forests that remained under the control of local communities.

Struggles over access to and use of government forests were common in the colonial period. Arguably, they became more common still in the postcolonial era, not least as more timber was removed from the hills to feed India's growing towns and cities. Timber mafias played a large role in the resultant deforestation. One of the best-known forest struggles in the 1970s and 1980s was the Chipko movement in Uttarakhand. Taking its name from the imperative form of the Hindi verb 'to hug', Chipko has been presented in some quarters as an essentially feminist movement. Women in Kumaun and Garhwal were lauded for opposing the alleged 'masculinism' of development policies based around big timber and big roads. Such policies failed to trust the wit or wisdom of local people and didn't respect an assumed fellow feeling for nature among forest-dependent rural women. In still other quarters, Chipko has been painted as a customary rebellion that mobilized long-standing ideas about the moral economy of the peasantry: about what men and women can legitimately expect of their rulers. In this discourse the forest is less explicitly gendered—although it is still often seen as a female space—and more explicitly made the property of a deliberative community.

Struggles over India's 'Unquiet Woods' in the 1970s and 1980s, as Ramachandra Guha once described them, led in the 1990s to Joint Forest Management (JFM) legislation. This required FD officials to regenerate India's degraded Protected Forests with the help of local user populations. JFM Committees have been formed in all states. They are expected both to replenish India's forest stock and to defuse difficult and sometimes violent relationships between forest beat officers and local communities. Committees vary in their composition and obligations, although most are expected to include a minimum number of Scheduled Tribals and women. A major study by Bina Agarwal has found that forest regeneration in Gujarat and Nepal is enhanced when significant numbers of women are party to decisions that enforce strict conservation rules, including rules that impose particular hardships on women (as, for example, in the collection of firewood). This is an encouraging finding, not least because it links the empowerment of women to environmental enhancement and sustainability. Whether or not some innate female 'nature' is in touch with nature more generally, it is certainly the case that women in India are crucially engaged in the management and hopefully regeneration of India's forests.

• See also *adivasi, commons*

Fundamentalism

Fundamentalism has loomed large in the minds of Indians, as of others across the world, over the final years of the twentieth century and early in the twenty-first. It is associated especially with Islam, first because of what was understood of the ideas of Ayatollah Khomeini in Iran in the 1980s, then the rise of the Taliban in Afghanistan, and finally because of the destruction of the Twin Towers of the World Trade Center in New York on '9/11' (11 September 2001) at the hands of al-Qaeda. Both the Taliban and al-Qaeda are commonly described as 'fundamentalist' political movements, and fundamentalism has come to be popularly associated with Islam. India, however, has also experienced the emergence in the 1980s of militant fundamentalism in the Sikh religious tradition, and what has been described as Hindu fundamentalism—while Muslim reformers in India have, from the eighteenth century, contributed very significantly to what has come to be known as Muslim fundamentalism.

'Fundamentalism' is a modern word that actually came into use first in the United States in the 1920s, in the aftermath of the First World War, when it referred to 'a religious movement, which...became active among various Protestant bodies...based on strict adherence to certain tenets (such as the literal inerrancy of Scripture) held to be fundamental to the Christian faith; the beliefs of this movement, in opposition to liberalism and modernism' (*OED*). Subsequently, from the 1930s, but especially from the 1980s onwards, the term has been used with reference to other religions as well, most frequently in regard to Islam, and to mean 'a similarly strict adherence to ancient or fundamental doctrines, with no concessions to modern developments in thought or customs'. The description given by the anthropologist T. N. Madan, who says that 'Fundamentalist movements lay claim to exclusive possession of "the truth" [and] brook no dissent', probably reflects very well what is generally understood to characterize fundamentalism.

Scholars trace the development of Islamic fundamentalism in India back to the eighteenth century, and it is widely held that the particular reform movement based in the seminary of Dar ul-Ulum, at Deoband near Delhi, founded in 1867—the adherents of which are described as 'moderate fundamentalists'—has exercised a particularly strong influence through to the present. The Taliban are thought to have been influenced especially by 'Deobandi fundamentalism'. Probably more significant, however, in the twentieth century, was the teaching of Abul ala Maududi (1903–79), described by Madan as 'fundamentalist *par excellence*', who sought expressly to 'return to the real and original foundations of the Islamic ideal', and was a profoundly influential exegist of the fundamentals of Islam. Paradoxically, in common with other fundamentalists, Maududi can be seen as having been in many ways an innovator—redefining tradition in the light of contemporary challenges from Western modernity.

Hindu nationalist organizations (*see* Hindutva) have commonly been described as 'fundamentalist'. The anthropologist Christopher Fuller, for example, describes the actions of the Sangh Parivar over the question of the replacement of the old mosque, the Babri Masjid, in the north Indian city of Ayodhya, by a Hindu temple dedicated to Rama, as 'the most dramatic saga of modern Hindu fundamentalism'. Whether or not Hindu nationalists themselves accept this description is doubtful, given their strong statements about Hindutva being not a religious concept but a form of cultural nationalism. Yet their association with a modern Hindu philosophical tradition—that was also a response to the challenge of Western modernity, and that looks to the Vedas as the foundation of Hinduism—makes it an appropriate description.

• See also *community, Hinduism, Hindutva, secularism*

Gandhi

Mohandas Karamchand Gandhi (1869–1948), known as the '*Mahatma*' (meaning 'Great Soul'), the most famous of all Indians, is described by the *OED* as a 'political leader and social reformer'. He was also a thinker who is seen by some philosophers as having developed a profound critique of Western rationalism—though by some other scholars, like the anthropologist Clifford Geertz, as having been confused and muddled, and a sham. He has been described as having articulated a postmodern critique of industrial society and of the modern state before there was a current of thought called 'postmodernism'. He was deeply religious without having had very much at all to do with any religion in the formal sense. He has been seen both as a revolutionary and as a deeply conservative traditionalist, who endorsed caste distinctions, failed to confront class-based oppression, and whose actions in regard to untouchability were at best ineffectual. His intimate though never uncritical follower, Nehru, described some of his ideas as 'unreal'. Yet he was a gifted organizer, and as a political leader it was he who transformed what had been a largely middle-class and upper-caste political association—which is what the Indian National Congress had been—into what was probably the greatest mass movement in history.

Gandhi is acknowledged as the father of independent India, and is represented in pictures—like those on some Indian banknotes—and in statues all over the country. Yet the efforts of the Nehruvian state to build a modern India, and perhaps even more the present-day pursuit by the state of 'growth-at-all-costs', fundamentally contradict Gandhi's vision of independent India. His idea of India as a state built up from the bottom on the foundations of the village community, though it was championed by some of his followers in the Constituent Assembly debates, had very little traction. The idea of local self-government through panchayats entered into the new Constitution only amongst the (non-justiciable) Directive Principles. His idea of the self-sufficient village and of village industry survives only in the state's continuing promotion of handicrafts and 'village industry'. Most Indian towns and cities have a 'Mahatma Gandhi Road'—but, as a famous cartoon once showed, with their shops and cinemas and advertising hoardings celebrating consumerism they could hardly be further away from the Gandhian ideal of asceticism. Gandhi was committed to religious pluralism, and to non-violence. Yet independent India was born amidst violence bred by communalism, and conflict between ethnic communities has been a recurrent scourge. Though pacifism has had some influence in India's stance in international politics, this has not stopped the country from becoming a nuclear power. So what have Gandhi's life and work and his ideas come to mean in contemporary Indian society and culture?

Gandhi's thought is not easily summed up, but it is widely considered that two ideas were of central importance for him: those of *'swaraj'* (meaning 'self-rule') and *'satyagraha'* (meaning 'truth force' but used to describe non-violent resistance). Gandhi's idea of 'swaraj' was laid out in the book *Hind Swaraj*, published in Gujarati in 1909 and in English translation in 1910, and it is there that Gandhi developed his critique of industrial society and of Western ideas of the state. Sometimes thought to have been just a 'nationalist tract', it actually argues for the transformation of Indians' whole way of life, based on the principles of restraint and self-control—or 'self-rule'—and finds the objective of political independence from colonial rule of any significance only in regard to this higher goal. There is evidently a connection between 'swaraj' in this sense and non-violence. It is the method of non-violent resistance that has perhaps been Gandhi's most important legacy, taken up most famously by Martin Luther King in the United States in the struggle there over civil rights.

Gandhi remains an ideal and a kind of a reference point in Indian political culture, but Gandhism has little practical meaning. His ideas and his memory are cynically invoked by politicians and others for their own ends; and they are at most a distant influence on those individuals and those actions that are described as 'Gandhian' in India today. There are still associations that claim to follow Gandhian principles, meaning that their leaders and members attempt to follow a relatively austere way of life and to carry on *'sarvodaya'* ('service on behalf of others')—in practice often some kind of community development work. Sometimes a particular figure is described as having taken on the mantle of Gandhi. This happened in 2011 when Anna Hazare, a sometime soldier in the Indian army, who had won a reputation for himself as a social worker in his native Maharashtra, emerged as the central figure of a popular movement against corruption. Hazare, who has a Gandhian style in his public persona—wearing, for example, what is sometimes called a Gandhi cap—led mass protests and called for civil disobedience against corruption. He also used the tactic of the threat of fast-unto-death, which Gandhi himself had deployed on some occasions, in order to bring pressure to bear on the government of the day to take action in regard to corruption. Hazare, however, also appeared sympathetic to Hindutva, and what he wanted the government to create to fight corruption would be in practice a bureaucratic monster, quite in contradiction with Gandhian principles.

It should be noted that Mrs Indira Gandhi, daughter of Jawaharlal Nehru and herself prime minister of India in 1966–77 and 1980–4, her son Rajiv, who was prime minister in 1984–9, his wife Sonia Gandhi, and their son Rahul—both of them contemporary leaders of the Congress party—have no kinship connection with Mohandas Karamchand Gandhi.

• See also *Ambedkar, community, congress, constitution, Nehru, panchayat*

Gender

The word 'gender' was once employed to indicate the class, order, or kind of something, but usually refers today to the cultural characteristics associated with being a man or woman (although, as the *OED* points out, gender is also sometimes used synonymously with 'sex' to denote 'male' or 'female'). Where 'gender' is invoked it implies a determination to expose the processes through which cultural attributes are attached to the different sexes and the arbitrary character of such ideas. Gender theorists show, for example, that there is nothing natural about the qualities and roles typically assigned to the two sexes. This point is especially pertinent to contemporary India, where patriarchal ideas about women's qualities—for example as diligent, caring, and vulnerable—are extremely persistent, and where the educational system, legal apparatus, police force, and other bureaucracies (as well as NGOs and the media) have tended to reinforce these assumptions and corresponding ideas about the roles appropriate for men and women in society. Society tends to expect that men will take major decisions within the household, control ownership of major assets, enter paid employment, and deal with public matters pertaining to the family, whereas women are imagined principally as homemakers and mothers. This is not to say that nothing has changed. The rise of an upper middle class in urban areas has been associated with new gender relations in parts of India, for example as young women find jobs in IT and couples absorb Western ideas about companionship and equality in marriage.

Gender inequalities are marked. The sex ratio is badly skewed in India and it is getting worse—from 972 women per 1,000 men in 1991 to 933 in 2011—reflecting the greater value that parents typically place on male children and, consequently, the higher level of care they provide to sons in cases of treatable disease. Among adults, a recent study based on data from the National Health Survey showed that between 1999 and 2006 malnourishment—especially anaemia associated with iron deficiency—increased for women from disadvantaged groups. The female literacy rate has risen from 9 per cent in 1951 to 65 per cent in 2011 but men's literacy rate (80 per cent) remains much higher. Far fewer girls are enrolled in schools than are boys, and parents are more likely to take girls out of school in the case of a family financial or medical emergency. Men are grossly over-represented among India's formal sector employees and among business leaders, and in the informal economy women typically conduct the poorest paid, most insecure jobs.

Gender violence is rife. There has been a substantial increase between the 1980s and 2000s in the murder of young women over dowry and the harassment of young brides on this question. Women are very commonly victims of domestic violence, and the intimidation and rape of women in public settings remains a pressing problem.

Aside from a thin urban upper middle class, wherein ideas about gender are beginning to change, men have a far greater capacity to spend time in urban and rural public space across India. They have more autonomy in terms of when and with whom they socialize and in their choices around leisure and cultural activity. Likewise, men have much greater freedom than do women to participate in the political life of the nation—from parliament, which remains heavily dominated by men, to district-level party organizations and representative bodies, down to the lowest levels of government in the village and urban neighbourhood.

Feminist scholars have recently stressed the danger associated with focusing solely on gender as a form of inequality. For all the points about women's vulnerability, gender cannot be imagined as the only, or even in many cases the most important, line of difference shaping social life in India. The hardships that mark the lives of women in India vary according to women's caste, class, religion, and age; women are often responsible for exploiting other women, for example in the case of mothers-in-law harassing new brides on the question of dowry; and it is often the manner in which gender intersects with another aspect of inequality, for example the status of a person as a Dalit, which renders them so vulnerable to poverty and marginalization. There is also an emerging gender literature on the particular difficulties faced by men in India, for example in relation to unemployment and associated 'crises of masculinity', and on the status of Hijras: transgender subjects who are often exploited in Indian society.

Post-structuralist feminist writers such as Judith Butler have also argued that in much of the mainstream gender literature the terms 'woman' and 'female' are prematurely and problematically stabilized, such that, for example, a person's status as a woman is taken for granted rather than analysed as a set of performances. One particularly troubling aspect of the 'work' that the term 'gender' performs in India is its tendency to subtly or directly attribute particular characteristics—such as vulnerability, victimhood, and marginality—to Indian women.

Another potential problem with gender analysis is its tendency to stereotype women as victims and men as aggressors. Since the 1980s in particular, women's organizations have become much more active in campaigning in India around a whole range of issues including alcoholism, rape, land rights, dowry, and domestic violence. Women have also been prominent in many rights campaigns. Further, women are often active at the local level, for example as representatives of their communities in everyday engagements with the state.

At the same time, and partly in response to such mobilization, the Indian state has made some efforts to improve women's political position. The seventy-third and seventy-fourth amendments of the Indian Constitution reserved 33 per cent of seats in village and town councils for women, and emerging evidence suggests that this may have had a positive impact on women's power and the manner in which government resources are disbursed in some regions. The Indian Government is currently engaged in legal reform around the issue of rape, and, at the local level, has made efforts to improve the responsiveness of the state to gender concerns, for example by introducing female-only police stations.

• See also *equality, feminism, masculinity*

Generation

Generation is a major axis of social difference and inequality in India, where patriarchal norms dictate that younger generations respect their seniors, and younger people often worked for older kin on farms or in household businesses. But the gradual movement of households outside agriculture, combined with rising education among young people, is slowly eroding such arrangements. Parents increasingly spend a large part of their incomes on education, and young people, who are more likely to be in school, have less time to do household and paid work. Attitudinal changes have accompanied this partial shift. Youth sometimes have forms of knowledge and experience that raise their status vis-à-vis older generations, even while parents continue to control major assets. There may therefore be a 'generation gap'—young people and their parents fail to understand each other's opinions and actions. There may also be a literal 'gap', as younger generations move to live outside the home. Reflecting these points, the English term 'generation' and Indian language equivalent words such as the Hindi '*pithi*' (generation) circulate widely in popular discourse.

Problems of social development and associated household crises with regard to education, childbearing, marriage, and work often manifest themselves in India as tensions between one generation and another. Such tensions and conflicts can take a wide variety of forms, but in many cases parents blame their children for failing to fulfil a household goal, while young people resent the pressures and restrictions placed on them by senior kin. Such scenarios are mentioned in numerous recent ethnographies of India as well as in novels and Bollywood films. Social change is occurring in other ways, too: novel alliances—between siblings or even across generations—are becoming evident, for example where young people join with grandparents in disputes with parents, and 'interstitial generations' are emerging, for example where young people in their twenties, well placed to advise on education and relationships, become mentors for younger youth.

According to Williams, 'generation' was first used in Europe in the thirteenth century to refer to offspring of the same parents—it was primarily a biological term and linked to 'the action of generating'. But he argues that the biological sense of generation slowly gave way in the late eighteenth and nineteenth centuries in Europe to social and historical uses of the concept. One aspect of this shift was the emergence of 'generation' used to denote a unit of time. A 'generation' corresponded to roughly thirty years—approximately the time it took for children to grow up, become adults, and have children themselves. Williams maintains that 'generation' in this sense—like the term 'period'—was used to refer to the distinctiveness of a particular portion of time, but in the context of general continuity. This use of the term is common among commentators writing about India, for example in accounts of India's 'next generation' of economic reforms. Such language is also connected to the idea that India is in a process of 'development'.

Much of the literature and public commentary on generation in India has concentrated on generation as a type of consciousness or identity. A generational consciousness may emerge as an effect of people's categorization by the state and other powerful institutions into age groups. In Europe in the nineteenth century the state became much more involved in regulating the lives of the population, for example through education. This process unfolded later in India, and is very much still ongoing. It is also possible that generational consciousness emerges because specific age cohorts encounter the same historical events at the same stages in their lives. Young people growing up in any particular place may be marked by their shared formative experiences to such an extent that they are predisposed to ally with other members of their generation. Where such a generational consciousness is strong—and when other conditions are propitious—generations may come to act as political units, sometimes even self-consciously referring to themselves as a generation. The *Jayaprakash Narayan* movement in the late 1970s and demonstrations against gender violence in India in 2012 are arguably generational movements in this sense, although they both involved a youth generation working alongside other sections of the population. Whether generation can 'trump' class, caste, and gender inequalities in the long term is a moot point in India.

One of the difficulties for analysts and public commentators in India, as in other parts of the world, is that it is practically very difficult to identify specific social generations; people are born continuously, not in clumps, and there are numerous logics that can be used for classifying populations into generations. This haziness allows institutions and individuals to dream up all types of generational groups. Perhaps the most famous such effort is Salman Rushdie's book, *Midnight's Children*, which reflects on the specific experiences of a fictional character—and his contemporaries—born at the precise moment at which India achieved Independence. Capitalist organizations are also involved in the invention of generations: 2G, 3G, and 4G mobile phones for example. India is often supposed to stand to benefit from a 'demographic dividend' because it has an exceptionally large younger generation, so that the numbers of those who can be productive greatly outweigh the numbers of those who depend on them (*see* population). The speed of social and economic change in India, however, means that generations—when applied to consumer goods and also to people—often topple over each other.

• See also *development, education, youth*

Globalization

Globalization—the proliferation and density of connections between different parts of the world associated with the development of capitalism on a global scale, new technological advances, and the increased movement of people across national boundaries—is conventionally dated to the later nineteenth century in the context of imperialism. These processes are often said to have retreated in the early to mid-twentieth century, before re-emerging and more vigorously so from the later 1970s. Certainly India, which had been pursuing a path of development that was marked by 'export pessimism' and detachment from international trade, has been much more tightly drawn into global circuits of capital and information since that time, and especially from the early 1990s onwards. Economic reforms since the 1990s have bolstered international trade and encouraged foreign direct investment, and the communications revolution has ushered in a period of intense international exchange in ideas.

In practice, 'globalization' commonly refers to India's emergence as a major service hub, for example in the processing of data for foreign firms—leading, of course, to growing concern in the West over offshoring and the loss of employment at home. Indian firms are now outsourcing some activities to other parts of South Asia and to China. Globalization is also used to describe the process through which India has been more tightly drawn into global networks of manufacturing. In addition, globalization refers to India's growing importance as a market for foreign firms, as they recognize the buying power of India's middle class—and even of those at the 'bottom of the pyramid'. The involvement of large foreign banks in the marketing of microfinance services to the Indian poor is a notable example of this trend. The interest of foreign universities in establishing branch campuses in India is another example, as is the importance of India as a market for military hardware. The key significance of India as a market can be measured in the seriousness with which the US and European countries woo Indian leaders through trade delegations, while the country has actually turned increasingly to trading relations with other Asian countries.

'Globalization' is also used in India to refer to the country's rising prominence, especially since the 1960s and accelerating in the 2000s, in networks of tourism and migration, circuits of international development aid, global cultural production (especially through the rising popularity of Bollywood movies), and networks of communication, as evident in a sharp hike in mobile phone ownership and growing access to the internet.

There is increasing recognition that the bundle of processes grouped under the term 'globalization' has had unequal effects, boosting metropolitan cities and leaving many other places behind. There are parts of India—such as remote regions of the Indian Himalayas—that may in certain senses be becoming less global rather than more so, reflecting the manner in which they have been marginalized within India economically. Nor does globalization result in some type of giant melting pot. Local people imbue iconic 'Western' products such as Coca-Cola with new meanings and utilize such symbols in ways that the manufacturers could not have anticipated: 'glocalization', as some would have it. Moreover, people's growing exposure to images and ideas emanating from outside India heightens their awareness of their distinctiveness vis-à-vis others, for example in terms of community, identity, and nation (*see* culture).

Globalization is often used to refer to the diffusion of ideas, people, and cultural practices from the West to other parts of the world: what is also sometimes termed 'Westernization' or 'McDonaldization'. This often mainly cultural understanding of globalization looms large in the collective Indian psyche, reflected in the subjects of Bollywood films and also occasionally the target of political opposition, for example from Hindu nationalists who want to protect a mythical Hindu India from the depredations of modernity: English-medium schools, Valentine's Day celebrations and Kentucky Fried Chicken have all been the targets for Hindu nationalist protests.

The West remains a major reference point for Indian citizens, but the notion that the West is gradually conquering India is a fiction. Most Indians are not learning to conform to Western practices, as the continued importance of arranged marriage shows. The notion of 'globalization as Westernization' also ignores how other non-Western places influence India, for example where city planners in India look to Singapore as a model, or where young people yearn to buy Japanese electronic goods and may have to settle for cheaper Chinese ones. Moreover, India is influencing the West as well as the other way round, as is evident in the popularity of Bollywood movies and Indian innovation in software—a point that has led some commentators to refer to a process of 'reverse globalization', but which instead simply indicates the multi-centred nature of globalization.

Globalization is sometimes used in the more specific sense of the spread of market-oriented approaches to the economy from Euro-America (especially the USA) to other parts of the world and the associated internationalization of corporate operations; globalization is a synonym for neo-liberalism. Some commentators and sections of the public in India welcome a new era of relative connectivity in the economy and market-centred economic planning, seeing in it the possibility for India to exploit its comparative advantage in terms of its population, spirit of enterprise, and natural resources. For powerful institutions such as the World Bank that advocate neo-liberalization, 'globalization' can be a useful tool of political discourse: it suggests newness and also a levelling of opportunities for participation in the economy over time.

But many oppose and resist neo-liberal globalization in India—from Gandhian NGOs to tribal villagers, socialist youth to environmental organizations. Anger at the involvement of foreign corporations in human and environmental catastrophes such as the Bhopal gas leak in 1984, Indian involvement in the Occupy movement, and also concern over the role of large corporates in the process of illegal land acquisition (land-grabbing) all attest to the force of such protest. Demonstrators often self-consciously style themselves as 'anti-globalization'. But interestingly the forces of anti-globalization are themselves highly globalized, often drawing on motifs of struggle from other parts of the world.

• See also *consumerism, culture, development, neo-liberal*

GMO

The acronym 'GMO' refers to 'genetically modified organisms', and in regard to agriculture, certainly in India, it has taken on a very negative meaning and become a symbol for all that environmentalists and the critics of neo-liberal economic policies seek to oppose. This is quite ironic, given that all agriculture, from the very beginning, has depended upon genetic modification, brought about by selective breeding carried on, initially, by ordinary cultivators. What have come to be labelled as 'GMOs', however, are varieties of plants that have been genetically *engineered*.

In genetic engineering, desirable genes (and their inherent characteristics) are transferred, in a laboratory, between organisms (and usually across species) so as to create desirable traits that it would otherwise be impossible to bring about through conventional breeding. An important example of such genetic engineering is that of the insertion of a gene from the soil bacterium *Bacillus thuringiensis (Bt)* into plants to provide them with insecticidal qualities—the resulting *Bt* protein, when ingested by certain pests, causes the insects to die. This particular process has been widely approved with cotton and maize (used for fibres and feed respectively—though *Bt* enters the food chain from both sources) but has so far been highly contested for use in food staples such as rice. The process involved is more accurately referred to as recombinant DNA (rDNA) technology, and the cultivars produced by it are better described as 'transgenics'. It may sound to be a difficult process, but in fact such genetic engineering is regularly carried out by ordinary college students of biology. It is not, after all, so very 'hi-tech'—and this is why, contrary to the arguments of anti-GMO campaigners, it has been possible for there to have sprung up a veritable cottage industry in parts of India, China, and Brazil, for the production of transgenics, often incorporating genetic material 'pirated' from big corporations (very much like 'pirate' film and music CDs).

Protagonists of the use of genetic engineering in agriculture argue that it has the potential to bring about a new agricultural revolution, comparable with the green revolution, and that it can deliver benefits to both farmers and consumers, for example by reducing the requirement to use plant protection chemicals, if pest resistance is built into plants genetically. Or it may make it possible to develop cultivars that are more drought tolerant, or capable of being grown in saline soils that are otherwise uncultivable. Or it may produce plants that give higher yields. But there is widespread fear of the technology as well, reflected in such epithets as 'frankenfoods'. The insertion of genetic material from another species into a plant is thought to be 'unnatural'. It is argued that the cultivation of GMOs involves unacceptable risks to human health and to the environment, and that—because the technology was developed initially by a small number of powerful, mainly American, chemical companies—it will be of benefit mainly to these corporations, which own patents to control the use of genetically engineered crops. The costs for small farmers in India of using these plants will impoverish them—or so it is argued. For these reasons there has developed powerful resistance to the application of genetic engineering in agriculture, mobilized around the 'GMO' acronym, in Europe and in both India and China.

In India, thus far, anti-GMO campaigning has been successful in restricting the use of the technology, except in regard to cotton cultivation. In this case, as one scholar has put it, 'farmers have voted with their ploughs', and have successfully resisted efforts by the central government to control the cultivation of *Bt* cotton. Such cotton, much of it grown using 'pirate' or 'stealth' seeds produced, not by the big corporations, but by local seed merchants, now accounts for more than 90 per cent of the cotton grown in India. Whether farmers have benefited from this, and in so far as they have, whether their benefits are sustainable, remains fiercely contested. And anti-GMO campaigning was successful in 2010 in causing the central government minister responsible to place a moratorium on the release of a *Bt* variety of brinjal (aubergine, or eggplant) in India—though this had been partly developed in public agricultural research institutions, and subjected to extensive testing. Resistance to the introduction of GMOs is powerful, while other techniques applied in agriculture such as mutagenesis (induced mutation) have largely escaped attention, and genetically engineered pharmaceutical products (such as insulin) have been very widely accepted.

• See also *environment, green revolution*

Green Revolution

This term seems to have been first used by the chief administrator of the United States Agency for International Development (USAID) in 1968, to refer to the impact of the introduction of new agricultural technology, based on the cultivation of what were then called 'higher-yielding varieties' (HYVs) of the major cereals. What he envisaged was an agricultural revolution in Asia and Latin America that would restrict the prospect of a

communist-inspired 'red revolution'. There continued at the time to be considerable concern among security analysts in the United States about the possibility that rural poverty in
Asia and Latin America, understood to be at least in part the consequence of inequality in
the distribution of land ownership, made for social conditions favourable to the spread of
communism. They also recognized, however, that efforts to address these problems directly,
through land reform, had generally—and certainly in India—been unsuccessful. The introduction of HYVs held out the prospect of a technological solution to these political
problems.

HYVs, or 'modern varieties' as they were later described, were the products of conventional plant-breeding carried on in research centres in Mexico and the Philippines, funded
by American foundations. They were bred to be fertilizer-responsive and proved capable of
much higher yields, if grown with adequate supplies of water. Such varieties of wheat began
to be introduced into India in 1966, in the context of severe shortages of food grains, and
what became known as India's green revolution took off, especially in Punjab, towards the
end of the 1960s.

But the green revolution, particularly in India, became the subject of fierce controversy.
Some observers believed that far from heading off the possibility of 'red revolution', the
introduction of the new technology, requiring as it did a package of purchased inputs,
including seed, fertilizer, pesticides, and water—often supplied by pumping up
groundwater—would end up by encouraging revolution. This was because the technological
package must often be beyond the financial means of smaller cultivators. It would, it was
believed, increase the advantages of the bigger cultivators and so increase inequality amongst
India's peasants. The possibility, then, that there would be political mobilizations of poor
peasants and landless people was a matter of concern for the Government of India by the
end of the 1960s. Would the 'green revolution' actually turn 'red'? Other critics argued that
the new technology would in the end be of most benefit to the mainly American corporations that (they said) supplied most of the inputs. The capitalist agriculture that the
technology encouraged would see the further impoverishment of a majority of the peasantry
and bring about the degradation of the environment.

As it turned out, the green revolution in India remained restricted largely to areas with
relatively good irrigation facilities, and smaller cultivators in these areas, as well as big
farmers, were able to take advantage of the new technology. Cereal production was successfully increased and India became self-sufficient in food grains. Poorer people, who depend
on purchases of food grains for their basic subsistence, benefited because of lower prices, and
in some areas because of increased wages that followed from the labour demands of green
revolution agriculture. The green revolution did not, however, supply the technical fix to the
problem of rural poverty that the administrator of USAID had hoped for.

• See also *development, environment, GMO*

Hindu (Hindustan, Hindustani)

'Hindu' is a Persian word, deriving from '*Sindhu*', the name in Sanskrit of the river Indus (that now lies in Pakistan), and it originally meant a native of 'the land around the Indus'. The *OED* records a similar use in English from the mid-seventeenth century, to describe a native of Hindustan, as in 'The inhabitants in general of Indostan were all anciently Gentiles, called in general Hindoes' (*sic*, 1655). Gradually, however, the term came to mean a native of India who had not converted to Islam; and now the current definition offered by *OED* is: 'An Aryan of Northern India (Hindustan), who retains the native religion (Hinduism) as distinguished from those who have embraced Islam; hence, anyone who professes Hinduism; applied by Europeans in a wider sense, in accordance with the wider application of Hindustan.' The term Hindu came to be applied to anything that was 'of India', or deemed to be 'native'. Thus there were references, for example, to 'Hindoo Muslims' and 'Hindoo Christians'.

'Hindustan', in turn, though it was surely in use much earlier, is first recorded by *OED* from 1801. It is now defined as follows: 'To its inhabitants Hindustan is "India north of the Narmada, exclusive of Bengal and Bihar", or virtually, the region covered by Hindi and its dialects. But from early times foreigners, Muslim and European, have extended it to include the whole of the peninsula...and this is the general geographical use.' The Persian term was introduced by the Muslim invaders of India to refer to the territory they had conquered across the Indus, and later to signify the heartland of the Mughal empire and, as the historian Christopher Bayly explains, a distinctive cultural realm, common to Hindus and Muslims, in the context of which forms of art, music, and poetry from both traditions were blended together. In the course of the eighteenth century this cultural term came to be identified with the greater part of the Indian subcontinent, existing alongside more or less strongly felt attachments to particular regional identities that Bayly describes as 'patriot-isms'. The language associated with it—Hindustani—became the link language across much of India, and it was described by European observers of India early in the nineteenth century as 'the national language' of the country.

Hindustani is defined by *OED*, which records its use in English from 1655, as 'The language of the Muslim conquerors of Hindustan, being a form of Hindi with a large admixture of Arabic, Persian, and other foreign elements; also called *Urdu*...(the) "language of the camp"...of the Mogul conquerors. It later became a kind of lingua franca over all India, varying greatly in its vocabulary according to the locality and local language.' This definition hints at the complicated relationship between Hindi and Urdu. There are only relatively minor differences of grammar between the two languages, and they are distinguished mainly by vocabulary and script, one a modified version of Persian and the other the Devanagari script of Hindi. They are generally mutually intelligible except in their higher, more literary forms. 'High Hindi' contains so many Sanskrit words, and the corresponding level of Urdu so much Persian and Arabic, as to render them mutually unintelligible. It was only as a result of a political struggle in the nineteenth century that Hindi became clearly established as India's major language—even though it is the language of only about half of the population.

• See also *Hinduism, language, nation*

Hinduism

Hinduism is now commonly regarded as one of the great religions of the world. This is not an idea that is shared by all contemporary religious leaders in India, however. Rather, they often refer to their religious belief and practice as the '*sanatana dharma*', meaning (roughly) 'eternal way of life', though sometimes translated as 'the eternal religion'; and they consider that all other theologies and religious practices are in some way encompassed by their own. Theirs is, simply, 'religion', not just one of a number of religious traditions.

This is one reflection of the extraordinary diversity of belief and practice that is found in what has come to be described as 'Hinduism', and it helps to explain why many Hindus, like Gandhi, believe that their religious tradition is distinctively and peculiarly syncretic, or inclusive, and encourages tolerance. As Islam spread into India, Muslims certainly thought of other Indians as practising a different religion. Then the British, first in Bengal in the later eighteenth century, confronted by a plethora of religious practice which they at first thought was largely incoherent primitivism, finally came to regard it through the lens of their own religious culture, and assumed that there must be a coherent system of beliefs that could be compared with those of Christianity. By the early nineteenth century they spoke of 'Hinduism', when Indians themselves may well still have thought of their religious identities in other terms, such as those referring to the followers of one or other major deity (of Shiva, or Vishnu, for example, or one or other of the goddesses who embody divine power), or of the sects created by particular religious leaders. Then some of the policies pursued by the colonial government, resting on the presumption that there was a distinct religion in India, helped to bring one into being. Meanwhile, reform movements developed amongst Hindus that sought to define and to bring coherence to their religion. 'Hinduism' is therefore often seen by scholars as a modern concept, formed as a result of what might be described as a process of reification.

The *OED* shows the word as having been in use by 1829; the Dictionary now defines 'Hinduism' as 'The polytheistic religion of the Hindus, a development of ancient Brahminism, with many later accretions.' There is something of a tautology here, given that 'Hindu' is defined as an Indian who 'professes Hinduism'. But if it was first the British who defined the religion of many Indians in such a way as to imply a structured coherence that it did not necessarily possess, Indians themselves began to use the term in the course of the nineteenth century, and to organize around it in various reform movements. In this 'reformed' Hinduism, the Vedas—four texts written down about 3–4,000 years ago that are the most ancient of Hindu scriptures—were generally identified as the foundational holy book. Hinduism was recognized as a 'world religion', associated—as are both Islam and Christianity, for instance—with a particular holy book on which religious authority is based. In 1893 Hinduism was represented at the 'World's Parliament of Religions', held in Chicago, by one of the most significant of the religious leaders of modern India—and a major influence on the Indian struggle for national independence—Swami Vivekananda (1863–1902). He taught that Hinduism, based on the Vedas, is a universal and tolerant faith, though he also believed that Hinduism is superior to other religions because of this.

Other religious traditions are characterized by diversity and difference, of course, but such are the inconsistencies and contradictions within Hinduism that in the words of one contemporary scholar, the German Indologist Heinrich von Stietencron, it 'certainly does not meet the fundamental requirements for a historical religion of being a coherent system [though] its distinct entities [the so-called "sects"] do. They are indeed religions, while Hinduism is not.' Among many points of difference, others of the major world religions are generally held to be much more highly organized than is Hinduism—within which there is nothing like 'the Church'—even though an eighth-century religious leader, Adi Shankara, founder of the philosophy of *Advaita Vedanta* (espoused by Vivekananda) created four monastic Orders which still have their *maths* ('*mutts*', or 'monasteries') today. Whether or not Hinduism is less 'organized' than other major religious traditions may perhaps be debated, but this perceived lack of organization was a matter of great concern for Indians who began to resist British colonial rule—which was associated with an evangelical form of Christianity—in the middle of the nineteenth century. They thought that Hindus must organize themselves as they had not before, and they began to do so through the formation of Hindu *sabhas* (or associations), brought together in 1915 in the *Hindu Mahasabha* (formed originally as a group within the Congress party), which subsequently played a significant part both in the struggle for independence and in the formation of a distinctively Hindu nationalism (*see* Hindutva). Hindu nationalism has come to project a notion of Hinduism as a unified religious tradition which is catholic internally (so it downplays differences between castes), but exclusive and intolerant in regard to those who are considered to be 'others', whose religions are held to be characterized by intolerance.

Religious scholars continue to debate the concept of 'Hinduism', even while very large numbers of people throughout India define themselves unconcernedly as 'Hindu'. Is there some coherent set of ideas that underlies the diversity in their religion? Some scholars argue, like Vivekananda, that there is unity deriving ultimately from the significance of the Vedas. To see these texts, however, as 'the canon of Hindu scripture' as they have been by some scholars, and as they are also regarded by many Hindu nationalists, is perhaps to reflect a Western frame of reference and a belief that there must be a foundational (or 'fundamental') text. It is also a reflection of the 'high' or Brahminical form of Hinduism, that defined by Brahmin priests, on whom the colonial rulers depended so much for their own information about those over whom they ruled—and, unsurprisingly therefore, referred to quite specifically in *OED*—when there may be no explicit reference at all to these scriptures in the rituals and practices of the popular or 'folk' forms of Hinduism that are its most common manifestation. In so far as there is unity in 'Hinduism', it perhaps derives most—as the anthropologist Christopher Fuller has shown—from similarities in such religious practice across the country, having to do with the everyday interactions of people, through *puja* (worship), with the multitude of deities who are held to have power over the world.

The Supreme Court of India has been compelled on a number of occasions to take a stance on what defines Hinduism. Several significant judgments by the Court have rested on an inclusivist view of Hinduism, holding that it is an all-embracing religion, but it also held in one case of 1966 that Hinduism 'may broadly be described as *a way of life* and nothing more' (emphasis added). The same argument led the Court thirty years later to conflate Hinduism and Hindutva, on the grounds that the latter too refers to the way of life of the Indian people. It cannot, therefore, according to the arguments of one judge, be equated with 'narrow fundamentalist Hindu religious bigotry'. The Court thus bridged the inclusivist view of Hinduism, propounded for example by Vivekananda, and the exclusivist arguments of Hindu nationalists. Both views, in holding that there is a unity in the religious traditions of 'Hindus', have the effect of homogenizing, and both proclaim the superiority of Hinduism to other faiths.

• See also *constitution, Hindu, Hindutva, secularism*

Hindutva (Hindu nationalism)

This word, which began to appear in writing in English early in the twentieth century (*OED* cites a text published in 1913), was originally understood, as the Dictionary says, to mean 'Hindu-ness' or 'the state or quality of being Hindu'. That it should go on to say 'In later use [Hindutva is] an ideology seeking to establish the hegemony of Hindus and the Hindu way of life; Hindu nationalism' is the result, largely, of the writings of Vinayak Damodar ('Veer') Savarkar. His two tracts, *Essentials of Hindutva* (c.1922) and the later *Hindutva: Who is a Hindu?* (1923), have a strong claim to be considered the foundational texts of Hindu nationalism. Savarkar (1883–1966) remains a hugely controversial figure in modern Indian history, one both admired and despised. As a young man studying for the bar in London at the beginning of the twentieth century, Savarkar became involved in revolutionary activities that led to his being imprisoned by the British in 1910. He wrote his texts on Hindutva while still in jail. After his release in 1924, he became for a long time the President of the Hindu Mahasabha (*see* Hinduism), a fierce critic of the Indian National Congress, and he was one of those accused of having plotted the assassination of Gandhi in 1948. It is a mark of the controversy that surrounds him even among Hindu nationalists that the English language website of the Bharatiya Janata Party (BJP), the party political arm of the broader movement for Hindu nationalism, the Sangh Parivar, does not cite him as an authority when it explains its use of 'Hindutva': 'Hindutva or Cultural Nationalism presents the BJP's conception of Indian nationhood ... It must be noted that Hindutva is a nationalist, and not a religious or theocratic, concept.' Yet this is exactly the idea of 'Hindutva' that Savarkar (an atheist) developed, in the context of controversy among Indians themselves over what defines a Hindu and should be the base for Indian nationalism.

Savarkar's answer to the question of 'Who is a Hindu?', given on the title page of the contemporary edition of *Hindutva*, is: 'A HINDU means a person who regards this land of BHARATVARSHA, from the Indus to the Seas as his Father-land as well as his Holy-Land that is the cradle land of his religion.' He goes on to say in the text that 'Hindutva is different from Hinduism'. Hindutva—and the Hindu nation—are defined by the two elements of common 'father-land', implying a territorial racialism, and common 'holy-land', or shared sacred geography. The first of these is important in that it suggests a fraternity based on common blood, so overriding caste differences. In this way Savarkar sought to overcome 'fissiparous tendencies' among Hindus (in the words of the contemporary Introduction to *Hindutva*) and to bridge the profound differences between the followers of the idea of 'sanatana dharma' (*see* Hinduism), which defends caste hierarchy as integral to Hinduism, and the Hindu reform movements that rejected caste differences. The idea of a common 'holy-land' suggests a set of cultural criteria that define 'Hindu-ness'. Savarkar speaks of shared Sanskritic 'rites, rituals, ceremonies and sacraments', and though he wants to argue that their significance is essentially cultural and not religious, religion is at best only partially displaced from his conception of Hindutva. Muslims, Christians, and some others cannot ever fully possess the attributes of Hindutva, because their holy places lie elsewhere. They cannot ever fully be part of the Hindu nation and must forever be 'others' to Hindus. The Muslim invasions of India were held to have been 'disastrous to the national virility', and were primarily responsible for the Hindu decline that it is the purpose of Hindutva to reverse. Hindutva implies xenophobic racism, and Savarkar and other Hindu nationalists (notably M. S. Golwalkar (1906–73), the second supreme leader of the Rashtriya Swayam-sevak Sangh) later celebrated both the actions of the Nazis in Germany against the Jewish minority, and the subsequent formation of a Jewish state in Palestine.

Savarkar's ideas provided what one writer refers to as a 'foundational vocabulary' for the leaders of the central organization of the Hindu nationalist movement, the Rashtriya Swayamsevak Sangh, founded in Nagpur in 1925 by K. B. Hedgewar (1889–1940) and led after his death by Golwalkar. This is now the core of a 'family' of organizations, the Sangh Parivar, that includes, as well as the BJP (though the political party, the Jana Sangh, that was its precursor was actually founded by the Hindu Mahasabha), the *Vishwa Hindu Parishad* (or 'World Hindu Council'), which is an organization of Hindu religious leaders, and other groups that are dedicated to the cause of Hindu nationalism, now defined in terms of the establishment of a 'Hindu *rashtra*'—a nation and a state governed by *dharma* (the Hindu way of life). Together they assert that the strength of the nation depends on Hindus being true to themselves as 'Hindus'.

Latterly, in the context of contemporary politics, the agenda of Hindutva has come to focus on three rather specific political objectives, which together define its popular meaning. These are the determination to establish a Uniform Civil Code (whereas at present Muslims and Christians are still allowed their own civil laws, grounded in religion: *see* secularism); to remove Article 370 of the Constitution that provides for the special status of Jammu and Kashmir (India's only state with a Muslim majority) within the Indian Union; and to build a Hindu temple, dedicated to the god Rama, on the site of the Babri Masjid, a sixteenth-century mosque at Ayodhya (in Uttar Pradesh in North India). The last of these provided a powerful focus for the political mobilizations of Hindu nationalists in the 1980s, and, despite the opposition of the central government, and in the face of an injunction against them by the Supreme Court, they succeeded in demolishing the mosque in December 1992. The construction of a temple on its site, however, has still not been accomplished, and the failure of the BJP to complete this task in the period from 1998 to 2004 when it headed coalition governments has been an important source of tensions within the Sangh Parivar.

• See also *community, fundamentalism, Hinduism, Muslim, nation, politics, secularism*

History

History has a range of connotations in English, though they converge around the ideas of 'narrative' or 'story' and of a chronological 'record' of events. Williams argues that the root of the English term is in a Greek word that had the early sense of 'inquiry' and then later that of 'an account of knowledge'. In their early uses in English, both 'history' and 'story' were applied to accounts both of imaginary and of real events; but the idea of history as organized knowledge about the past—involving 'inquiry', and the attempt to explain what has happened—became current from the later fifteenth century, and this remains the predominant use of the word. There are many different approaches to the way in which historical inquiry is conducted and historical narratives written.

English writers in the nineteenth century took it as self-evident that Indians altogether lacked historical sensibility. It was noted that while Muslims had at least produced chronicles of past events, Hindus hadn't even done that. The idea was even extended, as it was in some of his work by Marx, to the notion that India had no real history before the colonial era. For all the evidence of changes of dynasties, Indian society, it was held, had not changed at all in any fundamental sense. No contemporary scholar makes any such suggestion, but the idea that the lack of a sense of history—or ahistoricism—is one of the defining features of Indian civilization is accepted by some historians even now. Others disagree, referring to the existence, for example, of caste histories and family chronicles. One scholar, Peter van der Veer, has said that he finds the idea that Indians lacked a sense of history to be 'ridiculous'—though he also concedes that 'Hindu discourse often tried to avoid historical referentiality'. But whether Indians in the past lacked historical sensibility or not, there is no doubt at all that the writing of history has become an extremely important part of nation-building in modern India, as it has elsewhere in the world, and that the interpretation of the past, in school textbooks, and in regard to current events, is most intensely contested. And Indian historians have come to be recognized internationally as standing amongst the most influential members of their profession.

In the earlier nineteenth century Indians themselves responded to their own, and to their colonial rulers', understanding that they in some sense 'lacked history'. In 1838 a number of Bengalis formed a Society for the Acquisition of General Knowledge, in Calcutta, and the first lecture they heard was one 'On the nature and importance of historical studies'. From about this time Indians began to engage in history writing. Others, however, believed that India's rich religious and epic literature contained historical knowledge. The great epic, the *Mahabharata*, came to be treated not as an allegorical myth but as history, and it is still regarded as such by many Hindu nationalists for whom Krishna is a historical figure. In a similar way, many caste histories bring together myth and history. And the success of a political movement such as the Dravidian movement in the southern state of Tamil Nadu has to do in part with the skilful creation by some of its leaders, who were writers and film-makers, of a mytho-history of the Tamil people.

In the twentieth century Indian nationalists drew on contending interpretations of the past. Nehru's *Discovery of India*, published in 1946, sought to portray 'the essential unity' of India, for all its enormous diversity of language, religion, and culture, and provided a kind of charter for his conception of Indian nationalism—a multicultural conception as it might now be described. History teaching was, however, for a long time influenced by the work of R. C. Majumdar, which was solidly informed but included such ideas as that the period of Muslim ascendancy constituted the 'dark ages' of Indian history, and that Muslims and Hindus in India were two 'separate nations'. At the end of the twentieth century and in the present millennium, historical understanding has become an important battleground between Hindu nationalists and their secular opponents. Both sides have, for example, called historians to their aid in regard to the dispute over the site of the old mosque, the Babri Masjid in Ayodhya; and there have been bitter fights over the content of school textbooks, and over the writing of an official history of India's freedom struggle. It is perhaps hardly surprising that historians are now especially well represented amongst India's most notable public intellectuals. Among their peers across the world both India's left-oriented historians and those of the so-called 'Subaltern School', who offer fundamental criticism of postcolonial modernity, are very highly regarded.

• See also **colonialism, community, Hindutva, modern, nation, subaltern**

Identity

Identity is defined in the *Oxford English Dictionary* as 'the fact of being who or what a person or thing is'. But the notion that identity is usually associated with an individual 'person or thing' is relatively recent. Williams noted that before the seventeenth century, identity was imagined only in collective terms. It was not until the eighteenth and nineteenth centuries that commentators placed much greater emphasis on the individual and individuals' selves, lives, and qualities vis-à-vis other individuals. In India, questions of individual identity have been slightly less important historically, reflecting the greater social significance of group ties, for example based on family, location, and caste. But the notion of India as somehow fundamentally oriented towards the group is problematic, and the balance between collective understandings and ties on the one hand and individualism on the other is changing with the rise of individual, market-centric ideas and as a result of globalization.

The *OED* definition implies that identity is intrinsically linked to some underlying essence; 'identity' is what springs out of the core nature of a person or group. But scholars have argued that identities are better conceived of as fictional constructs. They reflect a human tendency to want to tell a particular story about an individual or collective and make these stories count as reality. Identity is therefore a means of constructing a narrative about oneself, one's group, or other people and other groups. The capacity of institutions and individuals to make particular identities stick often says a great deal about the distribution of power in society more broadly.

A person's identities—for example, as daughter, mother, friend, worker—may change during a single day and also over time as economic and social transformation takes place. Their sense of belonging to particular communities may also shift over time. This is especially the case in societies such as India in which people's lives are changing very rapidly in the context of urbanization, growing education, and new opportunities for communication. In such contexts it becomes very difficult to identify anything like a stable identity, and it is perhaps telling that some scholars—both within and outside India—have even abandoned the concept of identity altogether because of its tendency to suggest rather fixed cultural practices and processes of identification.

Implicit in many definitions of identity is the notion that identities spring—in and of themselves—out of the qualities of a person or thing. Yet identities are constructed in relation to one another: they emerge out of a sense of difference from another individual or group. They are also performed in relation to different audiences. For example, Hindu nationalists often define their own identity in relation to a Muslim 'Other', and with other Indians as their primary 'audience'. Likewise, the identity of a college student in Delhi may be formed in relation to her parents, other urban citizens, and students in other parts of the world, while the audience for her performances might be students, teachers, or a partner. Likewise, in the case of class, caste, and gender identities, the identity of a particular group—middle classes, Brahmins, women—always emerges partly from what they are not (poor, Dalits, and men) and in performances that take place in real-world contexts: at the water tap, in the bus, in the school playground. People's frame of reference—and the audience for their identity projects—is changing rapidly in contemporary India with the rise of cable and satellite television, increased travel, and greater exposure to foreign visitors and media. These changes in turn alter the extent to which and how people in India imagine their distinctive national, regional, group, and individual identities.

'Identity politics' is usually defined as politics based on the characteristics of a specific group, such as caste, class, gender, or some other particularistic quality, such as sexuality or place of origin. Identity politics is distinct from more ideological forms of politics, as well as from party politics and civil society action, and identity politics is strong in India, reflecting the power of group identities in the country and also the relative absence of broad cross-community understandings.

The Government of India's introduction of a new identity card (ID) scheme has politicized the question of identity. The Unique Identification Authority of India (UIDAI) was established in 2009 to provide all Indians with IDs. The scheme has the potential to improve people's access to core government services and banking, but has been criticized from the standpoint of civil liberties and with reference to issues of national security.

• See also *community, individual, modern, nation*

Individual

The notion of a singular person as an 'individual' is a central tenet of Western Enlightenment thinking, associated especially with the writing of Descartes. In this Western view, the individual human being is separable and discrete from other humans, with an independent capacity for thought, feeling, and action. The anthropologist Louis Dumont famously argued that this conception of the person—as a bounded, unique being with his/her own discrete centre of consciousness—is not widely applicable to India, although he suggested that a certain type of individualism does exist in India in the form of the 'renouncer', a spiritual figure who abandons society in favour of focusing on his own, individual, salvation. Dumont asserted that most Indians developed their sense of identity through relations with others, especially other members of their family, kin, or caste—the individual person was always subservient to these wider collectivities, and caste, in particular, formed the organic whole of which individual people were simply the part. McKim Marriott developed this idea, positing that people in India are better thought of as 'dividuals' rather than 'individuals'. Individuals are linked through the circulation of various substances—Marriott called them 'substance-codes'—such as blood, alcohol, and food, and these are transmitted between bodies, families, and castes.

The writing of Dumont and Marriott has since been challenged. The notion that India lacked an ethic of individualism is founded on a mid-twentieth-century vision of culture in which particular areas were imagined as having certain unchanging 'traits', such as an ethic of community. A more historical examination of the question of the individual in India would consider shifting concepts of personhood through time. It would entail acknowledging, for example, the importance of individualism within the *bhakti* tradition of devotionalism as well as within Buddhism, which emphasizes devotees' individual relationships to god. India has also changed a great deal since Dumont and Marriott formulated their theories. The spread of education and government efforts at development have had the general effect of loosening ties of family, kinship, and caste. For example, young people increasingly think about their marriages in 'individual' terms, and with reference to ideas of companionship and romantic love. After marriage, they place greater emphasis than did a previous generation on the satisfaction of individual goals and desires.

Another set of changes is bound up with the liberalization of the Indian economy since the early 1990s. Economic reforms ushered in a particular form of individualization based on an ethic of self-maximization through market consumption. Advertisements often encourage people to reflect upon the self and express individual difference through consumerism. Simultaneously, powerful institutions and organizations such as the World Bank enjoin people to take responsibility for their own individual lives, and 'individualism' (in English) or related Indian language terms such as '*vyaktivaad*' have gained increased currency. Another effect of modernization and liberalization has been the increasing personalization of religion and spiritual life. To a certain extent—and most prominently among the middle classes—temple worship has been partially replaced by the efforts of individuals to cultivate links with specific religious spiritual leaders. There are parallel shifts in the political sphere, again especially in the middle classes. People may be becoming less interested in collective mobilization than in individual efforts to shape society through organizational work. Others have argued that a broader process of political individualization is at work, wherein all forms of collective politics are withering away and people's political participation is increasingly limited to the individual act of voting.

But modernity and neo-liberalization are contradictory sets of processes; there has been no simple shift from community to individual understandings and practices. For example, in the social sphere, parentally arranged marriage remains predominant, even as young people formulate individual goals with respect to partners. In the economic sphere, many of India's microfinance organizations stress the importance of mutual responsibility with others, and enterprise is fostered within small self-help groups. Politically, India has witnessed many collective demonstrations over the past decade, and—in the cultural sphere—the idea of India as a society rooted in an ethic of community spirit and collective endeavour remains important in all manner of arenas, such as Bollywood films, novels, and advertisements. Moreover, some feminist scholars have pointed out that the notion of India's growing individual orientation is a product of gender power: women may not see the world in these terms. There is some anthropological work that supports this idea, showing that women are more inclined to view themselves as part of an organic, wider kin unit than are men in India.

In contrast to the *OED* definition, which pits the individual against the human 'group', the issue of the individual's relationship to the surrounding material and natural environment is also live in India. Some environmentalists would argue that the notion of growing individuality in the subcontinent underplays the extent to which people are part of the natural system they inhabit, and perhaps think of themselves in these terms to a greater extent than is the case in the West. Indeed, the growth of discourses critical of environmental degradation may result in new theories of people's 'relationality' that pit an 'individual West' against a supposedly more organically interdependent India.

• See also *caste, consumerism, family, neo-liberal*

Informal

When applied to economic activity, the *OED* defines 'informal' as 'carried on by self-employed or independent people on a small scale, especially unofficially or illegally'. Much of this definition does not apply very well to India and the global South, where the informal sector is sometimes regulated by the state or NGOs, straddles the boundaries between legality and illegality, and includes elites as well as the poor. The term 'informal sector' originates in the work of the anthropologist Keith Hart in the later 1960s in Ghana, and in its subsequent adoption by the International Labour Office (ILO) in a study of Kenya made in 1971. The ILO researchers saw that development in Kenya was not ushering in a process of smooth 'modernization' manifest in the emergence of large manufacturing units and formal service sector jobs, but was occurring more commonly through the growth of informal types of entrepreneurship—such as street vending, shoe shining, furniture making, and small-scale agricultural production.

This has been true, too, of India. In 2005, the National Commission for Enterprises in the Unorganized Sector in India defined the informal economy as 'all unincorporated private enterprises owned by individuals or households engaged in the sale and production of goods and services operated on a proprietary or partnership basis and with less than 10 total workers'. Other definitions in India place a similar emphasis on the informal economy being comprised of units: (1) operating at a low level of organization, (2) exhibiting little or no division between labour and capital as factors of production, (3) running on a small scale, and (4) involving people mobilizing capital on an individual basis and in situations where expenditure for production is often indistinguishable from household expenditure. According to a National Sample Survey in 2004–5, over 90 per cent of jobs in India are in the informal economy. Even in the non-agricultural sector, over 82 per cent of occupations are informal. In 2004 the informal economy accounted for roughly 50 per cent of GDP in India.

The precise connotations of the term 'informal' when applied to the economy vary according to one's perspective and political position. For many researchers in India, the informal economy is a realm of considerable exploitation (much of it self-exploitation), in which relatively marginalized sections of society work in difficult conditions to survive. Women, children, and low castes are over-represented in the informal economy, especially the least remunerative, most gruelling sectors of the informal economy such as garbage collection, street vending, and small-scale artisanal work within households. Recent research suggests that the informal economy is becoming more productive, but involves declining numbers of people. This suggests that some are leaving the informal economy in the face of poor returns—perhaps true especially for women—and also that those who remain are working harder. Several scholars have charted the hidden injuries of labour exploitation within the informal economy, highlighting the lack of effective state regulation of the sector, the absence of labour rules and guarantees, and the manner in which caste, class, and gender inequalities structure informal work. This is especially true in the context of the liberalization of the Indian economy, which has encouraged the outsourcing of multiple processes to small units in India, and has swelled the ranks of a vast 'surplus population' of informal workers. There is also a good deal of evidence to suggest that crime of various sorts—illegal intermediary work in the management of development projects, black market trade, and unregulated construction—constitutes a substantial section of the informal economy.

The informal economy is also sometimes represented and understood as a sphere of enterprise and innovation. Such an understanding can be traced at least as far back as Hernando de Soto's influential work on entrepreneurship in the informal sector in Peru in the 1970s, but it has received even greater attention in contemporary India with the emergence of studies and media productions stressing the enterprise of the poor. Moreover, much of the innovation, for example in areas such as telecommunications and IT, may engender productive and synergistic relationships with the formal sector and provide a measure of economic security. Commentators writing in this vein frequently stress that the informal economy arose in part as a result of the strictures and corruption associated with formal state regulation, rather than being straightforwardly a sphere of 'last resort'.

One interesting development in the Indian context is the growing involvement of the state, NGOs, and international organizations in coordinating positive forms of informal entrepreneurship. Much of this occurs through the activity of microfinance organizations and the small self-help groups that have emerged through small-scale financing. Relatively organized forms of informal work are also embodied in such initiatives as India's Self-Employed Women's Association, a trade union of women in informal work that has more than 1.4 million members. Another interesting development is the growing attempts by scholars and concerned citizens to map the contours of what the urban studies scholar Ananya Roy terms 'elite informality'. This term refers to the efforts of the rich to enhance their profits through such mechanisms as land grabs, tax evasion, and the construction of illegal property.

'Informal' is a term applied to other sectors apart from the economy, especially housing. Paralleling debates on the economy, commentators now often stress not only the poverty that can result in people living in informal housing, but also the enterprise associated with the construction of makeshift dwellings or slums. There is also an emerging literature on small-scale enterprise in India and the particular value that is attached to finding ways to 'make do and mend' in unpromising situations. In this literature, informality is sometimes elevated to a national point of pride: China has planning, but India has a type of what used to be described as 'Heath Robinson' ingenuity, after the name of an English illustrator who drew eccentric machines. It is what is now celebrated as 'jugaad' (*see* enterprise).

'Informal' is also an adjective that can be applied to politics. Partha Chatterjee has made the influential argument that the majority of the poor in India do not make demands on the state through formal channels, but rather through engaging in social protests, through navigating patron–client networks, or via engaging in corruption vis-à-vis individual state officials. This everyday politicking is informal in the sense that it is often illegal, violent, and does not take place within named, regulated political associations of a 'civil society' type. Recent work on the politics of those employed in the informal economy lends some credence to this analysis. Many of those employed in the unorganized sector draw back from trying to mobilize as labourers. Instead they form into alliances, often based on particularistic loyalties such as caste, to make demands on the state, frequently employing confrontational tactics.

• See also *corruption, development, enterprise, labour, poverty*

Justice

According to the *OED*, justice refers to 'the quality of being fair and reasonable'. Many scholars, commentators, and activists have taken what Amartya Sen terms a 'transcendental' approach to justice: they seek to identify perfectly just societal arrangements and campaign for a transition to this ideal, just state of affairs. Marxism is an example of a transcendental approach, founded on a vision of a perfect socialist society in which class divisions cease to be relevant. Likewise, Naxalite and Dalit movements in India have at their core a vision of total transformation to a just society. Sen has criticized transcendental approaches as being too black and white—a society might abolish slavery, but advocates of transcendental approaches might still diminish the achievement because the society remains 'non-just' from their perspective. Sen also argues that transcendental approaches unrealistically aim for complete agreement on what constitutes fairness and reasonableness, as if the meaning of 'justice' could be fixed for time immemorial and across the whole world.

A second approach to justice identified by Sen, and championed by him as more appropriate for the contemporary world, is comparative. It aims not at a watertight vision of what constitutes justice, but seeks to build up from below—and out of observations of notions of fairness in varied locations—a concept of what is usually regarded as just and reasonable by people in different places and in relation to various spheres of life. Sen urges people to think about justice by trying to imagine what their own society and social practices would be like to outsiders, and to reflect critically on those aspects of their social world that others would regard as unjust. Such an approach is attractive in part because it tallies with how people in South Asia actually discuss justice. In India, abstract ideologies are typically less significant in defining justice than practical concerns over educating children, obtaining food and medical care, or acquiring protection from the police or the courts. Moreover, people's approaches to obtaining justice in these spheres are increasingly comparative, since they are often travelling more than in the past and increasingly accessing electronic communication technologies.

Sen acknowledges that such a comparative approach will not lead to a definitive list of what is just and unjust for all people, in every society, across the range of people's activities. There will always be disagreement because 'justice' can be defined in very different ways in different contexts, people have different priorities with respect to justice, and individuals are also differently placed within societies and have varied interests. But a comparative approach is useful as a means to identify practices that most people in most parts of the world would regard as unjust: famine, widespread illiteracy, physical violence against women, and needless death from manageable diseases, for example. If agreement can at least be reached on these key points, it becomes possible to build and defend statements of minimum universal rights.

Contentious issues related to justice remain unresolved in India, reflecting the internal diversity of the country, for example along regional, ideological, religious, class, and gender lines, and also the sheer scale of the social injustices evident in the country. For some groups 'distributive justice' will be a rallying cry. Others will mobilize around calls for 'environmental justice' or 'justice for women'. In many cases these different visions of justice are in conflict. But there is nevertheless considerable agreement across the political spectrum about the need to tackle basic issues of injustice related to food, health, education, the environment, and political rights—Sen's pragmatic, comparative approach to justice seems to have been internalized by many citizens of India. The recent anti-corruption movement in India and campaigns around questions of rights are indicative of this point. More broadly, the Indian Constitution is a strong statement of universal minimum rights, and its survival, as well as the various amendments to the Constitution since 1950, stands testament to a shared sense of fairness among Indians.

According to the *OED*, justice can also refer to the administration of the law, or authority in maintaining a fair and reasonable society, as in the phrases 'system of justice' or 'criminal justice'. India has a highly developed legal system consisting of a Supreme Court in Delhi, various high courts at the state levels, and a complex network of local courts. But this system has long been a source of consternation to commentators and people on the ground. India's federal judicial system has a backlog of over 20 million cases and thousands of prisoners awaiting trial. The length of time people have to wait to obtain judgments has also risen rapidly in recent years. There is widespread bribery, cronyism, and other forms of nefarious activity occurring within the legal system, especially at the local and provincial levels. The twin problems of delay and corruption have especially negative implications for low castes, adivasis, Muslims, and women seeking legal redress.

As Pratap Bhanu Mehta has pointed out, another problem concerns the relationship between the legislature and the executive. The Supreme Court has acted as an important check on an increasingly corrupt and criminalized sphere of representative politics in India, and as the safeguard of democracy, but in the process it has expanded its role beyond that of interpreting and enforcing the Constitution to also scrutinizing legislation to determine constitutionality, creating law, and exercising policy prerogatives normally reserved for the executive. The most important mechanism for this expansion of juridical powers has been the institution of Public Interest Legislation (PIL). In PIL cases, the Supreme Court relaxes the normal requirement that only those directly affected can press charges, allowing any Indian citizen to approach it seeking correction of an alleged injustice. Judges have thereby come to play key roles in the governance of India, managing issues as diverse as the closure of polluting industries, the construction of new homes for slum dwellers, and the registration of tertiary educational institutions as universities. Whether such judicial activism is effective in terms of addressing injustice in the various spheres in which questions of fairness become relevant for Indian citizens, for example in relation to education and health, is a critically under-researched topic. But what seems clear is that the courts are increasingly arrogating powers normally reserved for the executive, and in the process undermining the reputation of India's state representatives (who are, after all, the ones who are directly elected). The gains to be had from the Supreme Court's purportedly just interventions may outweigh the loss of effective popular democracy—but, equally, they may not.

Another worrying development in India is the considerable assertiveness of bodies that are not part of the formal legal process. Most notably, *khap panchayats* (caste councils) in Haryana and western Uttar Pradesh have been involved in punishing people, especially youth, who are perceived to have contravened local caste norms. Young people have been ostracized, beaten, and even killed by panchayats that operate in the name of 'justice' but straightforwardly fail to abide by the criteria of fairness and reasonableness. 'Summary justice' and kangaroo courts are becoming depressingly common themes in the media and public discussion.

• See also *corruption, criminal, democracy, law, poverty, rights*

Labour

The original meanings of 'labour' in English (from around 1300) had the general sense, Raymond Williams tells us, of hard work and difficulty. The word still does carry these connotations. But from the seventeenth century it came to be used in a more abstract way to mean the activity of productive work, and then as a term of political economy—'labour' as a critical factor in the production of commodities, along with capital and materials. In the early nineteenth century the word also came to be used to refer to a social class, and in the course of that century a 'self-conscious and self-styled Labour movement' came into being, while the 'general sense of a political and economic interest and movement' was most specifically defined through the formation in Britain of the Labour Party (quotes from Williams).

In Hindi, the term '*kaam*' is analogous to labour, but people often use the term '*mazdoori*', which is more specifically associated with manual labour, and '*mehnat*', which also has the sense of 'toil' or 'burdensome work'. The English word has been used most commonly with reference to particular categories of employment or groups of workers, as in 'agricultural labour', 'bonded labour', 'contract labour', and 'casual labour'. There is still extensive child labour in India, in spite of the efforts of service organizations and of some NGOs to stop it. The term 'casual labour', commonly used to refer to workers who are employed and paid on a daily basis, is a more formal way of describing those who have historically often been called 'coolies'. This is a term, derived from a word found in several Indian languages, that came to be used in English from early in the seventeenth century, to refer to 'hired labour' or to porters, with the connotation, too, of their 'being of low status'. Agricultural labourers and coolies were, and still are, drawn disproportionately from the lower castes. 'Bonded labour' refers to those labourers who are bound in some way, usually through debt, to a particular employer, and whose freedoms in the labour market are consequently constrained. They may have to work for their employers at wage rates that are well below those currently prevailing in the market. This form of labour was very common in the past, in agriculture especially, where debt sometimes passed from one generation to another, binding a labourer's family to that of a particular employer. It is probably much less common these days in villages, but it persists in many occupations, and some scholars speak of 'neo-bondage' and argue that it remains widespread. 'Contract labour' refers to workers who are employed over a particular period of time to perform a specific task, their remuneration usually being for the completion of that task, rather than a daily or other wage or salary.

These are all forms of employment to which the ideas of 'hard physical work', of 'toil', and of 'pain' and 'difficulty' apply, and which account, between them, for a large share of the

Indian labour force. They are also forms of employment, offering very little in the way of stability, continuity, and security of income, that are particularly associated with vulnerable livelihoods that leave those carrying them on liable to live in poverty. They are forms of informal, or of what is in India often described as 'unorganized', employment, in which workers have no protection, as workers, under the law. For employers, employing casual labour or taking on workers on a contract basis is a way of keeping down labour costs, and in the context of India's liberalizing economy these have become ever more significant modes of employment. The participation of women in the labour force has increased, though this has been particularly amongst women with little or no education, who have entered occupations, often on a part-time basis and sometimes involving home-working, that offer no security. Contract labour is becoming more extensive in India's large-scale manufacturing industry. There is relatively less of what is often described, using the English word, by people speaking Indian languages, as 'permanent' employment, in which workers do enjoy protection under the law. Yet many economists argue that India's labour laws give rise to 'inflexibility' in labour markets—or, in other words, they say that it is too difficult for employers to hire and fire according to the state of the market—and that this is now an important constraint on the more successful development of the economy.

India has a labour movement, institutionalized in the form of several important confederations of trade unions. This is what is also referred to as 'organized labour'. Unions, and the confederations—which have often been at odds with one another—are, however, divided on political lines, and this fact, together with that of the relatively small share of the labour force that is unionized, accounts for the political weakness of the labour interest in the country. Still, the labour movement has been able to resist efforts by governments in the more recent past to reduce the scope of legal protection offered to those workers who do have access to it; and the courts have sometimes upheld labour rights, including even the right to gainful employment, which was legislated for in Part IV of the Constitution of India, among the (non-justiciable) Directive Principles.

The cultural meanings of 'labour' vary considerably across Indian society. High-caste status has been associated historically with avoidance of physical labour or 'toil'—and this is one reason why Bollywood film stars used to be well built, even plump, but not often muscular. On the other hand, the economic success of people from certain middle-ranking caste groups may be explained as being due to their capacity for 'toil'. This is the case among the entrepreneurs who have been responsible for the very rapid growth of the knitwear industry in Tiruppur, a small town in South India. They have worker-peasant origins, and their willingness to labour/toil alongside their employees in the companies they have set up has been instrumental in their success. 'Toil is capital', they say.

• See also *capitalism, informal, poverty, unemployment*

Land

The idea of 'land', in the several senses of the area ruled over by a sovereign, or in modern history the territory of the nation; of the natural environment; and of an area to be farmed or owned by individuals or communities, is very important for Indians, as it is for people generally—and especially for those who live in what are still substantially agrarian societies. In common parlance, 'land' most often refers to agricultural land—'*zameen*' or '*bhoomi*' in Hindi. 'Land' in the sense of the territory of the nation is an important aspect of nationalism in India, and perhaps especially so for those Hindu nationalists who hold to the idea of Hindutva, which may be understood as a form of territorial racism. Only those whose 'fatherland' and whose holy places are found in the Indian subcontinent can call themselves 'Hindu'. But association with 'the land' is quite generally of deep cultural significance, and particular qualities may be ascribed to groups of people according to what is understood to be the terrain from which they come. Even now, being able to 'eat one's own rice'—food from the land of the place to which one belongs—is important for some people.

Rulers in India have historically had sovereignty over a particular territory, implying some sort of superior right over the land, and both their political power and the economies of their realms have largely depended on how they exercised this right. It has been argued that whereas in the West, certainly by the eighteenth century, the significance of land ownership was for the profit that could be derived from it, in India what mattered was rather the power over people that command over land gave. As one scholar has put it, in India 'land is to rule', whereas in the West it was rather the case that 'land is to own'. Political power in India rested to a large extent on control over people, not land itself. What was of concern to a land controller (as we may say, rather than 'landowner') was to maximize the numbers of those dependent upon him.

The British, as rulers of India, relied heavily on revenue deriving from taxation of land (whereas the Mughals before them had generally taken shares of the crop), so they had to be concerned with land rights. They were often confronted by situations in which, it seemed, different people could claim rights over the same piece of land. There were, apparently, no clear rights of 'ownership'. So one of the first tasks of colonial government was to establish property rights and responsibility for the payment of land revenue. This was done in different ways in different parts of the country—so that different systems of land tenure (a term for the forms of property rights and the social relationships associated with them, which appeared in English first in the nineteenth century) were established. In much of the north and east the settlement of land revenue was made with individuals who exercised rights over large estates. The actual cultivation was carried out by tenant cultivators, from whom the estate owners (commonly referred to as *zamindars*) obtained a share of their product, a part of which was then handed over to the government. Elsewhere (in what is referred to as the *ryotwari* system), the colonial government reached a settlement of the land tax with those they presumed to be individual peasant proprietors (or '*ryots*'—a term which meant 'subject' in Mughal India, but which became synonymous with 'peasant'). Whether in zamindari areas, however, or in ryotwari ones, the level of assessment of the land tax was a matter of great contention, and there were many instances of rural protest against it. And the leasing out of land to tenant cultivators was found in ryotwari as well as in zamindari areas. The prevalence of share-cropping (in which the cultivator hands over a share of his produce to the landowner, rather than paying a fixed amount as rent), on terms that were generally onerous for them, meant that the cultivators usually had little or nothing left to invest in the land, while the owners had little or no incentive to do so. This sort of land tenure system became known as landlordism, a term which came into the English language in the nineteenth century, at first—according to *OED*—to describe the system of land tenure prevailing in Ireland. But Indians themselves were already debating landlordism and its implications by the 1840s, and collecting information on rack-renting and other practices of landlords.

Outside areas of commercial cultivation, some of it under British ownership, Indian agriculture generally saw very little development in the British period, and Indian nationalists argued that the core of the problem had to do not just with the land taxes levied by the colonial government, but also with landlordism. There was great inequality, they thought, in land ownership rights, and the tenurial conditions under which much cultivation was carried out meant that there were no real incentives for anyone to invest very much in agriculture. To address these problems, Indian nationalists, both some of those in the Congress party and the communists, argued that priority should be given to land reform. By this they meant that rights over agricultural land should be given 'to the tiller'. Shortly after Independence, the zamindari system was indeed formally abolished, but those who secured rights of land ownership thereafter were very often the larger cultivators who already had stronger rights—those who might be described as 'rich peasants'. The same people were very often those who ran the governing Congress party locally, and they used their positions of power successfully to resist subsequent efforts by governments to bring about land redistribution through the imposition of ceilings on the area of land that might be held by any one individual. Only in the states of Jammu and Kashmir, and in Kerala and West Bengal under the leadership of communist-led governments, has much redistribution taken place, though it has been legislated for by all the major states.

'Land to the tiller' remains of central importance in the programmes of all the major communist parties of India. The most important of them, the Communist Party of India (Marxist), for instance, continues to call in its programme for 'radical and thoroughgoing agrarian reforms that target abolition of landlordism, moneylender–merchant exploitation and caste and gender oppression in the countryside'. Latterly, however, the term 'land reform' has come to mean something very different in the context of India's economic reforms (*see* development). Supporters of these reforms look for the repeal of land ceilings legislation, and for changes in the law that will encourage large-scale capitalist investment in the agricultural economy.

Struggles over rights of land ownership and use have become even more intense in the era of the economic reforms. Urban land values have risen, and real estate is the basis of some massive fortunes among India's dollar billionaires. At the same time, what is seen as 'land-grabbing' by corporations or by government on behalf of corporations has given rise to popular resistance, no more so than in the areas of central and eastern India where there are large numbers of adivasis with traditional rights to forest lands, and in some parts of which there are very valuable mineral resources. The idea of 'land grab' has become (in the words of experts in peasant studies) 'a catch-all to describe and analyse the current explosion of large-scale (trans)national commercial land transactions'. It seems aptly to describe recent trends in India. Resistance to land-grabbing is sometimes articulated by India's Naxalites (or Maoists). On its part, in response to pressures from social movements, the Government of India has passed legislation—the Forest Rights Act of 2006—that offers more protection to adivasis, and new legislation to replace the colonial era Land Acquisition Act of 1894, which may provide for stronger guarantees of the livelihood rights of those who are displaced.

• See also *development, environment, peasant, village*

Language

The linguistic diversity of India is well known, and the Eighth Schedule of the Constitution of India recognizes as many as twenty-two languages (not including English). Hindi is the most widely spoken of them, being the language of most of the people of six major states that now account for more than 40 per cent of the population of the country as a whole. It has the status (under Article 343(1) of the Constitution) of being the country's 'official language... in Devanagari script'. Defined by *OED* as 'The great Aryan language of Northern India', it is considered to be an Indo-European language, spoken with very many dialects, and embracing distinct regional differences. In Bihar, for example, three different forms of the language—Maithili, Magahi, and Bhojpuri—are spoken in different parts of the state, each of them with large numbers of speakers.

Nationalist support for some form of Hindi as the national language predates the formation of the Indian National Congress in 1885; and a Hindi movement, involving a number of associations in different parts of North India, took shape in the later nineteenth century. The movement was driven by Hindu groups whose close association with Sanskrit and Hindi learning meant that their members found themselves at a disadvantage in competition for jobs in public service, for which familiarity rather with the Persian and Arabic vocabulary of Hindustani was preferred. The movement aimed to differentiate Hindi from Urdu, associated with Islam, and to make Hindi a symbol of Hindu culture. The adoption of slogans such as 'Hindi, Hindu, Hindustan' reflected the heightening of community awareness and the expression of a Hindu nationalism. In the early twentieth century the use of Hindi as the national language began to be proposed by nationalist leaders. By the time of Independence in 1947 there was widespread opposition to the continued use of English as the official language, but in the debates of the Constituent Assembly that drew up the Constitution of India, the fears expressed by members from those parts of the country where Hindi was not generally spoken led to the provision that English should continue to be the official language of the Union for fifteen years, up to 1965, when Hindi would replace it.

Language had also become important in sub-national political movements, especially in the South, where the four major languages—Kannada, Tamil, Telugu, and Malayalam—are recognized as members of the family of Dravidian languages, and are quite distinct from Hindi. Both Tamil and Telugu became transformed into objects of what has been described as 'devotion', as the social mobilization and political empowerment of their speakers gathered momentum. The historian Sumathi Ramaswamy describes how devotion to Tamil became so powerful as to have led some young men to set fire to themselves, while shouting such slogans as 'Death to Hindi! May Tamil flourish!' And it was the death from fasting of an obscure Congressman, Potti Sriramulu, in December 1952, that finally catalysed the formation of the state of Andhra Pradesh, as that of Telugu speakers. This was followed by agitation elsewhere for language-defined states. The central government was constrained to appoint a States Reorganization Commission, which reported in 1955, and—against the wishes of Nehru, who feared for national unity—finally to concede demands for the redrawing of other state boundaries on linguistic lines.

Opposition in the 1960s to the use of Hindi, seen as symbolizing north Indian and Brahminical domination, especially in the southern state of Tamil Nadu, meant that the constitutional provision limiting the official use of English has still not come to be fully implemented. English continues to be widely used in India for official purposes, and in the context of India's increased integration into the global economy to be spoken ever more widely. The numbers of those who are truly literate in English remain small—generously, perhaps 80 million people, going by the possible readership of English language newspapers—but the rapidly growing numbers of private schools offering tuition in English is an important marker of popular aspirations. So Hindi has still not finally become India's 'national language', even though it is now more widely acceptable and understood than at any time before. This is in part the outcome of the teaching of Hindi as a second or third language, and perhaps in part a result of national television networks and of the energy of Hindi films.

• See also *federalism, Hindu, Hindutva, nation*

Law

The idea of law, or of 'the law', is that of 'the body of rules, whether proceeding from formal enactment or from custom, which a particular state or community recognizes as binding on its members or subjects' (*OED*). It is very generally held that the most important function of the state is to maintain 'the rule of law', and widely recognized that the law is of great significance both as a reflection of established social order and as a potential agent of social change. But then where does 'the law' come from? Who decides on the body of rules that shall be deemed as binding, and how is its recognition as such established? Many of the particular problems of the law in India may be seen as having to do with the complex relations of formally enacted laws based on English law, with those based on actual or supposed Indian precedents derived from the Sanskrit *sastras* or Islamic *sharia* law, and with those deriving from local custom. Many of the British officials who ruled India in the colonial period believed that their greatest achievement was to have brought 'the rule of law' to India, in place of 'vague and fluctuating customs, liable to be infringed at every moment by the arbitrary fancies of the ruler' (in the views ascribed to one of them, Sir James Fitzjames Stephens, by his biographer). Indian nationalists, however, held to the contrary view that the British had imposed a legal system that was inaccessible to most people because of distance, cost, and language, inspired by ideas about law that were fundamentally different from those that lay behind their own systems of justice, and that the imposition of a body of law taken from Britain had many negative consequences. Indians today refer more commonly to individual 'laws' ('*qanoon*' in Hindi) than to 'the law' as an abstract idea. Their apparent litigiousness (though whether indeed people in India are more litigious than others, or are more so than they were in the past, is a matter for scholarly debate), the interminable character of court proceedings, and the vast accumulation of cases awaiting trial (now at least 20 million across courts at all levels), are problems that are still considered to have been created by the colonial legal system, and to mean that justice is in effect denied to many.

The British brought to India the ideas that law should be clearly set out in written documents, and judgments recorded; and that it should be based on universal, impersonal, and impartial norms (the idea of 'equality before the law', reflected in the common image of justice as blindfolded). In India, however, they confronted many different jurisdictions ruled by local custom, with no unified system of laws, and the relative absence both of written records and of professional lawyers. Then, as the legal scholar Marc Galanter has expressed it, 'in undertaking to administer the law in government courts, staffed with government servants (rather than to exercise [as they might have done] a merely supervisory control over the administration of law by [local] non-governmental bodies), the British took a decisive step towards a modern legal system'.

Even as they did so, however, there were some officials who recognized the gap between what the British government of India intended to establish and local ideas and practice. As scholars have expressed it more recently, the customary administration of justice through village and caste tribunals (or panchayats) depended on different principles, reflecting the fact that both the parties to a dispute and the members of the tribunal—who were not professionals—commonly came from the same place, and knew each other more or less well. In these circumstances, as modern ethnographic accounts have shown, the administration of justice was much more about negotiation, aimed at the resolution of conflict, than it was about establishing the 'truth' so as to rule in favour of one side and to declare the other the loser. Acknowledging these differences, some British officials sought to bridge the gap with the modern system by encouraging panchayat-like proceedings at local levels, and comparable ideas have animated the drive to establish the panchayat form of local government in independent India.

But colonial officials also sought to find a common body of law in India to which they could refer, and which would be accessible to them in a way that the orally based customary law of the villages was not. In doing so they elevated particular religious texts, and the

Brahmin scholars (or *pandits*) on whom they relied for their interpretation (until 1858, when the system was abolished), not recognizing that in doing this they were strengthening 'high culture' law at the expense of the customary law of villages and castes. It was argued by a scholar in the later nineteenth century, however, that 'before the establishment of British rule in India customary law used to be given more weight...than the Mitakshara or Dayabhaga' (the two most significant law texts applied by the British courts, and referred to still—the latter applying to Bengal and Assam, and the former to the rest of India).

Well before the end of the nineteenth century the British had extensively codified the fields of commercial, criminal, and procedural law, and these laws have generally remained in place to the present, with revisions and accretions. Personal law, however, is more complex, and family law in particular the British largely left alone, as a sphere of laws based on Hindu and Islamic texts. This entrenched a duality in the Indian legal system, and there continues to be tension between caste and religious particularism, ascriptive group identities, and recognition of duties relating to group membership, that are grounded in these personal laws, and the individual rights set out in the Constitution. The passage of the Hindu Code Bills in 1955–6, intended as a step towards the 'modernization' of Hindu society, was controversial at the time, and has given rise to the argument that Hindus are treated unfairly under the law by comparison with other religious groups. This has been one of the drivers of Hindu nationalism (*see* Hindutva).

In addition to these tensions in the law itself, which are in large part an inheritance from the colonial period, India's judicial system is recognized as being in desperate need of repair. A noted public intellectual, Pratap Bhanu Mehta, did not mince his words when he wrote that 'To describe the Indian civil justice system, especially at the level below the Supreme Court, as being in a perpetual state of crisis would be an understatement.' He drew attention to the inadequacy of the administrative infrastructure of the courts and of their means of organizing information; the reluctance of judges to impose court discipline; and the surprising lack—given the often very long delays in the judicial system—of institutionalized means for reaching out-of-court settlements of disputes. He noted, too, that 'the quality of the legal profession drops precipitously after the small cream of top professionals and it is the low median that has the most influence on the conduct of law'.

• See also *constitution, justice, rights*

Liberal, Liberalism

The adjective 'liberal', in English, conveys ideas such as those of being generous and magnanimous, of 'freedom from constraint', and, relatedly, those of open-mindedness and tolerance (*OED*). It is the idea of freedom from constraint that most clearly informs the political philosophy that is described as 'liberalism', and which is perhaps best considered to be an ideological orientation rather than a coherent political doctrine. Liberalism, according to the philosopher Bhikhu Parekh, emphasizes the supreme value of the individual, and offers 'a more or less coherent vision of man and society, characterized by the wish to free all individuals from arbitrary and unnecessary constraint'. According to *OED*, it is an idea that emerged at the beginning of the nineteenth century, and connotes 'support for or advocacy of individual rights, civil liberties and reform, tending towards individual freedom, democracy, or social equality'. It is also 'a political and social philosophy based on these principles'. The first of these definitional statements actually sets up one of the central dilemmas of liberalism, which is that of the tension between individual freedoms and the pursuit of social equality.

As a political doctrine advocating constitutional monarchy and parliamentary government, liberalism emerged in Spain and Portugal around 1800, and according to the historian Christopher Bayly reached the port cities of India and elsewhere in Asia not long afterwards, through the writings of British and French thinkers, and a few radical Europeans who were living in those cities. Some Indians began to argue for 'mixed constitutions', for a degree of popular representation, free trade, and a free press. Most important of all, to begin with, would be the jury system—then seen as being at the heart of the idea of representation—and the free press. In principle, jury rights extended to British subjects overseas, but this stood in opposition to British ideas of cultural and religious difference, and Asians were at first debarred from jury service. This restriction began to be challenged in the 1820s. The freedom of the press, however, remained an issue in the colonies throughout the nineteenth century.

Bayly argues that Indian thinkers did not simply take over European ideas. Rather, they reinterpreted them in the light of their own understandings of good government and of human well-being, changing the meanings of the European precedents. The great reformer, Raja Rammohan Roy (1774–1833), for instance, is described as having explored Sanskrit texts 'to create an historical genealogy for future representative government in India'.

Liberal values profoundly influenced Indian nationalists, who wanted to establish a regime of rights to life, liberty, and property—the last being challenged at first by only a few of them. The Constitution of India is founded on liberal principles, but it reflects very clearly the tension between individual freedoms and social equality. Part III of the Constitution provides for the individual rights and civil liberties that are necessary for equal citizenship. The members of the Constituent Assembly that drew up the Constitution relegated those clauses bearing on social equality, however, to the non-justiciable Directive Principles, in Part IV—statements of intent that fell short of establishing the economic and social rights that would have made for greater social equality. It was pointed out by Dr Ambedkar that this established a contradiction. As voters, Indians would be equal, but democracy would, he feared, be compromised by the sharp inequalities of Indian society. The Indian Constitution presents another problem, too, in regard to the principles of liberalism, because of the place that it gives to the rights of particular social groups such as Dalits and adivasis. The privileges that are accorded by the Constitution to these groups have been challenged in the courts because they are held to prejudice the individual rights that are also established in the Constitution.

Liberalism is deeply rooted in economic thought, and in this context is generally thought of as connoting advocacy for unrestricted trade, and as having been propounded most influentially by Adam Smith in his *The Wealth of Nations* of 1776. Economic liberalism stands for the principles that the operation of markets should be left as free as possible, and that the role of the state in the economy, correspondingly, should be severely restricted. These ideas have only recently come to be influential in economic policy in India, through the thinking and the practices of neo-liberalism.

• See also *citizenship, constitution, democracy, neo-liberal*

Marriage

The English word 'marriage' is widely used in India. Unlike in British Standard English, 'marriage' in Indian English refers to both the act of formalizing a relationship and the wedding itself—there is no separate word for 'wedding' (the word *shaadi* in Hindi also covers both the marriage and wedding).

Many predicted that the spread of ideas of individual choice and romantic love through the global media would lead to a shift to Western-style weddings and marriages in India: young people would arrange marriages themselves based on their own preferences. At the level of what happens inside a marriage there may be change. Social research suggests that young people are increasingly looking at marriage as a form of long-term companionship and basis for love. There are also increasing examples of 'love marriages' in India—unions not sanctioned by parents. But there is no straightforward movement towards Western-style marriages. What appears to have emerged instead in many parts of the country is a pan-Indian system of dowry marriage with four chief characteristics. First, senior kin arrange a union—this does not necessarily preclude young people from being involved in the decision-making but it means that parents are mainly responsible for marriage arrangements, and a key difference between India and the West is therefore that marriage in India typically refers to a contract between two families rather than an individualized union based around personal taste; second, marriages are usually caste endogamous; third, socio-economic considerations are primary in the choice of partner; fourth, dowry is used as a bargaining tool in families' efforts to secure a groom with valued qualities, such as secure work.

The word marriage in India is also linked to questions of caste. There has been some relaxation in caste rules around marriage, but most marriages remain in-caste. Indeed, in some parts of North India caste associations have emerged that police people's marriages and arrange violent punishments for transgressors.

Compared to the West, marriage in India is also a word relatively lacking in romantic associations and more thoroughly bound up with questions of interest, strategy, and mobility. Families often put considerable emphasis on social and economic considerations when making a match. Beyond the immediate qualities—education, job, physical characteristics—of a bride and groom, parents look for a family that is well placed economically and socially. A well-chosen marriage may provide benefits in terms of loans or assistance in getting a contract or job. The prevalence of dowries also heightens the common connection that people make in their minds between 'marriage' and questions of economic 'strategy'. A dowry may take several forms, frequently including expensive consumer goods. Dowries often amount to several times a household's annual earnings, and 'dowry inflation', as well as a more general rapid rise in the costs of marriage, has become a key issue in contemporary India—this in spite of dowry being formally illegal. For all these considerations of self-interest, issues of astrology and religious custom are often at the forefront of conversations about marriage.

The spread of this dowry system has meant that social activists, government agencies, and many NGOs have come to question the appropriateness of typical marriage arrangements. Dowry marriages may encourage youth to assess their appearance and achievements in narrowly instrumental terms. For example, in many parts of India it has become common for parents to construct price lists for grooms with particular occupations and educational qualifications. Likewise, parents sometimes refer to a need to pay extra in a dowry to compensate for a perceived shortcoming in a bride. In addition, the dowry system often draws young people into making comparisons between their own position and that of other, more successful youth. Young women may reflect negatively on their schooling and appearance, for example, and men may become conscious of their insecure work, poor education, and inability to fulfil norms of successful adult masculinity.

The dowry system may lead to social conflict too, such that 'marriage' is often a charged topic in many families. Conflicts may occur over parents' and young people's interpretation of the success or failure of past social strategies as these become evident at the time of negotiating a marriage. For example, young people may blame their parents for unsuccessful educational strategies, or parents and siblings may denigrate young people for their failure to acquire secure work. The period immediately after marriage may also trigger or expose conflicts. Spouses may become involved in quarrels over the ownership and use of a dowry and other property, and over reconciling competing expectations about work, companionship, and parenthood. In several parts of India, parents sometimes use harassment of a daughter-in-law to bargain for dowry payments after marriage. A groom's family may murder a bride after a dispute: dowry violence and dowry deaths are major social problems.

Marriage is a political issue in India. This politicization can be partly traced to what became known as the Shah Bano affair. In 1978 Mohammed Ahmed Khan divorced his 62-year-old wife, Shah Bano, under the terms of Muslim family law. Shah Bano had no means to support herself and her five children and therefore approached the courts in search of a monthly maintenance payment. The Supreme Court agreed that Shah Bano should receive such a payment under the terms of Section 125 of the Code of Criminal Procedure, but in 1986 the ruling Congress party responded to Muslim pressure by passing a new Act that nullified the Supreme Court's judgment. The Shah Bano affair sparked off demonstrations, both from Muslims keen to uphold their minority rights in India and among opposition parties who saw the Congress ruling as an affront to notions of universal citizenship. The politicization of marriage also takes other forms, however: efforts by caste organizations to enforce caste endogamy on reluctant youth, and protests against dowry by youth and women's organizations.

• See also *caste, family, individual, middle class, modern*

Masculinity

Masculinity is defined in the *OED* as 'the possession of the qualities traditionally associated with men'. Masculinity, like other forms of identity, is performative rather than a natural product of a person's sex, and masculinities are defined in part in opposition to what they are not. Masculinities are also diverse; there is no trans-historical vision of masculinity, even if there may be themes—such as physical strength and hard work—that surface with considerable regularity.

Scholars have pointed out that ideas of masculinity are based not only on their distinction from femininity, but also constructed in relation to the practices of other men. Moreover, these different visions of masculinity are often hierarchically ordered. The sociologist Raewyn Connell (né Robert Connell) has argued that in many places a 'hegemonic masculinity' serves as a marker against which men understand themselves. Those possessing the attributes of a hegemonic masculinity often protect their standing through labelling other male practices as being in some sense inferior.

In the colonial era, dominant British authorities often depicted Indian men as weak, effete, and superstitious in contrast to a vision of strong, virile, rational European men. At the same time, colonialists and Indian nationalists sometimes found common ground in their attempt to define a respectable masculinity distinct from a domestic, private world inhabited by women. What is particularly striking about postcolonial India is the continued importance of certain types of traditional, patrimonial masculinity, undergirded by men's control over land ownership, formal sector jobs, and political power. The force of a particularly narrow, pernicious vision of masculinity can be measured in a whole host of different arenas: the capacity of all-male caste organizations to inflict violent punishments on young women, the continued stigma attached to non-heterosexual relationships, the frequency of harassment by men and older women of young brides in the context of dowry, and—perhaps especially notable—the ubiquity of gender violence. The celebration of forms of militaristic, 'macho' masculinity in the mass media deepens such problems, even while various women's movements and rights organizations have done much to chip away at traditional masculinities.

There is an especially close connection between the reproduction of hegemonic visions of militaristic macho masculinity and the rise of Hindu nationalism in India in the twentieth century. The intellectual leaders of the Hindutva project placed great emphasis on the importance of Hindus as a martial race, and of the need for men, in particular, to revive their country in the wake of colonial rule and defend their homeland against Muslims. They were able to draw upon the popularity of wrestling, and the martial traditions of some groups of men, and they made '*lathi*' drill ('lathi' means 'stick' and refers to the canes used for example by the Indian police) part of the activity of the '*shakhas*' (local membership units) of the Rashtriya Swayamsevak Sangh (*see* Hindutva).

There are alternative traditions of masculinity in India, that sometimes intersect with hegemonic masculinities and sometimes present themselves as distinct or even opposed to dominant genres. The historian Joseph Alter, for example, has done much to track the history of visions of sexual abstinence and semen retention in defining a certain type of higher-caste masculinity; Gandhi embodies one particular and potent notion of the Indian male. Alter argues that such a vision of Indian masculinity is founded on self-control and a search for inner 'truth' rather than being straightforwardly about the pursuit of power. India's colonial and postcolonial history has also witnessed the emergence of 'oppositional masculinities', for example situations in which low-caste or minority religious leaders developed distinctive visions of manliness. For instance, the Dalit hero Dr B. R. Ambedkar promoted a particular vision of middle-class, respectable Dalit masculinity as a counterpoint to images of Dalits as degraded and downtrodden.

There is now a large body of anthropological work that examines how different masculine styles compete to become hegemonic in contexts such as the university campus, village, or shopping mall. Many of these struggles are played out among youth or reflect tensions between different generations regarding what constitutes an appropriate masculinity. Interestingly, marriage is often the point at which various different ideas of masculinity become objects of conscious reflection and are brought into conflict.

One of the difficulties with studying masculinity in India is its invisibility in public discourse. Masculinity is defined in part by its absence from everyday commentary; the apparently taken for granted nature of masculinity and masculine styles is precisely what gives dominant visions of masculinity such power to shape understandings of social order. This may be changing, however, and one important emerging question in India concerns the degree to which there might be a 'crisis of masculinity' occurring in the country. There are good reasons to suspect that this might be the case. Poor-quality education, rising unemployment, and increasingly intense competition among a large population of young men for female partners is sometimes creating social problems. Youth violence, alcoholism, and suicide are becoming features of contemporary Indian youth masculinities, and young women often complain that the rise of a large disenchanted male youth population increases their vulnerability to sexual violence. These reflections deepen the impression that India is 'no country for young men'.

• See also *feminism, gender, Hindutva, rape, violence, youth*

Media

Williams traces the idea of 'medium' to the early seventeenth century, when it primarily referred to an intervening agency or substance, especially language. In the eighteenth and nineteenth centuries two new meanings emerged: first, a modern, consciously technical sense of the word that distinguishes print from sound and vision, and second, a specialized capitalist sense in which a newspaper or radio broadcast is seen as the medium for something else—that 'something else' being, for Williams, advertising, and hence the reproduction of capitalism. In *Marxism and Literature*, Williams develops these ideas, making the important additional point that in the nineteenth century specific media in art, such as oils and watercolours, were reified: 'the properties of the medium were abstracted as if they defined the practice, rather than being its means'.

Williams fundamentally disagreed with Marshall McLuhan's technologically determinist claim that there was a direct causal relationship between, for example, the invention of print and such weighty historical events as nationalism, the Reformation, and the emergence of the industrial assembly line. Williams argued instead that technologies—media such as the radio or television—are social, and that social struggles and political economy profoundly shape their development.

The social and political perspective on media bequeathed by Williams is crucially important in understanding the history of media in India. India's foremost media theorist, Robin Jeffrey, identifies three stages of this history: a period of communication primarily via face-to-face contact in precolonial India; an intervening era of 'genteel print' lasting from the 1870s until the 1980s; and finally a recent period of mass print, television, and electronic communication. If the second period was one in which print media was increasingly diverse in India—the Congress reorganized itself into provinces based on language and promoted newspapers in regional languages, for example, from the 1920s onwards—the modern age is one of dizzying proliferation both in the content of media and media's technological forms.

The Constitution guaranteed the freedom of speech and expression to citizens, but of course this was only the start of the story, for woven into the question of media in India is the issue of its regulation, and especially the hoary dilemmas surrounding the appropriate role of the state in the provision and oversight of media productions. India has tried to steer a course between the Scylla of public control of the media (in the Soviet model) and the Charybdis of its rampant commercialization, but this has been difficult in practice. The recent entry of Reliance Industries, India's largest private corporate entity, into the country's media industry has heightened concerns about the corporatization of the media and the effects of this on heterogeneity and 'quality'. The fear, to put it bluntly, is that the media may serve a depoliticizing function, distracting the Indian population from pressing public issues and—directly or indirectly—legitimizing social injustice. Equally, political parties are notoriously active in the manipulation of the media in India, often through politicians' direct ownership of media outlets.

Weighed against such concerns, however, must be the very significant evidence that now exists for the democratizing function of media in India. One landmark study examined cassettes. In 1970s and 1980s India, people could use cassettes not only to listen passively to music, but also as a means of recording cultural products, precipitating the emergence of numerous stylized versions of regional folk music. 'Cassette culture', as Peter Manuel put it, lessened the social distance between producers and consumers, and had a decentralized structure, facilitating responsiveness to local prerogatives, including political demands. Another seminal contribution, written by Robin Jeffrey, accounts for India's 'newspaper revolution' in the 1980s and 1990s, tracing in the process the enormous democratization of print journalism during this period—a 500 per cent increase in the reading public and the proliferation of newspapers in regional languages. Yet another landmark study by Arvind Rajagopal tracks the changing dynamics of television ownership and programming in India. He charts the enormous cultural significance of the screening of the Hindu religious epics, the Mahabharat and Ramayan, on Doordarshan, India's public service (state) broadcaster, which was established in 1959, and, in turn, a steep decline in Doordarshan's audience with the entry of new private competitors since 1991 (although Doordarshan, or 'DD' as it is known, remains one of the largest broadcasting organizations in India in terms of infrastructure). Television ownership in India increased from 32 per cent in 2001 to 47 per cent in 2011, and three-quarters of urban households now own a television set.

Whether the rise of mobile phones in India will encourage democratization is moot, but it is absolutely clear that the boom in phone ownership—there were 4 million mobile phones in India in 2001 (and 32 million landlines), and a staggering 990 million in 2013 (and just 33 million landlines in 2012)—is of much importance. To a greater extent than even Williams anticipated in his warnings on the political economy of the media, mobile phones could become a vehicle for corporate powers to sell the ideas and practices of global capitalism. And yet, at the same time, it would be short-sighted to deny the democratic potential presented by people's widespread ownership of mobile phones—the practical benefits they provide, and also their political efficacy: youth and radical political parties have used phone technology to expose corruption and organize protests.

The rise of social media in India—notwithstanding the continued existence of a 'digital divide' in the country with respect to internet access—may have equally dramatic consequences. Blogs, Facebook, and Twitter, for example, were notoriously important in the mobilization of activists in the Middle East. Equally, new media are fuelling the rapid rise of pirated software, movies, hardware, and music in urban India—a grand re-enactment of an earlier round of cassette manipulation, but with viral, unpredictable (and possibly revolutionary) implications. The rise of social media also encourages reflection on Williams's point about the reification of media. The very act of participating in global forums of electronic communication may sometimes define people's identities, as for example where a person is a 'blogger'.

• See also *culture, democracy, politics*

Microfinance

Microfinance has tended to refer to small-scale financial services provided to the poor and those immediately above the poverty line—sections of the population who often lack access to the assets required for collateral and to information about how to save and obtain credit. In the popular imagination, 'microfinance' remains indelibly linked to the Grameen Bank, a microfinance institution (MFI) established by Nobel laureate Mohammad Yunus in 1976 to provide financial services to women in Bangladesh.

Microfinance did not enter the lexicon of development planners and ordinary people in India until the early 1990s. It was not until India's economic liberalization was under way that the Indian Government—through its National Bank for Agriculture and Rural Development (NABARD)—began to imagine the poor as potential 'creditworthy borrowers', who might contribute to economic growth. NABARD looked to women in particular, on the assumption that they were more likely to use the money in a responsible manner, and also partly out of a concern to address gender inequalities. In 1992 NABARD introduced a formal system of self-help groups (SHGs) in India. Each SHG typically consists of fifteen to twenty women, who usually live in close proximity and take on a measure of joint responsibility for saving and investing. The poor typically use their savings and loans for micro-enterprise, educational expenses, health emergencies, and marriage. Government banks and NGOs manage the savings of SHG members and extend loans on a not-for-profit basis. Members of SHGs may also lend and save among themselves; each SHG becomes a type of mini-bank in itself (in this respect SHGs differ from the Bangladeshi model, in which people can only save or take loans through the Grameen Bank). According to NABARD, there were 8 million SHGs across India, and 103 million households which received loans in 2012, with a concentration of microfinance activities in the South.

Since the late 1990s, microfinance in India has become less 'micro' and less narrowly 'financial'. The first shift came in 2000, when a number of NGO MFIs began to lend to SHGs on a commercial basis, becoming in the process non-banking financial companies (NBFCs) regulated by the Reserve Bank of India. NBFCs were allowed to make alliances with commercial banks, and they entered the microfinance business with alacrity. Commercial MFIs tend to lend larger sums than those lent to SHGs. Interest rates are also higher, and— unlike most national banks and not-for-profit NGOs—commercial MFIs will lend to clients in advance of their demonstrating a capacity to save. In addition, many 'start-up' MFIs have emerged, attracting funds not only from banks but also from venture capitalists in places as far away as New York. These companies continue to advertise their development credentials, stressing their commitment to reducing poverty and empowering women, but microfinance has become in many cases a fully fledged commercial enterprise. The total loans outstanding for commercial MFIs in India rose by around 500 per cent between 2002 and 2007, and it is commercial MFIs rather than SHGs that are now attracting most of the outside investment. At the same time as becoming more integrated into global flows of capital, MFIs have diversified, providing savings and insurance and assisting with money transfers. MFIs have also come to offer a range of non-financial services, including financial literacy training, health insurance, and skills development.

Within development circles, 'microfinance' has frequently been discussed as a kind of silver bullet, with the potential to change the fortunes of the poorest in India. In practice, the impact of MFIs in terms of poverty is difficult to trace, in part because of a lack of long-term data on the fortunes of those who have taken loans, and because of huge variations in the social contexts in which microfinance has been introduced. There is nevertheless some level of agreement among development scholars that MFIs have at the very least expanded the choices available to the poor and lower middle class, and moderately reduced the incidence of poverty, perhaps especially in rural areas. MFIs have also had a generally positive impact on women's capacity to make decisions and exercise control over household resources. Commentators have also noted, however, that microfinance on its own cannot alter the balance of power within local society, as reflected in patterns of land ownership and access to influential social networks. In the context of widespread corruption and poor-quality welfare services, access to credit and savings opportunities can only moderate adversity. Microfinance might be imagined as more of a 'safety net' than a 'ladder out of poverty'.

Similarly, MFIs cannot solve the problems that flow from women's lack of power within households over the use and ownership of productive resources.

As commercial MFIs with foreign backing become more visible and influential, the debate over the term 'microfinance' and its links to development has become more intense. Some have argued that the state's promotion of MFIs in a period of economic reform has provided a means by which government has shifted the costs of social reproduction from the state—constitutionally mandated to provide a decent quality of education to its populace, for example—to the poor. Another charge is that commercial MFI interest rates are too high—they are typically around 20 per cent per year. At least one development analyst has pointed out, however, that the interest rates charged by commercial MFIs are fair given the high administrative costs, and also that they are much lower than the rates charged by private moneylenders in India, which are commonly between 50 and 120 per cent a year. Others have claimed that senior management is sometimes placing considerable pressure on field officers to meet performance targets. These MFI field staff members have, in turn, been accused of treating their clients badly, especially where they are young educated men who are responsible for providing loans and other services to uneducated rural women. The pressure being placed on the poor by unscrupulous MFIs, and the associated proliferation of inappropriate lending practices, may even have contributed to a spate of suicides in Andhra Pradesh in 2010. There have also been defaults, partly because—unlike in the Grameen Bank system—Indian MFIs are not required to keep a portion of their clients' savings as an insurance against loss. An MFI (Development and Regulation) Bill is currently under consideration. But new legislation is unlikely to protect the poor from unethical practices.

At the same moment that commentators debate the relative merits and demerits of microfinance, the term has become increasingly politicized. Parties are using SHGs to try to woo sections of the populace, and political organizations are also taking sides in arguments about the appropriateness of commercial microfinance. Microfinance emerges not only as important in its own right, but as a means through which Indian citizens, political parties, and scholars are evaluating the social consequences of liberalization.

• See also *development, empowerment, gender, neo-liberal*

Middle Class

'Middle class' is a term that, while apparently straightforward, is very difficult to pin down analytically, in part because of the confusion over how precisely class itself should be defined, and in part because the adjective 'middle' is so vague. According to Raymond Williams, 'middle class' first appeared in the early nineteenth century in Britain and was counterposed to 'working class'. The concepts are really incompatible, as Williams points out: working classes being defined by their function and the middle classes by their position in a hierarchy.

There are a number of good scholarly and popular accounts of middle classes in colonial India and the immediate postcolonial period, especially of the 'bhadralok', a Bengali term meaning literally 'big people' but referring originally to an administrative elite that emerged under the British in the area of present-day Bengal. But the term middle class became much more popular in India in the 1980s and 1990s, in association with economic reforms and the wider social changes wrought by liberalization. The middle class in India was imagined in this period primarily as a consumerist class, a small upper fraction of the population capable of purchasing modern consumer goods such as a scooter and television. In other definitions, the middle classes were defined by their work or income. Those working primarily in non-manual employment could lay claim to middle-class standing, with the additional proviso that they earn a monthly salary rather than a daily wage. What also emerges clearly from studies of the middle class in India is that multiple dimensions of power tend to work in mutually reinforcing ways. As well as having a greater quantity of economic assets and a higher income than the poor, the middle classes also tend to possess better access to useful social networks and a higher volume of what Pierre Bourdieu termed 'cultural capital': educational qualifications and the capacity to speak English, for example.

Until quite late in postcolonial India the middle class, defined in terms of their purchasing power and salary, was very small. As recently as 1997, only 6 per cent of Indian households owned a television. Moreover, in a country where over 90 per cent of the population works in the informal economy, there are very few households that can rely on a steady monthly income, pension, and the employment guarantees historically associated with middle-class status in Western Europe and the USA. Reports of a middle class 250 million or even 300 million strong are inaccurate if the term 'middle class' is to retain any of the sense it has in a Western context. If one were to take English language ability as some sort of proxy for being middle class, one could note that in 2010 there were supposed to be 20 million English daily newspapers on the street every morning. Allowing perhaps four readers to each copy, one would then arrive at the 'comfortable-in-English' population as being perhaps 80 million at the most.

Middle class nevertheless remains an important aspirational category in India. It is possible that India is moving in the direction of the USA, where the terms 'lower class', 'working class', or 'poor' are rarely heard; everyone lays claim to being 'middle class'. This also reflects the fact that an increasing number of people engage in practices that have historically denoted middle-class status in India: ownership of a mobile phone and television, participation in formal education beyond primary school, and 'leisure' activities such as celebrating a child's birthday.

Members of the middle class in India—defined in terms of consumption, income, position with respect to the social relations of production, or in some other way—are more likely to be from middle- or higher-ranking castes. Caste and class overlap. Yet Dalits, Other Backward Classes, tribal populations, and Muslims have now entered the middle classes in India, often continuing to experience certain forms of discrimination, and thus in a certain sense constituting distinct blocs within a wider middle-class formation. There are also other vertical and horizontal divisions within the middle classes: between upper middle classes and lower middle classes; between professional, agricultural, and business sections of the middle class; between urban and rural middle classes; and between older sections of the middle class with secure positions in state bureaucracies—such as established members of the bhadralok in West Bengal—and newer sections of the middle class, whose claims to have risen above the masses rest more on their consumption power.

Unsurprisingly in this context, there has been nothing like a straightforward middle-class political lobby or mobilization in India, but rather fractured and complex assertions that reflect the interests of particular sections of the middle classes, often teaming up with the poor and/or the very rich. Upper sections of the middle classes in urban India have been important as a reactionary force, for example in their attempts to collaborate with the state to clear slums, or through their participation in Hindutva organizations. The middle classes as a whole have also been involved, perhaps to a slightly lesser extent, in broadly altruistic action, such as paternalist forms of NGO development in cities, environmental lobbying using public interest legislation, and anti-corruption mobilization. There are also many instances in which middle-class activists have formed alliances with poorer and less powerful sections of society to generate social movements, for example against the construction of large hydroelectric dams or in pursuit of the right to education. Research on middle-class politics in India also emphasizes the greater capacity of the middle class, as compared to the poor, to shape state policy or influence the operations of the local state via corruption. At a more social and economic level, an important achievement of recent studies of the middle class in India has been to show that remaining middle class itself requires a great deal of social and political work; class status is never guaranteed.

The rise of what some have termed a 'new middle class' in urban India is reflected in popular culture, for example in the increasing use of Western clothes, such as jeans; the rise of a restaurant and café culture in cities; new types of architecture; the proliferation of personalized forms of spiritualism; and Bollywood cinema, which serves as a stage upon which changing ideas about what constitutes a middle-class style are performed. But the Indian middle classes rarely just imitate a wider global middle class or Western middle-class style. There is considerable emphasis in scholarship and in the media on the distinctively Indian nature of middle-class cultural practices as well as regional middle-class cultures.

• See also *bourgeois, caste, class, culture, neo-liberal*

Modern, Modernity

Raymond Williams notes that 'modern' came into English from the Latin 'modo', meaning 'just now'. In many contexts—and certainly in popular speech—modern retains this sense of contemporariness. Yet since the sixteenth century in Europe, 'modern' also came to be associated with a particular period of history, first pitted against 'ancient' times and later against a 'medieval' period. In the eighteenth and nineteenth centuries, 'modern' carried with it the sense of a rupture from the past that needed to be justified. But in the nineteenth and twentieth centuries it generally suggested something positive: efficiency, productiveness, and cleanliness, for example. An exception was the discourses surrounding the 'modern girl' that started to circulate across the world, including India, in the first decades of the twentieth century, where the adjective 'modern' connoted ambivalence, even a measure of social danger. During the past century and a half, the word 'modernist' has also been attached to styles of experimental architecture, art, and fashion.

Modernity is a word freighted with political meanings, and powerful institutions have often deployed the terms modern and modernity in ways that reflect their own agendas. For example, the British justified colonial rule in India in part with reference to their own modernity relative to 'traditional' India, highlighting in the process the supposed superiority of Western technology, learning, culture, and society. The notion that India needed to 'modernize' in order to develop also underpinned Nehru's vision of socialism that dominated economic planning in the first two decades following Indian Independence. Indian planners emphasized the importance of catching up with the West and of emulating Europe's experience of modernity through the construction of industrial plants and encouraging urban migration (as laid out in the precepts of 'modernization theory').

Economic reforms in India from the mid-1980s onwards provided a further context in which dominant powers could promote visions of modern success. Large corporations and also local firms in India have used ideas of India's progress towards modernity as a central motif in their advertising and marketing strategies during the past thirty years. The idea promulgated by capitalist forces of being able to 'become modern' through the purchase of consumer goods also underpins the emergence of a new Indian middle class.

Certain parts of India and specific sections of the population are often labelled as being up to date and others, by contrast, as backward; the Indian landscape and Indian society has been temporalized in this important respect. For example, upper middle classes living in metropolitan India are commonly presented, or present themselves, as the face of 'modern India'. Meanwhile, tribal populations, Dalits, or those living in remote mountainous parts of the country are labelled 'traditional' or 'left behind'. Such judgements also characterize the legal language used to categorize the Indian population—'Other Backward Classes' being a case in point.

Scholars frequently associate modernity with a particular mindset. For Anthony Giddens, for example, a modern period is distinctive in large part because it is characterized by people who think of themselves as individuals, make strategic plans for their lives, and reflect consciously on the progress of their plans relative to the progress of others—as distinct, obviously, from a 'traditional' era in which such thought processes and reflexivity were putatively absent. For some early development theorists it was this modernity mindset that, above all else, needed to be planted in the heads of people in India and other parts of the global South. More recently, a broadly similar set of arguments has been rehearsed by those trying to encourage people in India to acquire education, save money, and avail themselves of loans. But there are flaws in Giddens's argument; even those in the most remote parts of India think carefully about how to manage their own lives and plan strategically with reference to long-term goals. But the spread of education, new communication technologies, and urbanization has certainly encouraged people to reflect on their individual lives and broadened their frame of reference.

Anthropologists have laid great emphasis on the plural nature of modernity as it evolves in different places. As for globalization, so for modernity: there is no one model, but multiple ways in which societies may break from a relatively static past and engage in reflexive processes of living. Alternative modernities surface in the efforts of Hindu nationalists or Islamic organizations to articulate a new vision of India, for example, even while such efforts also sometimes, and confusingly, come to be framed as anti-modern or traditionalist. The plural nature of modernity can also be charted in numerous arenas of economic and social life: architecture, film, urban planning, and fashion, to mention but a few. And people often meld practices imagined locally as traditional with those that have arrived more recently: they use computers to organize arranged marriages or mobile phones to communicate about an ancient religious festival. One conceptual response would be to argue that modernity in a place like India is always tangled up with the traditional, but a more proper response would simply be to observe that modernities everywhere are always composed of the fragments of previous eras.

'Modernity' is not a word used in common speech in India, but 'modern' certainly is, and much more often than—say—the Hindi word '*adhunika*'. The negative connotations of the word 'modern' sometimes surface—the term 'modern girl' is sometimes used to refer to young women assumed to be sexually available, for example. At a more general level, many individuals and institutions argue that the modern in India is a dangerous sham and that Indian citizens need to spend much more time focusing on traditional values. But 'modern' remains primarily an aspirational category, one that is used to describe someone educated, urbanized, au fait with happenings outside India, and in other ways 'up to date', and it is therefore no surprise that the adjective 'modern' is regularly appended to almost every conceivable service outlet in India, from schools to barbers, and from hospitals to design firms—as well as to bread made from refined flour.

• See also *development, globalization, middle class, tradition*

Muslim

Muslims constituted 13 per cent of the Indian population—160 million people—in 2001 (and estimated at 177 million in 2011, more than 14 per cent of the total), and they arrived in India from as early as the eighth century. The consolidation of Islam in the subcontinent occurred in the sixteenth and seventeenth centuries, when Mughal rulers developed a complex administrative structure in the region, encouraged trade, often with other Muslims outside the subcontinent, and boosted Muslim (especially Persian) forms of painting, dance, and architecture—the Taj Mahal being perhaps the most famous cultural product of this era.

'Muslim' is just one way in which those who believe in Islam define themselves; it may not be the most important aspect of their identity, and those who believe in Islam sometimes resent being bracketed in this manner in India. In addition, 'Muslim' is an umbrella category covering a wide variety of beliefs and practices. Most of the Indian Muslim population are Sunnis, who believe that the four caliphs are the rightful successors to Muhammad, as opposed to Shias, who argue that only the fourth caliph (Ali) is legitimate. There is also a substantial and increasing portion of the Muslim population who are Sufis, a mystical brand of Islam. In some parts of India there is a notable divide between Ashraf Muslims, said to have a superior standing derived from their Arab ancestry, and the Ajlafs, assumed to be converts from Hinduism and of lower status. There are also castes among Muslims, and sharp inequalities at the local level between social classes.

The Indian state has been partially successful in preventing widespread religious communal violence since the publication of the Constitution in 1950, where secularism was established as a founding ideology of the nation. At the everyday level, there is considerable evidence of neighbourliness, friendship, and unity among Hindus and Muslims in different parts of the country. Hindus and Muslims are often intimately linked together through processes of production and trade or within civil society, educational, or cultural institutions. In daily life the fact of a neighbour or co-worker being Muslim is rather unimportant or not important at all.

But 'Muslim' is a word which resonates powerfully in contemporary India, especially in the sphere of politics, reflecting the recent history of South Asia and the extent to which Hindu/Muslim tension and violence has periodically surfaced in the region. During the late nineteenth and early twentieth centuries, Muslim leaders in India were concerned about Muslims' lack of representation in the Indian National Congress and the rights that might be afforded to Muslims in an independent nation. In 1930, this concern precipitated a call for a separate Muslim state and, in the complex debates that surrounded the Partition of India in the 1940s, the plan to establish an independent and predominantly Muslim Pakistan won out. The violence associated with partition cast a long shadow over politics in independent India and partly explains the periodic upsurge in Hindu/Muslim violence since that time.

Paralleling Muslim concerns over rights, and intimately connected to those calls, were the concerted efforts of Hindu nationalist (Hindutva) forces in twentieth-century India to advance the argument that India is the spiritual homeland of Hindus. For Hindutva activists, Muslims are 'foreigners' or 'outsiders' in India, who pillaged the subcontinent historically and forcibly converted Hindus. In this view, Muslims are also unpatriotic and socially irresponsible, an idea encapsulated in the old canard that Muslims, because of their religious beliefs, are inevitably predisposed to have very large numbers of children. Hindutva forces have rewritten school textbooks to reflect a glorified Hindu past, and promoted their cause violently, through the destruction of the Babri Masjid mosque in Ayodhya in 1992 and by orchestrating riots and pogroms, such as those that took place in Bombay in the early 1990s and Ahmedabad in 2002.

The term 'Muslim' is also associated in the minds of many Indians with poverty. There is a substantial Muslim middle class in India, mostly in urban areas, and also a thin stratum of Muslims who are very rich indeed. But Muslims on the whole remain poorer than Hindus, as strikingly revealed in the government's Sachar Report, published in 2006. This report and subsequent analysis of the data contained in it has revealed that Muslims lag behind Hindus, and even the most disadvantaged of other social groups such as Dalits and adivasis, in terms of education. Indeed, Muslims seem to be falling further behind in the educational sphere. Between 1983 and 2000, the percentage of those completing primary school rose by 19 per cent for Dalits and 22 per cent for Adivasis, compared to 15 per cent for Muslims. These differences cannot be explained with reference to Muslims' poverty; Muslims with the same economic and social resources at their disposal as those available to Dalits suffer disproportionately from educational exclusion. The same applies to the sphere of work. Even controlling for Muslims' low education and other observable aspects of their social position, their disadvantage in terms of labour market access is much greater than analysts would predict. If Muslim men get educated, the extra earnings they can expect from this schooling are less than those of Hindus.

Scholars know little about why Muslims suffer disproportionately in the spheres of education and work—for example whether it is a matter of everyday social discrimination against Muslims or the Muslim community's own preferences. But it seems likely that the difference partly reflects the greater influence over the state of other marginalized communities, such as Dalits and Other Backward Classes, as compared to Muslims. Reflecting their political presence, Hindu Other Backward Classes and Dalits have received a greater amount of special government assistance, for example via reservations in educational institutions and public sector jobs, than have Muslims since the 1970s. At the everyday level, Muslims often have poorer access to schooling, health facilities, and other state services than do Hindus, in part because the mainly Hindu government officials and teachers are reluctant to work in Muslim-dominated areas of the countryside. Muslims commonly lack access to local state agencies, reflecting patterns of corruption and patronage, and even in districts in which there are Muslim majorities, returning Muslim representatives, political clout doesn't necessarily make for social betterment. The future prosperity of Muslims in India requires government to reflect on how Muslim-ness influences people's life chances.

• See also *community, Hindu, Hindutva, poverty, secularism, state*

Nation, Nationalism

'Nation' is an old word in English, having been in common use from the thirteenth century, when it had connotations of 'race' or 'breed' rather than of a political entity. Raymond Williams points out that there remains an overlap between these senses of the word, and he argues that it is difficult 'to date the emergence of the predominant modern sense of a political formation'. In current use, the core of the idea is given in the definition: 'A large aggregate of communities and individuals united by factors such as common descent, language, culture, history, or occupation of the same territory, so as to form a distinct people. Now also: such a people forming a political state; a political state' (*OED*). The earlier part of this definition has a long history in English, and this fact has been used by some scholars in support of the idea that the sense of distinct national identities—of 'national feeling'—has a very long history.

'Nationalism', however, is a word that has been in common use only since the mid-nineteenth century, having come into English from an eighteenth-century German term. *OED* defines it as meaning 'advocacy of, or support for the interests of one's own nation, especially to the exclusion or detriment of the interests of other nations. Also: advocacy of or support for national independence or self-determination.' Nationalism or 'nationalist feeling' is often regarded negatively, as Williams points out, because of the implication of exclusion or opposition in regard to others, whereas 'national feeling' has positive connotations, in common with 'patriotism', a word that appears originally to have been used more or less interchangeably with 'nationalism'. Now, however, the latter—in distinction from patriotism—'usually refers to a specific ideology, especially one expressed through political activism' (*OED*). The emergence of nationalism is thought by noted scholars to be a modern development (in distinction from those who see it as having a long history), and to have come about in the context of the development of market economies and then of industrialization and urbanization, which drew people out of the small communities in which they had lived. Then kinship and intimacy among people who had no real connections with each other came to be imagined in the idea of the nation, encouraged by monarchs and political leaders, who found in it a firm foundation of their own legitimacy and who used it in building strong states.

An Indian nationalist movement emerged, in the context of colonial institutions, in the 1870s and 1880s (*see* Congress)—in part in opposition to ideas of the British rulers such as that 'there is not, and never was ... any country of India ... no "people of India"' (the words of John Strachey, a distinguished civil servant in nineteenth-century India)—and it eventually became a powerful movement for national independence and self-determination. But what is 'the nation' in India? There was justification for the colonial idea that there was no 'people of India'. The adjective 'Hindu' only came to be used with reference to people throughout peninsular India in the nineteenth century—and indeed the establishment of a bounded territory called 'India' came only with an Act of the British parliament in 1899. What did exist were more or less strong feelings of identity among different peoples in different parts of the subcontinent—given partly by loyalty to rulers, perhaps by a particular devotional cult and a geography of sacred places, and by some sense of shared history, and ultimately in language. The historian Christopher Bayly describes these as 'old patriotisms'. Among the Marathas of western India, he says, 'an emerging sense of regional culture coincided with the creation of a regional language and the formation of a relatively strong state'. Another scholar describes the development of Telugu 'ethnicity' in the south between 1400 and 1600, while weaker forms of patriotism are distinguished, for example, among Tamils and Bengalis.

Such patriotisms did not immediately provide a foundation for Indian nationalism, and even at the end of the colonial period there was a strongly held view amongst some British officials that independent India would or should be a loose federation of independent nation states. Nations, they and others thought, are built around clear and distinct marks of identity, such as language, especially, or perhaps religion. And India was, and remains, famously diverse, with many different languages, different religious traditions, and various distinct cultures. Nationalists had to confront this diversity. One important approach was that of Hindu nationalists, some of whom drew on ideas that had constructed a unified, homogenized 'Hinduism', while others projected a form of cultural nationalism, Hindutva, which they sought to distinguish from religion, but which effectively excluded adherents to other religious traditions from 'the nation'. India had to be, they argued, a Hindu nation. Late in the colonial period, parallel sentiments developed amongst some Muslims, which led in the end to Partition and to the formation of Pakistan as a distinct (intended-to-be) nation state. The idea of the nation that ultimately prevailed in India, however, was a 'layered' one, according to the argument of Sunil Khilnani, in which people are at once 'Tamil' (say) and 'Indian', and which is based on universal citizenship and shared participation in a project of national development. It is a multicultural concept of the nation that draws on constructions of the past (those expressed notably—Khilnani suggests—in Nehru's book *The Discovery of India* of 1946), and on ideas of there being cultural forms, in mythology for example, that have long been common to the diverse peoples of the subcontinent. This construction, or 'imagining', of the nation has been threatened quite often, and it has been anticipated by some outsiders, and by some Indians, that the unity of the nation must be broken. It has been threatened, in particular, in struggles over the use of Hindi as the national language, and most recently by the resurgence of Hindutva.

Education has often been the forum in which governments have sought to construct a particular idea of 'the nation'—as happened in nineteenth-century Europe. Latterly, contending ideas of the nation in India have been played out in debates over the school curriculum and over the writing of history, between Hindu nationalists, in government between 1998 and 2004, and those holding to a secular vision, based on universal citizenship.

Thus far the Nehruvian conception of India has proven robust, but it cannot be taken for granted.

• See also *constitution, Hindutva, Nehru*

Naxalite

There is no word that is more significant in the political imaginations of Indians, across regions and social groups, than this one, which came into use after 1967. It was in February of that year that a breakaway faction of the Communist Party of India (Marxist) (CPI(M)) launched an insurgency in the Naxalbari region of northern West Bengal. This was in the context of intense debate within India's communist movement over strategy and tactics, which was of long standing but had been reignited in the circumstances of the Sino-Soviet split. One faction sought to pursue a Maoist line—following the example and the ideas of the Chinese leader Mao Zedong.

Maoism (a word that has been in use in English since the late 1940s) has come to be thought of as a distinct set of ideas about the nature and practice of communism. In India, however, the idea of Maoism has been particularly understood as meaning the mode of revolutionary practice developed by Mao in the course of the Chinese revolution, based among the peasantry, and aimed at first establishing rural 'base areas', which the Communist Party and its followers gradually expand so as to encircle the towns, and finally take over the state. This line of revolutionary practice, 'people's war', was first adopted by the faction of the Communist Party of India that was responsible for organizing insurgency in the Telengana region of the former Hyderabad state (and then of Andhra Pradesh) in 1948 (an insurgency that was finally put down by 1951 through action of the Indian army).

The Maoist line was taken up again by the Naxalites, led by Charu Mazumdar (1918–72), who had been a district organizer of the CPI(M). The Party, though supportive of China, was unsympathetic to militancy, and became part of a United Front government in West Bengal early in 1967, while Mazumdar and his followers held to the aim of bringing about revolution through guerrilla warfare based in rural areas. They organized sharecroppers ('*bargadars*' in Bengali) and agricultural labourers, who were mainly from lower castes and from amongst adivasis, against higher-caste landowners. They occupied lands, harvested crops, burnt land records and passed death sentences on oppressive landlords. The insurgency in Naxalbari was rather quickly crushed by police action but it continued elsewhere— notably in the Telengana and the delta regions of Andhra Pradesh—for much longer, though even there it was thought to have been overcome by the time of Mazumdar's death, in police custody, in July 1972. Still, Naxalbari is described by its chronicler, Sumanta Banerjee, as being 'no doubt ... a watershed in the recent history of India'.

In West Bengal the Naxalites, crucially, failed to build a mass base in rural areas—where the CPI(M) was by that time winning widespread support—and by the beginning of the 1970s their main supporters were mostly students from a middle-class background, their activities mainly urban, and often directed against the CPI(M). The movement was subject to the criticism that it was one of 'middle-class romantics', while the police action against the young supporters of Naxalism, many of whom were killed, created an enduring memory among Bengalis.

The Naxalites formed the Communist Party of India (Marxist–Leninist) in 1969. The Party, and the Naxalite movement, subsequently fragmented—as many as seventeen different groups were reported from central Bihar in the 1990s. But it survived underground, winning some support especially among low-caste poor peasants and agricultural labourers on the plains of Bihar, and more particularly among adivasis in the hills and forests of central and eastern India. At last, in 2004, the principal groups came together to form the Communist Party of India (Maoist), which reaffirmed the programmatic line of the Naxalites, of waging a 'people's war'. In the years since then, a Maoist/Naxalite insurgency (the terms 'Maoist' and 'Naxalite' having come to be used interchangeably) has gathered strength across a large swathe of the centre and east of the country, coming to be described by the prime minister, Manmohan Singh, as the gravest internal security threat that India has ever faced. Whether the insurgency should be seen as being driven by 'middle-class romantics', or whether it should be seen as a genuinely popular movement (when it may well have an element of both); and whether it should be treated primarily as a security problem, or rather as a development problem, are critical questions on which Indians are divided.

• See also *adivasi, commons, communism, terrorism*

Nehru

Jawaharlal Nehru, the first prime minister of India, was born in 1889 to a Kashmiri Brahmin ('pandit') family already prominent in the law and nationalist politics. His father, Motilal Nehru, would serve twice as the President of the Indian National Congress (INC). One of Nehru's sisters, Vijaya Lakshmi, would later become the first female president of the United Nations General Assembly. After an education at Cambridge, and the Inner Temple in London, Jawaharlal returned to India in 1912, and shortly thereafter he engaged with the INC. Radicalized in part by Tilak and Annie Besant, Nehru is commonly said to have apprenticed himself to Gandhi through the critical decade of the 1920s. Unlike Gandhi, Nehru never expressed any deep religious feelings; indeed, it has commonly been assumed that he was an atheist. Like Gandhi, however, Nehru was alert to the threat posed to the nationalist movement by communalism (Hindu–Muslim tensions, predominantly) and the stoking up of religious hatreds both by the colonial power, which proposed separate electorates for India's major religious communities, and by the Hindu Mahasabha. Like Gandhi, too, Nehru would spend much of the 1920s, 1930s, and 1940s in British jails. Nehru's major book, *The Discovery of India* (*see* history), was written in Ahmednagar Fort, where he was imprisoned from 1942–6.

Within six months of India's Independence on 15 August 1947 Gandhi was dead, killed by a Hindu fanatic, Nathuram Godse. The death of Vallabhbhai Patel in December 1950 consolidated the leadership of postcolonial India in the hands of Nehru, a position that would last to his own death in 1964. Along with Bhimrao Ambedkar, Nehru was the principal architect of the Constitution of India, which was promulgated in January 1950. He helped to ensure that governance in India would be fundamentally liberal, democratic, and federal. Nehru shared many of Ambedkar's intuitions about the need for the proactive empowerment of India's Depressed Classes—especially its Dalits and adivasis. He nonetheless proved unwilling to insist on land reforms that would directly empower the Scheduled Castes, much to Ambedkar's chagrin. Nehru instead oversaw the development of a Constitutional Framework which added to various Fundamental Rights a broader set of Directive Principles of State Policy that were non-justiciable. Nehru believed that India's poorest communities would be empowered by economic modernization and secular education. He put particular faith in the delivery of new formal sector jobs and new attitudes that would throw off ideas of *karma* and *dharma* (loosely, fate and duty) and a biologized account of hereditary worth (the caste system).

Central to Nehru's vision for independent India was the process of planned economic growth that began with the First Five-Year Plan (1951–6). Although the Constitution of India did not speak directly of socialism and secularism (the focus was on democracy and federalism), it was widely understood in the Nehru–Gandhi years—the reference here is to Nehru's daughter, Indira Gandhi, and his grandson, Rajiv Gandhi, both later prime ministers of India—that the country's founding mythologies of rule embraced all four of these compass points. Evidence of a socialist turn in India is more apparent in the first two prime ministerships of Indira Gandhi than in those of her father, but there can be no doubting that India's Second and Third Five-Year Plans (1956–66) proposed a dirigiste model of economic development that placed considerable resources at the disposal of the Planning Commission, which Nehru chaired. The Nehru–Mahalanobis model of rapid industrial development sanctioned massive state investments in heavy manufacturing, power, and infrastructure. Food production was expected to grow through the 1950s and 1960s mainly by virtue of institutional reform: higher output of grains was expected following the removal of zamindars and other apparently unproductive superior landlords or rent-takers. Nehru advertised his own faith in a new industrial future for India when he commended the Bhakra-Nangal dam to local labourers and other residents as a 'new temple of resurgent India' that they could look upon with pride and awe.

Nehru's reputation was badly tarnished in the years before his death due to growing signs of agrarian distress—seen by some, such as Charan Singh (the rich peasant leader from Uttar Pradesh who was briefly prime minister in 1979–80), to be a result of Nehru's 'urban bias'— and to India's ignominious defeat at the hands of China in the war of 1962. Nehru's reputation rose again when his daughter Indira imposed Emergency Rule on the country (1975–7), and sadly once more in 1984 when Indira was assassinated by her Sikh body-guards, following an ill-advised assault on the Golden Temple in Amritsar which she had authorized (Operation Bluestar). Nehru's rule was lauded on both these occasions precisely for not having threatened democracy and for not fighting religious fire with fire, as Indira misguidedly chose to do. Nehru was not averse to imposing President's Rule during his time as prime minister—not least in communist Kerala, although in this case the action seems to have been driven more by the then President of the Congress party, Mrs Indira Gandhi. It is widely considered that Nehru did his best to uphold each of India's founding myths in a way that his daughter did not.

Nehru's reputation came under attack again through the 1990s, and most sharply when the country examined itself, and was examined from outside, in 1997, fifty years after Independence. The word 'Nehruvian' was now used as a synonym in some quarters for fifty years of failure. Neo-liberal economists suggested that Nehru was as much to blame as his daughter for the development of a Planning and Licence Raj that had stymied economic growth and poverty alleviation. Meanwhile, an increasingly assertive community of Hindu nationalists blamed Nehru for appeasing—or privileging—India's Muslims within a landscape they described as 'pseudo-secularist'. It is perhaps only in more recent years that Nehru's reputation as one of India's greatest sons has begun to re-emerge from this twin-pronged attack. More reasonable observers of contemporary India note that it was Nehru, more than anyone else, who kept India together in the first twenty years after Independence, when many were predicting that the country was bound to fall apart. (Churchill, recall, had once said that India, with all its religious, ethnic, and linguistic diversity, was no more a country in the making than was the equator.) Fair-minded commentators also accept that Nehru's economic model in the 1950s was entirely in line with economic thinking at the time (which generally promoted import-substitution industrialization in developing countries) and laid the foundation for some of India's recent economic successes. Nehru has now been dead for fifty years. His legacy, and what it means to be Nehruvian, continues to be re-evaluated in the light of contemporary anxieties.

• See also *congress, constitution, democracy, development, federalism, Gandhi, secularism, socialism*

Neo-liberal, Neo-liberalism

Neo-liberalism refers to an approach to the economy and society that prioritizes market freedoms and reduces state involvement in and funding for public goods (*see* liberal). Under a neo-liberal regime, it is expected that the state should spend relatively little on welfare, such as education and health, and attempt to curb forms of social mobilization, such as trade unions, that might interfere with the principles of free-market capitalism. The term is often said to have first appeared in the 1960s in Latin America but it gained common currency in the 1970s and 1980s with the rise of Thatcher and Reagan, both of whom moved their respective countries in more neo-liberal directions. The term neo-liberalism is often also linked to the phrase 'Washington Consensus', coined by the economist John Williamson in 1989 to describe the market-driven tenor of the package of reforms promoted by the World Bank, International Monetary Fund, and US Treasury Department for developing countries in the 1980s.

Neo-liberalism is sometimes counterposed to classical liberalism, with its emphasis on free trade and individual liberty, but the extent to which the 'neo' of neo-liberalism refers to some modification of classical liberalism or liberalism reapplied in a new era is somewhat open to debate—the *OED* favours the former interpretation defining neo-liberalism as 'a modified form of liberalism tending to favour free-market capitalism'.

Neo-liberalism in the West is specifically associated with a move away from the Keynesian approach to the economy and society in which the state—since roughly the 1940s—played a major role in the provision of basic services to the poor, a model which continues to dominate public policy in many parts of continental Europe. The extent to which the notion of neo-liberalism can be applied to India is therefore open to doubt; India lacks any period in which the state effectively provided for the masses in terms of health care and education, for example, in a manner that would parallel the National Health Service in the UK. Barbara Harriss-White has made a version of this argument, pointing out that many sectors of the Indian state were in a certain sense already functioning according to market logics before India's economic liberalization, as reflected in endemic corruption.

There is also the thorny question of quite how far India's embrace of the market has actually occurred. It is true that India's economic reforms involved a raft of measures that can be construed as broadly pro-market. But the reforms were not especially radical and left many key areas untouched. Chronic underfunding of government health care and education has given rise to numerous new types of private schooling and health care, but this may be the unwitting outcome of government neglect rather than a conscious process of neo-liberalization.

The Indian Government introduced new measures early in the twenty-first century to support the poor population, most notably a vast employment guarantee scheme (the Mahatama Gandhi National Rural Employment Guarantee Scheme), and the state's spending on development increased markedly at this time. Increased state spending in certain sectors can be construed as consistent with a neo-liberal strategy—neo-liberalism is about rolling out the state as well as rolling it back. But the massive extension of government funds to India's poor and lower middle classes—and through corruption to regional and local brokers—complicates any attempt to brand India straightforwardly as 'neo-liberal'. Moreover, there has been no straightforward withdrawal from the state with respect to the provision of basic services. Rather, recent years have witnessed the emergence of new institutional forms in which the state partners with private interests, local NGOs, and large international donors in the delivery of goods—a phenomenon by no means unique to India but which, again, makes the country an awkward case of neo-liberalism.

David Harvey has characterized actually existing neo-liberalism in many parts of the world, including India, as associated with 'accumulation by dispossession', whereby corporate capital extends its advantage at the expense of the poor. This argument has considerable force in India, where strong-arm tactics such as land-grabbing are common.

Neo-liberalism is also an ideology, associated especially with an ethic of individualism and success through participation in capitalist production and consumption. Governments and other powerful organizations, such as the World Bank, try to generate consent for market-driven approaches and stifle resistance through encouraging people to imagine themselves as entrepreneurs and consumers. Whether such a neo-liberal ideological programme can succeed in India is a topic of considerable debate. There is evidence that youth increasingly look to the market rather than to government as a source of employment and basis for mobility. But equally the notion of the state as a guarantor of rights, locus of decision-making, and source of development and services remains very powerful in the Indian collective psyche, including in the minds of youth. There is also growing evidence of popular resistance to neo-liberalism, including Naxalite insurrections, rights movements, and the demands made by civil society groups for strong state regulation of capitalist markets.

• See also *development, globalization*

NGO

This by now familiar acronym stands for 'non-governmental organization'. Organizations 'not belonging to or associated with government' (which is how *OED* defines 'non-governmental organization') have been in existence for very much longer, but the term 'NGO' came into general use only with the establishment of the United Nations in 1945. From its early days, the UN has wished that non-state agencies should attend and have observer status at some of its meetings, and the expression NGO is used in a document of the UN Economic and Social Council published in 1946. From this time NGOs have become increasingly significant actors in public affairs, and especially so from the 1980s onwards. They are now sometimes very influential in decision-making in some areas of public policy, both internationally—as they are in some of the deliberations of the World Bank—and at national and local levels, in India as they are elsewhere in the world. It is estimated that India had as many as 3.3 million NGOs in 2009. Yet the idea of the NGO is controversial in the country, and very many organizations in India's civil society very deliberately resist being described as such.

A simple definition of an NGO is that of 'an organization that is not part of government and not a for-profit business'. NGOs are often described as constituting, or being part of, the 'not-for-profit sector', or as being an essential constituent of the 'third sector', outside both state and market. But these definitions embrace an enormously diverse range of organizations, and it may be important to distinguish between (among other possible examples) 'community-based organizations' such as local residents' associations, and other membership organizations, and those organizations that though definitely 'non-governmental' are nonetheless professionalized, with bureaucratic hierarchies and a paid staff. Employment in NGOs of the latter type has indeed become an attractive career option for highly qualified young people in India and in other countries. Many such NGOs are involved in operational work, notably in the delivery of different social services, even perhaps under contract to government. Others are involved in campaigning and advocacy—and some, of course, in both operational and campaigning work. No matter what their field of work, however, such organizations cannot properly be described as being 'voluntary' or 'membership' organizations.

India has been the home of a good many notable NGOs since well before the time that the concept became prominent. The voluntary service organizations that sprang up around the nationalist movement, such as the Ramakrishna Mission founded in the mid-1890s, the Servants of India Society founded in 1905, the Seva Samiti Society founded in 1910, and many others, can fairly be described as 'NGOs'. The work of Gandhi's Constructive Programme was a non-governmental activity, and the historian Carey Watt has listed as many as eleven organizations connected to this Programme as 'NGOs'. As Watt has shown, India had a growing associational culture and voluntary sector through the first half of the twentieth century.

Much has come to be expected of NGOs over the closing two decades of the twentieth century and in the early years of the present one. It is still widely believed that NGOs can do a much better job than bureaucratically run governmental agencies in delivering different services, because those who work in them are dedicated to the goals of their organizations in a way that bureaucrats commonly are not, and driven by commitment to those whom they are serving. NGOs are thought to be more in touch with people and capable of encouraging them to participate more actively in public affairs. They are held to be more innovative and more flexible. All of this may be justified in some cases, but certainly not in those of all NGOs. Some assessments have reached quite negative conclusions, and there is an increasing tendency, certainly in India, to see NGOs as being subject to very many of the same limitations as governmental organizations. Professionalized NGOs are seen as serving the interests of those who are employed in them, rather than of those whom they are supposed to serve. Further, the idea that NGOs can and should replace government is understood as being part of the agenda of neo-liberalism, and to be part of the 'rolling back of the state' that it advocates. It is feared by many in India that allowing this to happen will be to diminish universal rights of social citizenship. In other countries in which there has been considerable devolution of responsibility for delivery of educational or health services to NGOs, there are reports of a kind of patchwork quilt effect, with very different levels of provision in different regions. There are questions about the accountability of NGOs, other than to their funders. It is for these reasons that many civil society organizations in India react forcefully against being described as 'NGOs'. They identify NGOs with neo-liberalism, with dependence on foreign funding, and hence on agendas set by outsiders, and with self-serving on the part of those who work in them.

• See also *charity, empowerment, enterprise, environment, middle class*

Panchayat

'Panchayat' is a Hindi term, with a Sanskrit root, the word for 'five'. Its literal meaning is 'the assembly (or council) of five', and it has entered into the English language literature on modern India with reference to the idea of a village council. Contemporary India has a system of decentralized local democracy, 'panchayati raj', in which the primary unit is the panchayat, which is now an elected council for a village or a small cluster of villages.

The idea of the panchayat as a village council is actually controversial. It seems that it became linked with the idea of the Indian village as a community, which loomed large in the imaginations of some colonial administrators in the nineteenth century, and the social life of villages was presumed to be controlled by such councils. Yet when the attempt was made in the census of 1911 to study village panchayats, it proved hard over much of the country actually to identify them. The census of Bombay went so far as to pronounce that the idea was a myth. The reaction of others to the negative findings of the census was to conclude that these—it was thought—significant instruments of local democracy must have been destroyed because of the impact of colonialism.

Subsequent studies of Indian villages report, most clearly, on the existence of caste panchayats, though there are also references to village panchayats. In some cases the reports show the existence of quite formally constituted bodies, but very often it seems that the idea of the panchayat is that of a gathering of respected men whose authority in the resolution of disputes is accepted by others. They do not necessarily all come together at one time and place, but they deliberate amongst themselves, aiming to reach consensus. Panchayats seem usually to have operated according to principles of deliberative, consensual decision-making, rather than the adversarial practices and majority ruling of many Western councils. Whether or not a village panchayat is at all representative of different castes and social groups is a matter of some dispute, and it certainly appears that local panchayats were commonly gatherings of members of what sociologists have described as the 'dominant caste'. The dominant caste is the caste community that, by virtue of some combination of numbers, control over land and labour and other resources, is able to exercise power over a locality. It is possible, therefore, that what were represented as village panchayats were actually deliberations of the dominant caste, supplying rulings over village affairs. There are some recent reports, however, of 'traditional' local panchayats in which different caste groups *are* represented.

The existence of these institutions of what he saw as self-government, and the principle of non-adversarial decision-making were an inspiration for Gandhi. His idea was that independent India should not have a Western-style state at all, but that it should be governed through a decentralized 'bottom-up' system, founded on 'village swaraj' (self-government). He envisaged a hierarchy of panchayat institutions, with the village panchayats at its base, and a national panchayat at its apex. There would be no political parties. The idea, as an alternative to parliamentary democracy, attracted no support at all in the deliberations of the Constituent Assembly, but the idea of local self-government was eventually adopted, mainly as a way of encouraging rural development, through an article of the Constitution. This is among the non-justiciable Directive Principles, which are expressions of objectives that the state should seek to achieve; Article 40 says that the government should 'organize village panchayats and endow them with such powers and authority as may be necessary to enable them to function as a unit of self-government'. Attempts to implement this objective were, however, very largely frustrated—by the opposition of state-level politicians who saw in local councils a threat to their own powers and privileges—until the passage in 1992 of the 73rd Amendment of the Constitution. Since that time, panchayati raj institutions have been established throughout most of the country, though with varying degrees of commitment in different states. The base of the system is the election of representatives to the village (or 'gram') panchayats, with one-third of seats being reserved for women, and the position of chairman (*pradhan*) being reserved in some cases for women and in others for Scheduled Castes. The village panchayats then elect representatives to the second tier of the system, at the level of the Development Block (the basic unit of the development administration, covering a number of villages); the block panchayats, in turn, elect representatives to the third tier, at the district level. Panchayati raj has become well known internationally as a system of democratic decentralization of government, though how well it works varies considerably.

• See also *community, constitution, Gandhi, village*

Patronage

In the *Oxford English Dictionary* a 'patron' refers to either a person who gives financial or other support to another person; a customer in a shop or restaurant; a provider in relation to a client, often with the additional sense of 'protector'; or a person or institution with the right to grant a benefice to a member of the clergy. Patronage therefore refers to the act of serving as a patron and can mean providing financial services, other resources, physical protection, or some type of spiritual assistance or favour. As the different meanings of 'patron' also suggest, patronage can be granted out of goodwill or, more commonly, reflects institution-alized relationships of mutuality, based for example on money (as in a shop) or ritual practice (as in the case of a Roman slave owner), and linked to larger regional cultures and political arrangements. Integral to most discussions of patronage, certainly in India, is the vexed question of precisely how to evaluate the phenomenon from a normative standpoint. Patronage has connotations of resource provision in a situation of inequality, and it suggests exploitation. But patronage also connotes an ethic of care, mutual responsibility, and respect.

In India in the mid-twentieth century, anthropologists and political scientists reported on the existence of a so-called 'jajmani' system among different castes, wherein a high-caste patron (jajman) would provide grain or money to low-caste service providers (*kameen*). This system was underpinned by complex rules about appropriate ritual interactions between jajmans and kameens, for example regarding the sharing of food. On a wider scale, princes in India were widely regarded by their subjects as patrons, who could be depended upon for assistance within a regional moral economy.

At the same time, many political scientists studied the existence of patron–client relationships in local politics. During the colonial era, the British bolstered the position of local 'big men' by giving them additional titles and authorities, for example to act as local tax representatives for the colonial power. In rural and urban areas, people tended to interact with authorities via a locally trusted patron with knowledge of the colonial authorities. Both before and after Independence, the Congress party enrolled precisely this class of local big men in its own organizational structure. Ordinary people could get some access to government largesse via the pressure they could exert on local bigwigs, who now boasted Congress party titles. Far from being some hangover from the past, patron–client networks actually allowed Congress—and many succeeding governments in India—to win votes and maintain consent for rule; India is therefore sometimes labelled a 'patronage democracy'.

The jajmani system has declined in India. But patronage relations are being revived in modern arenas. Political parties in India, as well as politicians, manage their relationship to populations mainly through developing personal relationships with locally important figures. Politicians give feasts to their supporters—food and patronage are closely linked—and supporters engage in rituals of obeisance to their political protectors. The vast size of the Indian electorate means that this patron–client system is enormously complicated and multilayered, and brokers and go-betweens occupy numerous niches in the system.

Patronage has also emerged in universities, international migration networks, and the competition for white-collar service work. For example, in universities junior students often survive in their institution through cultivating a relationship with a senior student. This relationship is often developed through humiliating and sometimes physically violent initiation ceremonies on campus—called 'ragging'—in spite of such practices being illegal. In this context, and in many others, a patron is expected not only to act as a bridgehead for certain kinds of resources and as an advocate, but also as protector; having been humiliated and beaten by one's patron in university, you can fully expect that the patron will in turn protect you from similar violence in the future. Another sphere in which patronage has been studied closely in modern India is that of the market. Scholars such as Barbara Harriss-White argue that patron–client relations are absolutely central to how the economy works in provincial India.

It is also evident that some of the conventions associated with patron–client relationships in the past colour people's everyday interactions in the present. As in politics, so in other spheres of life in India, people create personalized relationships of trust and reciprocity within institutional contexts that are—at least in theory—supposed to be rational and formal. Thus, for example, people make gifts to their doctor in the hope that he or she will act as a patron in the future; they develop special relationships with particular teachers in school; or they cultivate patron–client-type relationships with specific lawyers or judges. Outside of bureaucratic spheres, the rise of spiritualism in India has been associated with the emergence of personalized religious relationships between clients and religious gurus.

The emergence of new forms of know-how and authority associated with the growth of formal education and new technologies may be redistributing opportunities for acting as a patron, while eroding some older patron–client ties based for example on age or ritual authority. Whether this marks an end to patronage or just the emergence of new types of specialist patron or broker—the 'technical wizard' for example—is a moot point. Certainly, the spread of notions of universal citizenship and rights in India over the past twenty years amounts to a challenge to the personalized relationships on which patronage is based. The anti-corruption movement in India, the Right to Information Act, and such phenomena as the formation in 2013 of the Aam Aadmi ('ordinary man's') political party point to popular opposition to the continued existence of patronage in politics and public bureaucracies. These dynamics are lending fresh urgency to the question of how to evaluate patronage from a normative standpoint.

• See also *caste, colonialism, congress, corruption, democracy, faction, politics*

Peasant

The general understanding in English of the word 'peasant' is that it refers to someone who lives in the countryside, usually working on the land. More specifically, it refers to small working landholders and agricultural labourers. The term was in common use in England certainly by the fifteenth century, but given the transformation of English agriculture over the succeeding centuries it became increasingly redundant, as capitalist relations of production became established and the categories of 'landlord', 'tenant', and 'labourer' more apt. By the nineteenth century, Williams tells us, the word was described as a *new* name, used in a derogatory way by townspeople to refer to country labourers. The older meaning of the word—that of smallholding agricultural producers working with their own and family labour—seemed to apply more appropriately in other countries such as France, Russia, and Ireland. Perhaps for this reason it does not seem to have been a term very much used by the British in India in the nineteenth century. Baden-Powell, for example, in his classic work on land tenure in India (*see* village), does refer to 'peasant proprietors', but not at all frequently.

The word has no strict translation in any Indian language, though the Hindi term '*kisan*' has come to be used in place of the English, as it was by an early authority on the agrarian economy of independent India, Daniel Thorner. In lectures he gave in 1955, Thorner took the word '*kisan*' to mean 'working peasants'—defined as 'those villagers who live primarily by their own toil on their own lands. They do not employ labour, except briefly in the ploughing or harvest season, nor do they commonly receive rent.' At the same time, in the mid-1950s, the word 'peasant' was not used very much at all by sociologists of India. A classic collection of village studies, for instance, includes reference to the idea of the peasant very rarely, except in an essay on 'peasant culture' by an anthropologist who had previously worked in Mexico. The idea of 'peasant culture/society' had by then become current amongst scholars studying Mexico, thanks in large measure to the influence of the anthropologist Robert Redfield. It came into more general use amongst Indian scholars only much later. One of them, André Betéille from the University of Delhi, wrote in 1974 that the term 'peasantry' is 'most meaningfully used to describe a more or less homogeneous and undifferentiated community of families characterized by small holdings operated mainly by family labour'. He went on, however, to question the use of the word in India, given what he saw as the highly differentiated character of rural society in the country.

The idea of the peasant has become current in Indian thought thanks in large measure to the influence on communist activists and left-wing intellectuals of the writings of both Lenin and of Mao Zedong. These communist leaders were both much concerned with the question of which groups of rural people would be most likely to support proletarian revolution, and undertook analyses of the rural economies of Czarist Russia and earlier twentieth-century China, respectively, in order to answer it. Both argued against the idea that rural society was any longer, if it ever had been, characterized by homogeneous communities of families operating smallholdings largely with their own labour. With the development of capitalism, they both showed, rural society became increasingly differentiated. A process of class polarization seemed to take place, so that the rural economy saw the establishment of capitalist farms operated by wage labour, with few working peasant smallholders. Based on their empirical work, scholars and political activists (in India and elsewhere in the postcolonial world) began to distinguish between 'rich', 'middle', and 'poor' peasants, according to their employment, or not, of wage labour and their capacity to produce a surplus. Thus rich peasants, sometimes labelled using the Russian word 'kulak', are those who operate their holdings mainly through the employment of wage labour and who produce a surplus over the immediate subsistence needs of their households; while 'poor peasants' are those who, while cultivating some land and having some resources of their own, are unable to produce a surplus, and must rely to a significant extent on carrying out waged work for others. Only the 'middle peasants', probably a small and shrinking group, correspond to Thorner's idea of the 'working peasant'. These categories have come to be used very commonly in both scholarly and popular writing in India over the last forty years, initially in the context of a controversy over whether or not capitalism was developing in Indian agriculture.

While the idea that rich peasants became politically more powerful in the 1970s—partly as a consequence of the green revolution—was current at the time, in the course of the following decade there developed what were described both in English and in Indian languages as 'farmers' movements'. The change of terminology reflected the recognition that the category even of rich peasant was hardly appropriate to describe the highly commercialized cultivators of the richer agricultural regions of the country. Now, in the twenty-first century, when it is well known that very many rural people across much of India depend upon a whole range of activities outside agriculture, whether carried on locally, or by migration to other areas and to towns and cities, the appropriateness of the peasant idea is less and less apparent. It seems likely that, just as happened in England in an earlier time, the word will become increasingly archaic.

• See also *green revolution, land, village*

Police

According to the *OED*, 'police' refers to 'The civil force of a state, responsible for the prevention and detection of crime and the maintenance of public order.' Policing denotes 'The duty to maintain law and order within an area or at an event.' The precise boundaries, however, between the 'civil force of the state' and private citizenry in India are often blurred. For example, high-ranking police officials routinely make use of police vehicles to ferry relatives to social events; students often act as informal police snitches; and low-ranking police officers shade ambiguously into a wider nexus of authority holders, for example where they act as hired security guards alongside private individuals.

There are at least three different bodies of personnel that come under the broad title of 'police' in India: 'general-purpose police forces' with full powers of access, arrest, and investigation for any criminal offence throughout India; special-purpose police, such as the Border Security Force, holding powers of enforcement in connection with a narrow range of offences; and general-purpose police whose jurisdiction is limited to particular territories, such as the Indian Railway Protection Force. When people refer to the 'police' in India, they most commonly mean the first category of general-purpose police (referred to henceforward simply as 'the police').

The Indian police has one of the most elaborate command hierarchies in the world, with six levels—headquarters, range, district, subdivision, circle, and station—and four basic ranks of lateral recruitment: Indian Police Service Officer (the only rank recruited and trained nationally rather than at state level), Provincial Police Service Officer, Sub-Inspector, and Constable. For the vast majority of the police, there is little or no upward mobility through the ranks. Even within the ranks promotion can be slow. Constables comprise more than 90 per cent of the police in India.

The broad terms of police action were set out during the colonial period under the 1861 Police Act, which emphasized the maintenance of law and order over and above issues of public service and criminal investigation. Under the British, the police were initially charged with protecting European society in India, but gradually became the protectors of propertied classes in general. While policing is formally a state subject, all states broadly follow the guidelines provided by the Police Act.

After Independence, the police continued to protect the rich rather than create an environment conducive to the upholding of the law. Other problems also persisted in the postcolonial period. The police in India are notoriously inefficient and poorly trained; there is very little oversight or review of police activities; malpractice and rent-seeking are endemic; and the police are unresponsive to the needs of local communities, especially the poor.

'Police' is a word that conjures fear in the minds of many ordinary Indians. The National Project on Preventing Torture in India found that 1.8 million people fall victim to police torture each year in India, most of them women, low castes, or Muslims. Likewise, the Justice Verma Committee Report of 2013 found evidence of institutionalized sexual aggression perpetrated by the police and paramilitary forces in conflict areas. The failure of the police to prevent—or its active encouragement of—riots and pogroms is also well documented. Aside from such egregious police malpractice, the police are typically arrogant, impolite, and intimidating in their interactions with the public.

'Police' and 'corruption' are words commonly heard together. State governments and politicians routinely interfere in the activities of the police, for example using transfers as a system of reward and punishment, co-opting police officers to act as private guards for VIPs, and compelling police officials to pay illegal rents on the basis of what they can earn in bribes and kickbacks. Low-ranking officers are expected to accumulate large side incomes, a small portion of which they keep themselves, the remainder being passed on to superiors, criminals, and politicians. Equally troubling is a tendency for the police to be hired by criminal gangs or politicians to carry out extra-juridical killings, which are falsely recorded as having occurred in 'encounters' with criminals. Large corporations also wield considerable influence over the police, as became glaringly apparent in May 2012 when the Haryana police assisted corporate bigwigs in suppressing a legal demonstration by the Maruti Suzuki Workers Union.

In the media, books, and films the police are usually depicted as weak—the foolish lackeys of more powerful figures—or as jumped-up thugs. A three-year intensive study of the Rajasthan police carried out by the Massachusetts Institute of Technology and the Rajasthan Police in 2006–8 found that 71 per cent of people did not report crimes because they believed that the police could not or would not do anything, and would ask for a bribe to register a First Information Report. Morale is very low inside the force, too, and police officers do not even trust one another. An anthropologist recently asked police officers whether they would trust their co-workers to take care of a vulnerable female family member; the majority said no.

Since the late 1970s, there have been repeated efforts to reform the police. After the Emergency of 1975–7, the Janata Party committed itself to reducing police corruption and appointed a National Police Commission to investigate aspects of police functioning. None of its recommendations were implemented, however. Further committees were established in 1998 and 2002, but again their recommendations were left to gather dust. In 2005, the central government appointed the Soli Sorabjee Committee to draft a new model police bill, which was presented to government in October of that year and is still pending.

The Supreme Court has stepped into the breach in some respects. In 2006 it ordered state governments to professionalize the police force, by limiting transfers, instituting new procedures for the appointment of a Chief Commissioner, creating separate departments and staff for investigation and patrolling, establishing a Police Establishments Board to monitor selection and promotion, and setting up a Police Complaints Authority. But, again, the states have resisted implementing the Supreme Court's directions.

• See also *corruption, state, violence*

Politics

Politics is conventionally defined as 'the activities associated with the governance of a country or area' (*OED*), particularly the relationship between parties competing for power. During the nationalist movement in India, and even more so during the postcolonial period, increasing numbers of Indians were drawn into politics in this sense. During the first two decades of Indian Independence the Congress party, under the leadership of Nehru, dominated political life and held power in New Delhi. But in the mid-1960s political parties representing regional and sectarian (especially agricultural) interests challenged Congress dominance. In the 1980s and 1990s, marginalized sections of society emerged more prominently within formal politics across India, as evident in the political ascendancy of the Bahujan Samaj Party in Uttar Pradesh, alongside a backlash from wealthier sections of society embodied in the electoral success of the Hindu nationalist Bharatiya Janata Party. In the most recent phase of Indian politics, the Congress party has become just one among a number of competing political parties, and since 1989 India has experienced a series of minority and of coalition governments.

Paralleling this democratization, the government has made increasing efforts to decentralize power, and elections at the district, subdistrict, and village and urban neighbourhood levels have been important in drawing people into the political process. Also feeding into this story of an increasingly plural politics is the rise of social movements reflecting particularistic concerns: women's movements, communist mobilization, student and youth protests, religious and separatist movements, caste movements, and protests around rights and corruption. While much of this activity is positive from the perspective of democratization, a troubling aspect of India's recent political history has been the rise of religious communal violence, for example in the early 1990s in connection with a project to build a temple on the site of an old mosque in the north Indian city of Ayodhya. In several instances the Indian state has been complicit in communal pogroms—for example in 1984 after the assassination of Prime Minister Indira Gandhi when Sikhs were targeted, and in western India in 2002 when government forces in Gujarat sided with Hindus in attacks on Muslims.

At the same time as becoming more democratic in terms of elections, representative politics, and social movements, Indian public policy has—to a certain extent—become more attuned to the needs of the people: 'politics' to a certain extent has yielded 'development'. The Indian Government has launched ambitious development programmes focused especially on the provision of food, health care, education, and credit. These efforts have contributed to a reduction in the proportion of the Indian population living in poverty.

There is nevertheless a new scepticism in India among ordinary people regarding the nature of politics. This disillusionment partly reflects the Indian state's failure to engage in the radical redistributive measures (such as land reform) that would threaten the entrenched power of India's upper and middle classes. And endemic corruption and bureaucratic inefficiency have prevented the government from implementing innovative development programmes and obstruct the ordinary citizen's access to key services. In addition, politics in India has become increasingly criminalized, through the absorption of criminals into political assemblies, and also because of widespread looting by the political elite. One response to government corruption, criminalization, and underinvestment in services has been a general feeling among citizens in India that politics ('*rajniti*' in Hindi) is inherently somehow 'dirty' and unattractive. In some cases this is a discourse primarily heard among India's middle classes, who prefer to channel their efforts into NGOs and voluntary associations rather than engage in the relatively grubby business of politics proper. A type of public culture of anti-politics exists in India in which elected officials and public representatives of the state—and indeed any type of participation in politics proper—are held in low regard. This partly explains the establishment in 2013 of the overtly anti-political Aam Aadmi Party ('ordinary person's party').

But this retreat from Politics with a capital 'P' has been associated with the proliferation of activities that are political with a small 'p', beneath the level of involvement in representative politics and participation in large-scale social movements. Negatively, this proliferation is associated with the continued importance of often violent and predatory forms of clientelism in India—what Partha Chatterjee calls 'political society': caste groups using bribes and coercion to seek resources from the state and the strong-arm tactics of powerful criminals, for example. On the positive side, however, there is also growing evidence that Indian citizens have absorbed notions of universal citizenship and are demanding government assistance and accountability at the local level. People are becoming more involved in petitioning government officials for services, complaining about corruption, and trying to pressure the state into guaranteeing their rights. This is reflected, for example, in the increasing use of the Right to Information Act (2005), which allows members of the public to lodge enquiries about different aspects of state functioning. There is also evidence of a large number of young people and older citizens being involved in writing letters to officials and using the internet to complain about government. This politics is not only about the allocation of scarce resources; it sometimes results in the creation of new services and goods, as for example where slum dwellers demand a new hand pump or villagers manage to club together to pressure the state into providing electricity to their settlement. People often see these various forms of everyday struggle as forms of politics.

• See also *civil society, class, democracy, state*

Population

The British carried out the first national census in India in 1871. But it neither reflected nor encouraged a clear set of colonial policies on the issue of population. Colonial authorities generally believed that a sizeable population was the sign of a healthy nation, and were not overly concerned about India's size. It is true that in the 1920s and 1930s Indian economists, influenced by emerging ideas of modernity, began to link India's alleged overpopulation with a type of 'civilizational deficit'. Yet population remained for the most part a minor theme.

This changed dramatically in the two decades after 1947, when population became a fierce topic of debate. The population of the world was rising quickly and scholars feared that population growth would outstrip the capacity for emerging economies to provide food, and so would trigger social strife. Building on such ideas, state officials in India began to view population growth as a cause of poverty, and organized concerted birth control campaigns. But the results of the census of 1961 showed much more rapid population growth than had been expected, stimulating further action. The slogan 'We are two. Ours are two' appeared very widely, in all the major languages, in campaigns intended to encourage confidence in contraception. Subsequently, of particular note was a move in 1976 by the Indian Government to offer financial and other incentives to citizens to be sterilized. The sterilization procedures were simpler for men, who received vasectomies, than for women, who had to undergo tubal ligation—and yet women were the main targets of the campaigns. The sheer ham-handedness of their implementation, influenced by the prime minister, Indira Gandhi's younger son Sanjay, rendered them largely unsuccessful. Concerns over the size of the Indian population have continued, however, to have the effect of making the family a crucial aspect of social policy. The state in India, as well as NGOs and corporate bodies, are increasingly involved in shaping intimate aspects of family life, often with reference to tropes such as 'overpopulation' and the 'modern family'.

A Malthusian-type development disaster did not come to pass in India in the years after Independence, in part because the existence of a vibrant democracy has served as a bulwark against famine. The public distribution system established in India in the mid-1960s, after two bad cultivation seasons and in the context of stagnation in the agricultural economy, offered the state a means of preventing widespread starvation. At the same time, fears about the consequences of India's rapidly rising population have assumed new forms. Many emphasize the negative effects of rapid population growth on the environment.

During the 1960s, some commentators argued that population increase can be an opportunity. Esther Boserup, for example, claimed that large numbers of people serve as a type of 'resource', spurring innovation. Likewise, a prominent argument in contemporary India is that the country's large population—1.2 billion according to the 2011 census—can benefit society. It is the structure as well as the overall size of India's population that is seen as a boon. There has been a decline in fertility in India since the 1980s, associated with increased use of contraceptives and rising education, and a consequent rise in the proportion of the population in young adulthood. According to the census of India for 2011, the proportion of the population in this age group is now 46 per cent. Economists have argued that such a 'youth bulge' can generate increased personal savings, which in turn can lead to growth in per capita income. Moreover, a large young adult population can encourage positive social change, for example through promoting new attitudes to education and gender empowerment. Just as China is said to have gained from its 'demographic dividend' in the 1980s and 1990s, India might be able to do so in the 2010s and 2020s. But India will only benefit from this dividend if the state improves the institutional environment and creates work opportunities for youth—the prospect of a 'demographic disaster' of mass youth underemployment also looms.

It is not only the issue of the overall size and structure of the population that generates political heat in India, but also a host of complex questions about the relative numbers of people belonging to different religious, gender, caste, and other social categories. Hindu nationalists have stoked a popular myth that Muslims have large families, in spite of widespread evidence suggesting that Muslims do not usually have more children than one would expect given their economic standing. Highly charged language about Muslims 'flooding the country' with their offspring is often institutionalized within Hindutva. The middle classes often mark their position in society through reference to their small families relative to the urban and rural poor, and higher-caste laments about 'teeming' populations of low castes are often heard in India.

Gender and population are intimately linked too. The child sex ratio (0–6) worsened in India from 927 girls for every 1,000 boys in 2001 to 914 in 2011. These figures can mainly be explained with reference to the relative neglect of female children in the first years after their birth and their death from treatable diseases such as diarrhoea. The figures also reflect the continuing existence of female infanticide, and especially the growing use of prenatal diagnostic techniques and sex-selective abortion. Tackling these problems is likely to require concerted action on the issue of preference for sons, which is linked to the rising costs of dowry and continued inequalities in how men and women are perceived in India.

India may benefit from a type of political demographic dividend. The demographer Tim Dyson argues that in many Western societies, the demographic transition from high fertility rates and high death rates to low ones has historically been important in these societies' democratization; autocratic regimes find it increasingly difficult to survive where there are large adult populations. In India the transition to democracy occurred in advance of the demographic transition, but Dyson suggests that an increase in the median age in India from about 20 in 1951 to 25 in 2011 is likely to increase political stability.

• See also *development, family, feminism, poverty, state*

Populism, Populist

The terms 'populism' and 'populist' are derived from the word 'popular', which in turn has its root in a Latin term meaning 'belonging to the people'. By the sixteenth century the ideas of 'popular estate' and 'popular government' were current, referring to 'a political system constituted by or carried on by the whole people, though there was also the sense of low or base'. Then, Williams tells us, the transition to the modern meaning of 'widely liked' or 'widely favoured' contained 'a strong element of setting out to gain favour', and the word was often used in a derogatory sense. Even now concepts such as 'popular literature' or 'popular press' carry connotations of being of inferior quality, or of work that sets out to win favour, as well as the more positive sense simply of being 'well liked'.

These different shades of meaning are reflected in the political concept of populism, which has been applied to, or in some cases claimed by, a number of political parties in different parts of the world. It is often used quite loosely, but its core meaning is given as being 'the policies or principles of any of various political parties which seek to represent the interests of ordinary people' (*OED*). It came into use towards the end of the nineteenth century with reference to the People's Party in the United States, and also to a political movement in Russia that represented the peasantry. The term 'spread quickly, and is now often used in distinction from socialist, to express reliance on popular interests or sentiments rather than particular (principled) theories and movements' (Williams). Leaders labelled as 'populist' are generally political outsiders who—as the political scientist Tariq Thachil has put it— 'craft appeals that attack the political establishment for being deaf to the needs of the ordinary citizen'. Populist ideology frequently carries a connotation that 'the people' have been discriminated against or cheated by those who have been in power, often involving the invention of the idea that they have a common enemy. Populist leaders use such anti-elite appeals in the interests of establishing direct links with voters. Populism/populist are also terms used critically, however, especially by scholars and politicians on the left because of the suggestion that 'the people', or 'ordinary people', are an undifferentiated whole, whereas the reality is that there are class differences, and differences of class interest among 'the people' of every society. Indian Marxists, for instance, argue that the peasantry of the country has its own class divisions. They, and others, point out that the pursuit of populist policies screens differences of class interest, and discourages political mobilization by working people in pursuit of their own interests, usually to the benefit of power-holders and the middle and upper classes.

The adjective populist is used very generally in India, therefore, as elsewhere in the world, to refer to politics and policies that are intended to be crowd-pleasing and so to offer electoral advantage, often involving the use of public resources to give away goods to voters (or, in other words, policies focused on redistribution rather than on growth). Examples are promises by political leaders, in different states of India at different times, to make rice (say) available at 'two rupees [or other subsidized low price] per kilo'; or, even more blatantly, the giving away of sarees, colour television sets, food-mixers, and latterly laptop computers by the competing political parties in Tamil Nadu, when they have been in government. These policies are described in the press and by some scholars as populist ('intended to appeal to or represent the interests of the ordinary people'—*OED*), and in this context the term has a negative and even derogatory sense, because these sorts of policies are held to be an unproductive drain on the public purse. Better that the state shouldn't subsidize anything at all, according to some, or that it should subsidize public education and health, according to others, rather than seeking to secure voters' loyalties with giveaways. Thus the Food Security Bill that was passed by the Indian parliament in 2013 was castigated in the business press as being 'populist'—as prioritizing redistribution over growth, and being driven by narrow electoral calculation. The use of the term veiled and drew attention away from what may be seen as perfectly legitimate objectives of a government concerned with meeting the expectations of those who had voted it into office.

Several significant political parties in India use an Indian word meaning 'the people' in their titles, and propose policies that are distinctly populist (rather than socialist). The regional parties of the southern state of Tamil Nadu, for example, which have vied with each other for political office over the last half-century, both claim to speak for 'the Tamilian'. This is the idea of the 'ordinary Tamil person', or—originally—of the middle- and lower-caste 'Dravidian' people (though excluding the Dalits), who had been robbed of their due by upper-caste people who were supposed to have come from North India. Historically, their ideology projected the idea that Brahmins were the common enemy of the (lower-caste) 'Tamilian'/'people'. This is a classically populist kind of argument.

• See also **democracy, politics, socialism**

Poverty

There are few English words that are of greater significance in the culture and society of modern India than 'poverty', and the equivalent term in Hindi—'*garibi*'—is also in wide circulation. It is widely known, within the country and outside, that India is home to the largest number of poor people in the world. The relief of poverty has become a constant preoccupation of Indian governments and the focus of a myriad of official programmes, and it is the concern of many groups in India's civil society. At the same time, many other Indians seek to avoid confronting the visible facts of their country's persisting poverty, and even more so its possible causes. Middle-class Indians may see poverty as a threat to their own way of life. This is especially so when they are confronted by the slums in which a majority of the urban population lives, and one response, from the colonial period to the present, has been to seek to remove the poor physically from urban spaces through slum clearance.

Poverty has been a factor in Indian politics since the colonial period, when economic nationalists—notably through the writings of Dadabhai Naoroji (1825–1917), one of the early leaders of the Indian National Congress, in his book *Poverty and Un-British Rule in India* (1901)—argued that British rule had impoverished their country and its people. There is a definite echo of these arguments in Nehru's words in opening the first debate of the Constituent Assembly, when he said 'The first task of this Assembly is to free India through a new constitution, to feed the starving people, and to clothe the naked masses, and to give every Indian the fullest opportunity to develop himself according to his capacity.' This remarkable statement also seems partly to anticipate the later arguments of the Nobel prize-winning Indian economist Amartya Sen about the way in which poverty can best be conceptualized. Nehru's governments did not, however, give priority to poverty in their policies, and it was only after the first serious attempts to measure its incidence in the country, around 1970, that poverty reduction rose up the policy agenda. Indira Gandhi, then the prime minister of India, made the Hindi '*garibi hatao*' (meaning 'abolish poverty') her slogan in the 1971 general elections.

But how is poverty defined? *OED* offers a definition that certainly reflects everyday understandings: 'The condition of having little or no wealth or few material possessions; indigence, destitution.' The same ideas of 'lacking' or being 'deficient', and of being 'deprived' (of something of value), recur in the *OED*'s definitions of related words such as 'poor'. And in the main, 'poverty' or 'the state of being poor' is understood as meaning 'lacking' or 'being deprived', particularly of income. This is the principal way in which economists, not only in India, have gone about measuring poverty. But what level of income should be taken as indicating that a person is poor? Is there some absolute standard that can be used? The standard approach has been first to take it as axiomatic that a certain level of intake of dietary energy (calories) is necessary for life itself to be sustained and for people to be active; then to ask what 'basket' of basic commodities is required to supply that amount of energy on a daily basis; then to calculate how much this basket costs in the relevant economy (so defining the 'poverty line'); and finally to measure what proportion of the population does not have sufficient income to secure the basket (or in other words, lacks the income to live above the poverty line). This is what is meant when it is said that x or y per cent of the people are poor/live in poverty. Poverty measurement in India has become increasingly refined, beyond this basic approach. Yet it remains the case both that many assumptions have to be made, and that the survey data on which so much reliance has to be placed are highly imperfect—depending substantially on people's willingness or ability to recall their consumption expenditure over a period of time. It is for these reasons that the definition of poverty, and of the poverty line, and assessment of trends in the incidence of poverty over time, have become so controversial in India. Further, whether or not a certain level of income will supply a person with an adequate basket of commodities will be influenced by many other factors, such as whether or not he or she suffers from chronic illness or a disability, or has access to adequate amounts of clean water. Early in the twenty-first century different official bodies have come up with widely divergent estimates of the incidence of poverty in the country, ranging between about 25 and as much as 80 per cent of the population. This very wide gap should be a reminder that poverty, thus understood, in terms of income deprivation, is only a construct, depending on more or less arbitrary judgements.

The severe limits of the conventional construction of poverty in the sorts of measurements on which government depends have been recognized in arguments about the need to take account of dimensions of poverty beyond income, including assets—such as the quality of housing (which is more easily observed than income or expenditure)—and access to public goods such as water and proper sanitation; and in the view that account must be taken of the perceptions of the poor themselves, in which, for example, self-respect may matter as much as material possessions. This latter position resonates with Amartya Sen's argument that the conventional way of understanding poverty rests in any case on a very narrow view of what constitutes a worthwhile human life. Mere survival is hardly an adequate goal. Rather, should we think in terms of people's 'capabilities' for leading lives that they have reason to value (which seems to go back to Nehru's wish that Indians should be able to develop themselves 'according to their capacity'). These ideas have contributed to the greater emphasis that has been given by Indian governments to 'human development', taking account of life expectancy—and hence, in principle anyway, of the quality of health care—and of access to and levels of education, as well as of income. The main priority of government remains, however, to reduce poverty as income deprivation, both as a matter of ethical principle and in the interests of political legitimacy.

Successive governments have introduced a wide range of policies and programmes intended to reduce income poverty, including efforts to provide poor people with some assets, or with gainful employment—as in the Mahatma Gandhi National Rural Employment Scheme introduced in 2005—as well as direct subsidy of consumption through rations of essential commodities supplied through the Public Distribution System, or most recently through cash transfers. Debate continues about whether or not these schemes and others should be made universal, or be subject to targeting. Latterly (as in the Food Security Bill passed by the Indian parliament in 2013), the principle of targeting has been adopted, and this has given great salience to the category 'Below the Poverty Line (BPL)', which is used as a basis for adjudicating on who should be entitled to state subsidies. But how is the state to identify those who are living below the poverty line? Measuring individuals' incomes is extremely difficult in what is still predominantly a rural society, and there is reason to be concerned both about 'errors of exclusion', when those who need assistance miss out because they are not listed as 'BPL', and on the other hand 'errors of inclusion', when relatively wealthy people have been counted among the poor. Poverty programmes may be subject to massive 'leakage' through various forms of corruption.

• See also *development, land, politics, state*

Rape

The Indian Penal Code of 1860, drafted by Thomas Macaulay, identified rape as an offence and made it punishable under Section 376. Rape was defined as sexual intercourse with a woman against her will, without her consent, where consent had been obtained forcibly, where the woman mistakenly believed herself to be married to the perpetrator, or where the woman is under ten years of age (this age limit has since been raised to sixteen).

As several feminist commentators have argued, this definition of rape has in practice allowed many perpetrators of violent sexual offences to escape justice. Until recently, marital rape was not recognized in India, and rape was a crime that could only be committed by men in relation to women. Moreover, vaginal intercourse was a precondition for rape; there have been several cases in which very young girls have been sexually violated but in which sexual intercourse has not been proven, and so aggressors have escaped justice.

Over the past forty years a series of government-sponsored law reports have recommended changes to the Indian Penal Code on the issue of rape, usually without having much effect on the overall prosecution rate. Most recently, the 172nd Law Commission Report (2000) proposed the substitution of the definition of rape with that of 'sexual assault', the definition of which goes beyond penile penetration to include penetration by any part of the body and by objects. The commission also suggested that the law relating to sexual assault be made gender-neutral: under the new proposed rules, men and women could be charged with the rape of men, women, and children. These recommendations were included in a draft Criminal Laws Amendment Bill produced by the Ministry of Home Affairs in 2010, but have yet to be brought before parliament.

At the time of the partition of India, large numbers of women from both sides of what became the border between Pakistan and India were victims of forced abduction and rape. But it is the ubiquity of sexual violence in rural North India in the postcolonial period that has made 'rape' such a major topic of national debate. In rural areas of the north Indian states of Haryana and Uttar Pradesh, where caste and class inequalities are especially evident and patriarchal dominance is marked, rape is often institutionalized. Higher-caste men frequently use rape as a means to bolster their dominance, stave off unrest, and teach 'lessons' to lower castes. It is difficult to measure the incidence of sexual violence because of chronic under-reporting, but figures collected by India's National Crime Bureau suggest that the number of Dalit girls and women who were victims of rape rose from 27 in 2007 to 56 in 2011 in the Indian state of Haryana, reflecting a broader national increase; in September 2012 alone, nineteen cases were recorded of Dalit women having been raped in rural Haryana. The higher-caste perpetrators of rape often intimidate the families of their victims to prevent them pressing charges, or else they bribe the police and judiciary to avoid prosecution. In some cases, khap panchayats (caste-based extra-constitutional bodies) adjudicate on rape cases at the village level, invariably allowing higher-caste men to escape justice. In certain instances these cases reach the media, creating considerable regional furore over particular rapes, especially where Dalits have access to some form of NGO support or links with human rights organizations in major cities. But stories of young women being raped in North India often go unreported. At the same time, khap panchayats sometimes falsely label premarital affairs among consenting adults as 'rape' as a means to police the boundaries of caste-monogamy—rape is a word weapon in struggles to defend local notions of honour.

The shockingly brutal gang rape of a female student on a bus in Delhi in December 2012 placed questions around gender violence at the forefront of public debate, and it became a symbol for the inability of the Indian Government to initiate legal reform and address long-standing gender discrimination within modern institutions, such as the courtroom, police station, and university. Women's organizations have pointed out that the burden of proof in most rape cases continues to fall upon victims rather than perpetrators, that no one involved in rape during communal riots has been successfully prosecuted, that there is no effective witness protection scheme in India, and that gender discrimination occurs in courtrooms. Veena Das argues that senior government officials, lawyers, and judges use rape trials to emphasize women's appropriate role as mothers and wives; until very recently, women were quizzed on their sexual history during the course of rape trials, and their sexual conduct could be used as evidence bearing on the case.

Some feminist commentators argued that the Delhi rape was not a straightforward reflection of India's patriarchal past but rather indicative of a contemporary global cultural regime of female vulnerability. Others have pointed out that rape in India is often closely entangled with issues peculiar to the country; 'rape' in the Indian subcontinent frequently reflects the intersection of multiple forms of inequality—including gender, caste, class, and age—perhaps to a greater extent than in some other contexts.

• See also *caste, feminism, state, violence*

Reservations

The term 'reservations' refers to a system of positive discrimination in India, usually in educational institutions and public sector undertakings and bureaucracies. Although reservations now exist for many different marginalized groups, they remain indelibly linked to questions of caste. During the three decades leading up to Independence there was a series of debates involving British administrators, the Dalit leader Dr Bhimrao Ambedkar, and other leading political figures in India regarding the degree to which low castes should receive special dispensations. During this period, it was generally established that reservations should be on the grounds of a combination of economic and social disadvantage (caste) rather than on economic grounds alone (class), partly for the practical reason that a huge proportion of the Indian population was poor. It was also agreed that untouchable castes and tribes should receive some special assistance. In the 1930s, the colonial government created lists (or 'schedules') of castes imagined as deserving of affirmative action: the so-called 'Scheduled Castes' (SCs) and 'Scheduled Tribes' (STs).

Ambedkar drafted the terms by which reservations in educational institutions and employment would be granted to SCs and STs, particularly through his role in writing the Constitution. There were debates at this time regarding the difficulty of imposing time limits (reservations were imagined to start with as temporary) and concerning the danger of stigmatizing low castes through granting them separate quotas. But concerns over SC/ST reservations in educational institutions and public sector undertakings subsided somewhat after Independence. Attention shifted, rather, to the question of reservations for so-called 'Other Backward Classes' (OBCs)—castes putatively above SCs and STs in the caste system, but nevertheless suffering from forms of social and economic backwardness.

Two government commissions were established to look into the possibility of OBC reservations. Nehru put aside the recommendations of the first commission in the mid-1950s, leaving it to individual states to decide on reservations for the more than 2,000 caste groups that had been identified as 'backward'. But in 1990 V. P. Singh acted on the recommendations of the Second Backward Classes Commission (which originally reported in 1980 under the chairmanship of B. P. Mandal) and introduced a 27 per cent national-level quota for OBCs in educational institutions and public sector undertakings. This came on top of an existing 15 per cent reservation for SCs and 7.5 per cent quota for STs, bringing the total reserved quota to 49.5 per cent. Upper castes reacted furiously to this measure; according to some reports more than 150 students attempted to immolate themselves in different incidents of protest across India.

Those critical of caste reservations have been more concerned about OBC reservations than about SC and ST reservations, and more critical of employment reservations than positive discrimination in the educational sphere. A first common criticism is that reservations are inherently unfair, interfering with principles of 'merit'. A variant on this argument is that reservations are in principle acceptable as long as class rather than caste is the guiding principle of differentiation. Another criticism is that reservations only assist a 'creamy layer' of wealthy low castes, something that governments have sometimes tried to address by proposing sub-quotas within the OBC, SC, and ST categories. A more fundamental critique is that reservations serve to highlight and politicize caste difference and are therefore intrinsically paradoxical, as well as being in some sense unconstitutional and anti-secular. In addition, critics maintain that reservations, although only meant to be temporary measures, inevitably become permanent, because powerful political constituencies are created that defend low castes' rights to special privileges. Two further critiques have received some attention recently: that reservations deprive low castes of political leaders, because it is a condition of public sector employment that workers do not engage in formal politics; and that reservations have resulted in the selection of poorly qualified candidates, thus compromising government functioning. The supporters of affirmative action counter that reservations do benefit a portion of ordinary SCs, STs, and OBCs; that they create a new cadre of leaders in local societies; and that reservations have a powerful symbolic effect.

There are some who do not object to reservations per se but rather to the manner in which parties highlight and strategically deploy the issue. Another concern is that some castes, such as the Jats in Uttar Pradesh (UP), have been able falsely to portray themselves as 'backward' in order to qualify for OBC reservations. Yet another issue is that the reservations system may be subverted in practice, with higher castes seizing positions meant for low castes.

Since the early 1990s, affirmative action has taken new forms. In 1993, a constitutional amendment in India called for a random one-third of panchayat (village council) leader positions to be reserved for women. The *Rajya Sabha* passed a Women's Reservation Bill in March 2010 that would extend these quotas to state and national assemblies. Reservations have also been extended to Muslims, at the central level and in at least two states (Andhra Pradesh and Kerala). In an interesting move, in 2007 the UP government introduced reservation in promotions within government employment in order to counteract the glass ceiling effect (but this was repealed in 2011 because it was deemed unconstitutional). There have also been calls for reservations in private sector institutions, especially since 2006, although fierce opposition from the corporate sector has stymied such a move, at least in the short term. The cumulative effect of these various moves has been to create new fronts upon which those for and against reservations line up, and as in an earlier period it appears that youth are often both the most vocal critics and supporters.

• See also *caste, equality, gender, politics, youth*

Rights

According to the *OED*, a 'right' is a moral or legal entitlement, especially one accruing to the citizen of a country. Part III of the Indian Constitution set out a range of Fundamental Rights: the right to equality, including equality before the law and the abolition of untouchability; the right to freedom, including of speech and expression; the right to freedom from exploitation, such as forced labour, child labour, and human trafficking; the right to freedom of religion; and a set of cultural and educational rights. Further, the Constitution's Directive Principles deal with social and economic rights, including the right to education, the right to work and a living wage, and the right to a decent standard of health care.

Several scholars have pointed out that, in practice, many people in independent India have not been accorded equality before the law, either as a result of their low caste standing or because of their gender or religion. In work, forms of extreme exploitation persist, including the employment of children in dangerous occupations and child trafficking. Muslims, Sikhs, Christians, and other religious minorities have faced periodic violence in independent India—pogroms in Delhi (1984) and Ahmedabad (2002) being notable examples; and, from a development perspective, many people lack access to good-quality education and health care. Amartya Sen has been among the most prominent intellectuals highlighting the 'democratic deficit' in India and arguing for a new definition of development, based on people's capacity to fulfil personal freedoms and underpinned by the existence of civil and personal 'entitlements' or 'rights'.

At the same time, there has been growing mobilization around the question of rights, a word sometimes translated as '*haq*' in Hindi and Urdu but which has also entered Indian languages as a loan word from English. Rising enrolment in education, the growing influence of NGOs, and increasing penetration of the state into people's everyday lives have together contributed to a growth in people's awareness of their political, social, and economic entitlements and a concomitant upsurge in popular political action with respect to specific 'rights'. This has led to a Right to Education movement: a group of nine NGOs and over 2,000 voluntary organizations that successfully campaigned in the 1990s for a constitutional amendment that would make it incumbent on the state to provide free and compulsory education to all children aged six to fourteen—a 93rd Constitutional Amendment Bill establishing this right was passed in 2001. It has also led to a Right to Work movement led by voluntary organizations and focused on increasing people's pay and job security, and culminating in the establishment of the National Rural Employment Guarantee Scheme, via an act passed in parliament in September 2005. A Right to Food Campaign in the 2000s and early 2010s also unfolded through public interest legislation and NGO activity aimed at the expansion and improvement of the Public Distribution System.

Another arena in which rights discourse has been prominent is in the field of subaltern political resistance: Dalits have mobilized regarding their right to freedom from exploitation and violence, much of this occurring in the aftermath of specific 'atrocities' and involving India's National Commission for Human Rights; the All India Democratic Women's Association and linked organizations are fighting on gender issues; Muslims' rights organizations are highly active; and there are increasingly prominent organizations defending the rights of youth, students, children, and the physically and mentally challenged. Much of this energetic politicking is directed towards civic rights, but sometimes—as in the question of rape—questions of personal rights are at stake.

There has been rather less mobilization on political rights in India, for example around questions of police injustice and the criminalization of politics. One exception is that of the campaigns seeking to bring to light human rights abuses in Indian-administered Kashmir, where Human Rights Watch reported extrajudicial killings, torture, and disappearances in the 1990s. Another area where political rights came to the fore was in the opposition to the Prevention of Terrorism Act (POTA) in India in 2002. POTA allowed the detainment of a suspect for 180 days without charges being brought. It was repealed in the face of popular and elite protest in 2004. Protests regarding political rights are likely to become more frequent over the coming decades because a growing population schooled in notions of universal citizenship is encountering a social and political landscape characterized by the widespread abuse of power, clientelism, and social inequality.

In 1976, the 42nd Amendment to the Indian Constitution saw the introduction of ten 'Fundamental Duties' for the Indian citizen, such as the duty to protect the nation, and it is interesting that Hindi terms such as '*haq*' mean both 'rights' and 'duties' simultaneously. But the Indian state has not (yet) shown much enthusiasm for linking the question of rights to the one of 'duties', nor for promoting the idea of connecting rights with the related term 'responsibilities', as currently stressed by the UK government, for example, in its definition of citizenship.

• See also *citizenship, constitution, democracy, state*

Roads

India has long been at a crossroads. It was centrally placed on one of the Silk Roads that connected Persia with eastern Asia, and excavations in cities in Bangladesh suggest intensive trade and cultural exchange along the Silk Road between what is now India and China from at least the first few centuries BC. The Grand Truck Road (GT Road)—that 'broad, smiling river of life' as Rudyard Kipling described it—was another major conduit connecting Afghanistan with Bengal, dating back some 2,300 years. The British constructed large numbers of Indian roads as part of their wider drive to modernize India, too.

Road-building continued in the postcolonial period, and became especially intense after 1995. By 2011, India had a road network of over 4 million kilometres—the third largest such network in the world. But the quality of Indian roads is often woefully poor. Only 49 per cent of the country's road network is paved. Judged against its population, India has a weakly developed system, and pitifully few national highways. This partly reflects the Government of India's wider failure to foster equitable, inclusive development.

Roads in colonial India were a symbol of imperial power and facilitated the deployment of troops. Focusing on the last few decades of Empire, the historian David Arnold has argued that roads were places where state authority was also put on show through the display of motor vehicles ('modern transport'). Subaltern groups contested state power, in part, through disrupting this official traffic: bringing processions into the street, for example, or simply 'getting in the way'. Certainly, the roadblock (*rasta roko* in Hindi) was an important tool of Gandhian non-violent mobilization, and it continues to be a highly significant means of protest today.

In the postcolonial period 'roads' feature heavily in political debates, from parliament down to local levels. The compulsions of post-Independence democratic politics—the need for votes, for example, or the requirement to 'reward' a loyal local bigwig—are often paramount in decisions around the construction and siting of new highways and smaller roads. Increased road construction has also created a class of '*tikedaars*' (contractors), often those from higher-caste backgrounds, who embezzle funds earmarked for construction with the help of politicians and bureaucrats. The social implications of such corruption are evident in many parts of India. In rural areas, villages in which lower castes or Muslims are numerically dominant are often poorly connected to major urban centres compared to those in which higher-caste Hindus predominate. The environmental costs of widespread political interference in road construction and the mass embezzlement of funds at the local level are equally apparent, for example in Himachal Pradesh and Uttarakhand, where deforestation and the inappropriate siting of roads is causing sometimes catastrophic damage. The question of whether an ongoing shift in India towards the private financing of large road-building projects will help address these social and environmental problems is moot.

'Road' is also a word that connotes danger in India. According to the National Crime Records Bureau, 135,000 people died on Indian roads in 2009—roughly fourteen an hour. No country in the world has more road accidents. This is partly a problem of infrastructural planning, when the needs of the car-owning middle classes are usually placed above those of pedestrians and cyclists, as they were in 2013 in Kolkata—cycles were banned from some city roads in the interests of solving the problem of congestion. The frequency of accidents also reflects a huge problem of drunk driving, speeding, and the lack of an effective system of driving tests.

The everyday social and economic significance of roads to ordinary Indians is enormous. Along with the railways, roads are the means through which people gain access to markets, schooling, health care, development resources, and numerous other social and economic goods. They are crucially important in terms of facilitating business and entrepreneurialism. Road construction alters local marriage practices, allowing families to form unions at a greater distance. Roads are also major hangouts and places of public discussion, sometimes sites where social inequalities are marked and, at other moments, places where new types of interaction become possible.

Indian citizens are often ambivalent about roads. The coming of a road to a village, or improvements to an existing road, can increase crime and create new unsustainable consumption patterns—even while it provides many benefits. Roads may dissolve certain types of community solidarity and interaction, even as they frequently create identities and provide occasions for new types of exchange. Roads offer, then, a powerful metonym for 'development' itself, embodying in miniature the possibilities and contradictions of economic growth and social change.

Roads are woven into popular culture in India, as in most other places in the world. They are the subject of novels in India, from Rudyard Kipling's *Kim* to Shrilal Shukla's *Raag Darbari*, to R. K. Narayan's writing on South India. Roads feature in poems, such as Tagore's 'Lover's Gift', and in many Bollywood movies, for example Ram Gopal Varma's (2002) Bollywood flick, which was entitled simply '*Road*'. The road, or 'the street', is also a crucial site for public performance, pilgrimage, and everyday sociality. The word 'road' (*rasta* or *sarak* in Hindi) is also commonly used as a metaphor and applied in all manner of conversational contexts—'this is the road I will take in life' is the type of phrase often heard in India.

Secularism

The adjective 'secular' was in use in English by the thirteenth century. Amongst a range of meanings, the one that perhaps best defines it is: 'belonging to the world and its affairs, as distinct from the Church and religion; civil, lay, temporal'. The noun 'secularism' became current only from 1851, when it meant: 'the doctrine that morality should be based solely on regard to the well-being of mankind in the present life, to the exclusion of all consideration drawn from belief in God, or in a future state' (*OED*). Webster puts it more pithily as: 'indifference to or rejection or exclusion of religion and religious considerations'.

The idea—and the ideology—of secularism derive in large measure from the Enlightenment philosophers, who questioned religious authority over human affairs; it was expected by early sociologists that the effects of industrialization, urbanization, and the spread of formal education would be to bring about progressive secularization in society. As the English historian Owen Chadwick put it, there was thought to be 'a growing tendency in mankind to do without religion'. These expectations have been largely confounded by the historical experience of the last century and a half. In regard to the state, however, a fundamental influence has been that of the American Constitution which, in the words of Thomas Jefferson, builds 'a wall of separation between the Church and the State'.

The Constitution of India in its preamble proclaims that India is a 'secular', as well as a 'socialist' and a 'democratic', republic, though it has done so only since the introduction of the 42nd Amendment in 1976. In the debates of the Constituent Assembly that drew up the Constitution, the question of whether or not India should be described in this way was a matter of controversy—and debate has not ceased in the many years since then. The political rise of Hindu nationalism in the later twentieth century has meant that questions about the meaning of secularism in the Indian context have acquired particular salience, and it has been much discussed by India's most prominent intellectuals.

In the Constituent Assembly debates there were those who sought the adoption of the Jeffersonian 'wall', and advocated the strict separation of the state from any concern with religion. Ranged against them, however, were a good many Hindu traditionalists, who argued that account must be taken of the religiosity of Indians, which renders the whole concept of secularism problematic, and also of the encompassing, tolerant character of Hinduism. In the end the position that was adopted was one of 'equal respect' for all religions, or what one political philosopher, Rajeev Bhargava, has more recently described as 'principled distance'. As Nehru put it on one occasion, 'A secular state does not mean an irreligious state; it only means we respect and honour all religions, giving them freedom to function.' The particularly Indian conception of secularism is set out in Articles 25–30 of the

Constitution. The position that they set out falls short of what some scholars have argued defines a secular state: adherence to the principles of freedom of religion, of equal individual citizenship, and of the separation of state and religion. The Constitution of India, however, while it sets out the principle of religious freedom, also empowers the state to intervene in the affairs of religious institutions—as it has done, for example, in legislating for freedom of entry to Hindu temples for 'untouchables' (as Dalits used to be labelled); it provides for affirmative action for certain social groups (such as Dalits—though the practice of untouchability, grounded in religious ideas, was forbidden under Article 17 of the Constitution), which may be seen as being in conflict with the principle of equal individual citizenship; and it has allowed for 'minority' groups to retain the personal laws defined by their religious traditions. In Article 44, however, among the Directive Principles, there is a reference to the establishment of a uniform civil code, and in the light of this some of the traditional family practices of Hindus were reformed. Divorce was legalized, for instance, and polygamy prohibited. That Hindus should have been made subject to secular laws while others have not been is anomalous in regard to the principle of equal citizenship, and as some politicians recognized at the time it opened up the state to charges of communalism. It has indeed been on the matter of the civil code that Hindu nationalists have claimed that the secularism proclaimed in the Constitution is a sham ('pseudo-secular', they say), since it allows Muslims and Christians to retain their own family laws while Hindus have been required by law to relinquish theirs. The establishment of a uniform civil code with which *all* Indians must comply remains an important part of the platform of Hindu nationalism.

Some of India's most influential intellectuals argue that the ideology of secularism—which one of them, T. N. Madan, describes as a 'fuzzy' concept—is inappropriate in the Indian context, given the significance of religion in the everyday lives even of Indians who are not especially 'religious'. Loyalties and practices relating to religion—as in regard to personal law—render even the notion of equal citizenship problematic. Others argue that the ideal of secularism has been fatally compromised by the failure of the state to keep religion and politics apart. The attempt to impose a version of secularism has ended up, therefore, by causing a great deal of harm, manifested in communal violence. All these thinkers are concerned with the defence of minority rights in the face of the permanent majority of Hindus. Whether this can be done, and a nation that is modern in its own particular way be created through mobilizing 'resources of religious tolerance' in India's 'supremely spiritual culture', as some argue, remains highly controversial.

• See also *community, constitution, fundamentalism, Hinduism, Hindutva*

Slum

English writers, including Charles Dickens, began to use the word 'slum' in the earlier nineteenth century, in the context of industrializing cities, to refer to 'a street, alley, court, etc. situated in a crowded district of a town or city and inhabited by people of low class or by the very poor . . . a thickly populated neighbourhood or district where the houses and the conditions of life are of a squalid and wretched character' (*OED*). There has been a strong tendency subsequently, in India and elsewhere in the world, to tie these traits to the further idea that such city spaces lack social organization, and are centres of criminality—or, these days, are hives of terrorism. It is telling that the Hindi word for slum—'*basti*'—is often heard in popular discourses alongside the word for 'dirty', which is '*gandi*'. Slums are seen to be dangerous places. In this way, town planning documents from northern India in the later colonial period both held the poor responsible for disorder and for insanitary conditions in towns, and suggested an opposition between 'the poor' and 'decent people'. Similarly, the Maharashtra Slum Areas Act of 1971 defined a slum as 'any area [that] is or may be a source of danger to the health, safety or convenience of the public of that area or its neighbourhood, by reason of the area having inadequate or no basic amenities, or being insanitary, squalid, overcrowded or otherwise'.

From the point of view of social elites, therefore, slums are a danger to society and an affront to modernity. They ought not to be there. They reflect the lack of rational planning and must be 'upgraded' using planning tools. India's first prime minister, Jawaharlal Nehru, once said, 'It is scandalous that a city like Bangalore should have slums. Don't allow them to grow here. Root them out. Once they grow they have a tendency to stay.' At the time he said it this injunction was probably understood as meaning that it was the responsibility of government to bring slums into the modern city by upgrading their housing and civic amenities—and this was the approach generally adopted in the 1950s and 1960s. But 'root them out' might also justify slum clearance, as had happened in north Indian towns in the inter-war period. It has taken place ever since, but increasingly so latterly, when it has been justified by recourse to the legal idea of 'public nuisance' but frequently driven by the interests of urban real estate and of property developers concerned to create 'world-class cities'. The word 'slum' now has strong connotations of illegality, and may be used interchangeably with 'encroachment'. Those who 'encroach'—who squat and try to make lives for themselves on publicly or privately owned land—may be seen as being as much common criminals as any pickpocket, rather than as citizens who have a right to somewhere to live. Illegal encroachment, however, is also carried on in some cases by agents working for large companies that have found sites for business developments. Encroachment is not undertaken only by the poor, and may be defended by politicians. Somewhat ironically, slums may also be seen as undesirable by middle-class people, because they are known to be the 'garrisons' of votes for frequently corrupt politicians.

There is an alternative understanding of the slums that house a large (50 per cent or more) and probably increasing share of the populations of all of India's large cities, and of what 'slum' means. This is an understanding partly reflected in the popular film *Slumdog Millionaire*, set in Dharavi, in Mumbai—and which, with Hindi films too, has made the slum or shantytown the icon of modern India. This is a representation of the slum as the site of an alternative form of urban sociality and economy—based on a strong sense of community, and a place of opportunity and of hope for labouring poor people—rather than the site of danger and despair.

• See also **city, development, modern**

Socialism, Socialist

Socialism refers to a broad and diverse current of political ideas that became powerful in Europe from the mid-nineteenth century, which is when the word itself came into use. It has also had a significant influence in Indian politics. The Constitution of India, in its Preamble, describes the country as 'socialist'—though only following an Amendment passed in 1976. Political parties calling themselves 'socialist' won about 10 per cent of the popular vote in general elections through the 1950s and 1960s, and self-described socialists fighting elections in parties with other names have continued to be significant political actors to the present. Indian planning of the 1950s and 1960s was commonly identified with 'a socialist model of development'. But whereas through most of the later twentieth century the idea that India was or should be in some sense 'socialist' was very widely accepted, this is no longer the case. Indeed, the idea is anathema to many of the country's political and business leaders, who blame India's economic failures of the past on the attempt to pursue socialist policies. It is also striking that there has been no substantial critique of India's shift towards neo-liberal economic policies from a socialist perspective.

The idea of socialism has long been contested, certainly from the later nineteenth century. As Raymond Williams points out, two radically different conceptions of social reform underlie the many different versions of socialism that have been propounded at different times. One is a project of reform of the capitalist social order, but based on the extension of liberal values, political freedoms, and social justice ('conceived as equity between different individuals and groups'); the other presents an alternative to capitalism, based on cooperation and social equality, in opposition to a competitive, individualistic form of society, and depending on social ownership and control. It has been in the latter sense that communist parties have claimed to pursue 'socialist' objectives, and have often included the term—or that of 'social democrat'—in their formal titles. On the other hand, the 'socialism' (for example of the British Labour Party) drawing on the ideas of the Fabians—committed to advancing the principles of socialism via gradualist and reformist rather than revolutionary means—seeks rather to reform the capitalist order than to establish an alternative form of society.

Both conceptions of socialism became influential in the nationalist movement in India in the 1930s, and Nehru among other leaders of the Congress became committed to broadly socialist objectives. The Resolution reached at the annual session of the Congress of 1931, held in Karachi, extended the definition of freedom to include an 'end to the exploitation of the masses', and Gandhian ideas of class conciliation were openly attacked. Subsequently the Congress Socialist Party (CSP), a caucus within the larger organization, was formed in 1934, and joined by Indian communists in 1936. Some of the leaders of the CSP were Fabian socialists, others were Marxists, so there were big differences amongst them. But together they were successful in moving the Congress as a whole to the left, reflected in commitments to radical agrarian reform, until a countermove was made from the right, influenced by Gandhi, in 1939.

In 1948 an amendment to the rules of Congress, moved by leaders from the conservative wing of the party, prohibited the continuation of organized groupings such as the CSP within it. This move successfully weakened the influence of the socialist left in the party. The CSP became the Independent Socialist Party, which thereafter went through a number of different combinations, and some splits, eventually to merge into the Janata Party in the later 1970s. Indian socialism then perhaps reached its apogee in the Janata Dal government led by Prime Minister V. P. Singh in 1989–90. Singh himself acknowledged only India's earlier socialist leaders—of whom perhaps the most influential was Ram Manohar Lohia (1910–67)—as his mentors; and the decision of his government to implement the recommendations of the Mandal report concerning the extension of reservations for members of the Other Backward Classes marked the culmination of long-running efforts by one faction amongst India's socialists to raise the status of the lower castes.

Given the general climate of ideas in the 1940s, and in the light of the commitments made by the Congress in the preceding decade, it is not surprising that in the debates of the Constituent Assembly that drew up the Constitution of independent India in 1946–9 there should have been speakers who offered strong support for socialism. In his speech proposing the Resolution of Aims and Objects, at the commencement of the debates, Nehru said explicitly, 'I stand for Socialism and, I hope, India will stand for Socialism.' He explained, however, that while the objectives that were laid out for the country were inherently socialist, actually to have used the word in the Resolution would have been divisive, so it had been avoided. Dr Ambedkar, among others, did not agree. He said that, quite to the contrary, he had expected the Resolution to state explicitly 'that in order that there may be economic and social justice in the country, there would be nationalization of industry and nationalization of land'. But the Resolution, when it was passed, contained no such wording. Though, subsequently, India's industrial policy reserved some sectors for state-owned enterprises—and these enterprises remain a significant part of India's industrial economy in the early twenty-first century—nationalization of industry has never been attempted at all systematically (though some sectors—coal mining and banks, for instance—have been nationalized); neither has nationalization of land ever been seriously considered. Private property rights are guaranteed in the Constitution.

In practice, according to Nehru himself, in the 1950s and 1960s, India pursued a 'third way', neither capitalist nor communist, but combining directive planning and accommodative democratic politics: at most Fabian socialism, of sorts, and a long way from what Nehru himself had seemed to promise in the 1930s. There was certainly no attempt either in his time, or in that of his daughter, Indira Gandhi, as prime minister in the 1970s, when she made some moves to the left, to develop an alternative to capitalism; and even milder reform of the capitalist social order was severely constrained above all by the failure of redistributive land reform. Indian socialism has been more a matter of rhetoric than of substance.

• See also *communism, constitution, development, Nehru, politics*

Society

The first meaning of 'society' in the *OED* is given as 'the aggregate of people living together in a more or less ordered community'. This notion is not inherently linked to any particular scale—it is possible to talk of 'European society', 'British society', and 'London society', but it tends to be most associated with people living in a relatively large area, and 'society' is especially linked to the nation. This point is implicit in Raymond Williams's first definition of society: 'a body of institutions and relationships within which a relatively large group of people live'.

Some maintain that this notion of society has limited relevance to India. Sudipta Kaviraj argued that the British in India and Congress leaders after Independence—rather than fostering a sense of belonging to 'Indian society'—deepened fissures in the social fabric, especially caste and local divisions. '[The Nehruvian elite's] basic failure', Kaviraj writes, 'seems to have been the almost total neglect of the cultural reproduction of society, a common thicker sense of we-ness.' In a similar vein, Partha Chatterjee argues that people in India characteristically mobilize with reference to ideas of locality, caste, and kinship—what he terms 'political society'. In Chatterjee's view, 'civil society'—founded on the notion of the existence of a large body of like-minded individuals—is too abstract a principle for the masses, and exists only in the minds of India's upper middle-class elite.

But Kaviraj and Chatterjee perhaps underestimate the existence of 'society feeling'. Broad-based notions of belonging to 'Indian society' have probably coexisted with caste, local, and other sectarian loyalties for a long time. The rise of education (citizenship education is a major part of the curriculum) and the emergence of new technologies, especially the television and internet, have strengthened people's sense of belonging to something like a 'society'. There have been several movements recently in India that have attracted broad-based support among people who see themselves as part of 'Indian society', such as the Anna Hazare anti-corruption movement of 2011 and 2012 and the large-scale women's and students' demonstrations that took place in December 2012.

'Society' can also mean a club or association, as can the related terms '*samaj*'—perhaps the most direct translation of 'society' in Hindi—and '*sabha*', which can mean 'society' but more often refers to a particular forum or meeting, as in Lok Sabha (literally: people's forum, and the name of the national parliament in India). There are very many such societies—or 'samajs' or 'sabhas'—in India, from those associated with education, such as the Delhi Public School Society, to ones that reflect specific sporting or cultural interests, such as chess societies and drama societies. The number of such societies has been growing rapidly as a result of the expansion of education and urbanization.

There is a complex politics surrounding how the word 'society' is deployed in India. Political parties, NGOs, or associations use 'society'—or the words 'samaj' or 'sabha'—to advertise their inclusivity and support base. For example, the 'Bahujan Samaj Party' (literally 'the majority of society party') has traded on its capacity to represent the masses during a series of elections since the early 1990s in Uttar Pradesh.

Another aspect of the politics of 'society speak' is the manner in which the word is often defined asymptomatically as everything that happens outside the sphere of the state and state power. The growing presence of the state in people's lives in India since Independence—either as a source of development, a mode of disciplining the population (the police), or in the form of political parties and politicians vying for attention—has therefore been important in raising people's consciousness of belonging to 'Indian society'. At the same time, a decline in the legitimacy of the state has encouraged people to view Indian society as a type of bulwark against the excesses of politicians, or at least as less governed by self-interest and corruption.

Raymond Williams argued that society is often used to refer to a force, as in the phrase 'society's norms'. This is a very common way in which the English word 'society' or 'samaj' are used in India. People complain at the everyday level about the weight of society's 'expectations' or about society as a type of barrier. 'I would have got married to him, but I was worried about what society would think.' This sense of being oppressed or constrained by society is often especially keenly felt among historically subordinated groups, and it is linked to the way in which relatively powerful sections of society try to lay claim to being representatives of society. For example, Hindu nationalist leaders have tried to equate 'Indian society' with 'Hinduness', and especially upper-caste forms of Hinduness.

There is a much older meaning of 'society', from the Latin 'societas' meaning 'companionship'. India is imagined by scholars such as McKim Marriott as a place of 'society' in this sense, somewhere where notions of the individual and individuality are relatively muted and where life is lived, as it were, in public. Yet economic and social change has frayed some of the social ties binding people together, for example on the basis of joint families and extended kinship groups, and notions of individuality are becoming more marked. Alternatively, it might be argued that new forms of 'society'—in the sense of companionship—are replacing others. Anthropologists have noticed a novel emphasis on companionship in many circles when families assess the suitability of a bride or groom for their son or daughter, and have also noted that ties of friendship are becoming important in generating social collectivities, especially in modern settings such as universities and using new technologies such as the mobile phone.

• See also *family, individual, state*

(The) State

The state refers to both 'a nation or territory considered as an organized political community under one government', and 'the civil government of a country' (*OED*). The modern state in this sense is conventionally dated to the Treaty of Westphalia in 1648, which brought the Thirty Years War in Europe to an end and marked the emergence of a new European order of sovereign states. These new political arrangements transformed a situation in which populations were subject to a variety of overlapping sources of authority into one in which rulers were acknowledged as governing a specific territory within a wider set of European states. Postcolonial states were established on the same basis—subject to the rule of a single governing authority and an equal member of a larger system of states.

The state in India therefore refers to the main organs of democratic government, including legislative, judicial, and parliamentary institutions at different scales, as well as bureaucracies. But 'the state', in a more anthropological sense, is also distributed across social life, embodied, as it were, in a government jeep, a police file, a truncheon, or perhaps something as intangible as the particular swagger of a visiting official or the manner in which he drinks his tea. 'Stateness' is a term sometimes used to indicate how aspects of state functioning blend into everyday practices.

India is a country with a huge state machinery and in which stateness inveigles itself into people's lives in numerous subtle and not-so-subtle ways. For a child in school, the state ('sarkar' in Hindi) might be the public bus, the stick used to beat children, the textbook, and the midday meals which are distributed free of charge across primary educational institutions in India. For the university student, the state might manifest itself in the police officer patrolling the campus, the government sweeper cleaning a hostel corridor, and the examination paper for the state's provincial civil services. For a poor rural Muslim labourer, the state might be constituted mainly as an absence: the lack of an effective port of call after being harassed by a higher-caste Hindu official, or if the derelict local village health centre is choked with weeds and garbage.

Much of the debate on the state in India has focused on the upper echelons of government—politics, political parties, and questions of rights and citizenship—and the question of power. Scholars have often adopted a Marxist perspective to show how powerful capitalist forces influence state policy. Feminists have made parallel arguments in relation to gender. Others focus on the implementation of state programmes, showing how clientelism and corruption shape people's access to goods in ways that reflect social inequalities. There are often fewer teachers posted in villages with high proportions of Muslims in North India as compared to Hindu-dominated villages. A higher-caste land revenue officer will tend to favour another higher-caste over and above a low-caste labourer. Women often find it difficult to engage in the nitty gritty of negotiating with state officials in public offices.

Other commentators have concentrated to a greater extent on the enabling power of the state, showing for example how affirmative action based on caste and gender can sometimes improve the position of previously subordinated groups. Where low-caste leaders come to power at the state level, a measure of caste empowerment may occur. The state, more generally, may at the very least have staved off mass famine in India since Independence and it has been a fairly effective guarantor of many basic political rights. For all its failings, the state, too, has raised people's educational levels, increased life expectancy, and reduced poverty, albeit not as fast or as effectively as many hoped.

An important line of work in this regard is that which focuses on the state as a public keyword—a word used regularly on the ground. For all the evidence of the state's inability to fulfil people's aspirations in modern India—and notwithstanding evidence, too, of the frequent violence and corruption of the state—most people in India continue to believe in the idea of the state and cling at some level to the belief that 'the state' can and should work better. Other commentators have examined how certain qualities become associated with the state, which is often imagined as a circle of institutions 'up there'. It is interesting to note that the Hindi word for state—'sarkar'—also means authority in general.

The rise of neo-liberalism and globalization is throwing the question of the appropriate remit of the state into some doubt, generating fresh debates about the state's role in development. For some, the priority in India is the continued rolling back of the state to make way for market forces, and in a related move many lower middle-class and middle-class parents and young people are increasingly looking outside the state sector for educational and employment opportunities. Others emphasize the importance of the state as a countermanding influence on market liberalism, for example as a guarantor of rights, or stress the significance of various types of state/corporate/third-sector collaboration in the delivery of services, such as education and microfinance.

Paralleling these debates, and interrelating with them, is a growing body of anthropological writing on the manner in which the stuff of the state circulates within and beyond government bureaucracies—paper files, photographs, technical equipment, and the like—which serves in turn to enumerate, discipline, and control local populations—or 'governmentalize' them, in Foucault's memorable terms. Also crucial to this literature is the point that the state can only reproduce its authority through frequent performances of power.

'State' and 'society' are often imagined as distinct. But society is not the opposite of the state in India but rather a setting in which stateness is enacted: for example, where police business occurs in a tea stall or a land revenue officer brokers a deal in a rich farmer's front room. In such examples, state practice often departs wildly from official protocols and the letter of the law. In the economist Lant Pritchett's terms, India is a 'flailing state' wherein a rational head is disconnected from its out-of-control limbs.

• See also *constitution, corruption, democracy, justice, rights*

Subaltern

Literally 'a position in the army below the rank of captain' but commonly referring to a 'person of lower status' (*OED*), subaltern is a term widely used in South Asian studies to refer to a person oppressed within power regimes, especially colonized subjects during the period of imperial rule. The word was popularized through the work of both Indian and English historians who came together first in Britain in the late 1970s to discuss how to rewrite South Asian history 'from below'. Oxford University Press published their first collection of articles under the heading of *Subaltern Studies* in 1982.

Subaltern studies academics set out to revise how scholars and popular audiences would imagine the history of South Asia by challenging Eurocentric accounts. Historian Ranajit Guha was the leading figure in the movement, gathering together a number of younger scholars including Partha Chatterjee, Dipesh Chakrabarty, David Arnold, David Hardiman, and Gayatri Chakravorty Spivak. Subaltern studies scholars rejected analyses of the Indian nationalist movement that emphasized the role of bourgeois leaders. They also challenged a tendency in some historical circles to imagine peasants primarily as members of factional networks linking them to local and regional elites. In the view of the subaltern scholars, peasants mobilized a great deal among themselves (horizontally) to express their own world view.

The question of who, precisely, constitutes the 'subaltern' was left somewhat open by the subaltern studies group, but the peasant was usually the emblematic figure, and the overall criterion appeared to be that the person or people concerned should be 'counter-hegemonic': opposed to the dominant culture, which in South Asia's history meant the culture of imperial rule. This definition reflects the influence on subaltern studies scholars of the Italian Marxist Antonio Gramsci, and his argument that power is expressed partly through cultural 'hegemony'—the production of potent ideas that come to frame how people imagine their relationship to the state. In Gramsci's view, and in the views of subaltern studies scholars, this hegemony is always liable to be critiqued by the subject population, and Gramsci was especially interested in the existence of an oppositional peasant culture manifest in folklore and everyday speech. Aside from Gramsci, the emphasis placed by the subaltern group on active resistance to the violence of the state/colonizers reflected the particular conjuncture in which the group formulated their ideas: the aftermath of India's Political Emergency (1975–7).

The Subaltern Studies Collective produced a series of landmark volumes over the 1980s, 1990s, and into the twenty-first century. They were typically fairly eclectic in their theoretical borrowings, but a strong interest in the work of Gramsci, and later Michel Foucault and Michel de Certeau, have been hallmarks. And subaltern studies scholars shared a desire to recover the lost voices of the downtrodden through the use of sources, such as vernacular newspapers and songs, which had not previously been accorded the status of historical evidence. Further, subaltern studies scholars were united in viewing this recovery of forgotten perspectives as a means of giving agency to the marginalized in South Asia. Among the classic works of subaltern history are Shahid Amin's account of law and violence in colonial North India and Ranajit Guha's work on peasant uprisings, but subaltern scholars have delved into issues as diverse as the history of religious communal tension, food riots, forest struggles, and the genealogy of Dalit mobilization, among many other topics. Since the 1980s, scholars have increasingly used the term subaltern as an adjective, meaning something akin to 'radical', 'alternative', or 'grassroots'. The rapid growth of postcolonial studies in universities in the West has fuelled this appropriation of the term.

Vivek Chibber has recently launched an excoriating critique of the work of the Subaltern Studies Collective. Chibber argues that subaltern scholars such as Chakrabarty and Chat-terjee have exaggerated differences between South Asian peasants and their European counterparts by stereotyping Indian subalterns as fundamentally 'community minded', and that this has discouraged subaltern studies scholars, particularly those writing in recent years, from employing Marxist analysis. In Chibber's view, peasants across the world have historically had similar concerns over food, material security, and freedom of expression, and this observation suggests the value of a universal theory of exploitation and resistance of the type provided by Marx. The very term 'subaltern' might, in Chibber's reading, be unhelpful analytically because of its specific association with communities in the global South.

Among the many other critiques of the use of the term 'subaltern' are the arguments that it obscures differences within excluded groups in South Asia, for example those based on gender, that it draws attention away from regional and subregional differences, emphasizes textual production over other practices, and places too great an emphasis on violence, confrontation, and tension as opposed to agreement, compromise, and negotiation. Use of the term can have the unintended consequence of suggesting that people's oppression is always experienced as a product of national dynamics. Feminist scholars have argued that subaltern studies scholars fetishize a space of male 'resistance'. And use of the concept 'subaltern', because it is underpinned by an understanding of history as interplay between the colonial power and the colonized masses, has the perverse effect of bolstering the binary categories of elite historical analysis. There are also problems associated with transposing historical discussion of subalterns to the present. Today's South Asian 'subalterns' more commonly embrace the state as a source of development than reject it as an instrument of power.

It is perhaps partly for these reasons that social groups in India have not very often used the term 'subaltern' in their protests. Either they have employed the term 'citizen' or they have mobilized around more descriptive categories such as 'Dalit', 'youth', or 'women'. For all the influence of the Subaltern Studies Collective—there is now a Latin American Subaltern Studies school, for example—it is not a term that ordinary activists across India readily understand.

• See also *citizenship, Dalit, history, state*

Terrorism

While the sorts of actions that are now described as 'terrorist' have a much longer history, the word came into use in English only at the end of the eighteenth century, following the experience of what came to be called 'the Terror' perpetrated by the then ruling group in the course of the French Revolution, in 1793–4. It meant government through the use of violence and intimidation, and this was the original way the word terrorism was used—with reference to the use of these means by a government or a ruling group in order to maintain its control over a population. *OED* refers to the employment of paramilitary or informal armed groups, by a government, as being possible means to this end; and India has, early in the twenty-first century, experienced the formation by a state government of such forces. This was through the formation in 2005, by a senior Congress leader in the state of Chhattisgarh, of the *Salwa Judum* (meaning 'purification hunt' in the tribal Gondi language)—a militia of tribal youth, later armed and (supposedly, at least) trained by the state government, aimed at countering the Naxalite/Maoist insurgency in the state. Widely criticized for violations of human rights, the Salwa Judum was declared illegal and unconstitutional by the Supreme Court in 2011.

Generally, however, terrorism has come to mean the clandestine but systematic use of violence and intimidation, intended to instil fear in others, in the pursuit of political aims. Understood in this sense, terrorism has a long history in India. Those who were described by British officials in the later nineteenth century as 'Hindustani Fanatics'—followers of the fundamentalist form of Islam known as Wahhabism—were held responsible for a number of attacks, that may have included the assassination of the Viceroy of India, Lord Mayo, in 1872. Somewhat later, at the end of the nineteenth century, there was a reaction within the Indian nationalist movement against what was thought of as 'Moderate' agitation. One form that the reaction took was that of revolutionary terrorism, 'which sought a short cut to freedom via individual violence and conspiracies', as the historian Sumit Sarkar has described it. Revolutionary terrorists carried out a number of attacks on British officials in Bengal around the turn of the century, and a small Tamil group of revolutionaries was responsible for the murder of Robert Ashe, the acting Collector of Tirunelveli District, in 1911. There was activity—under the leadership of Veer Savarkar (*see* Hindutva)—in London, too, while the revolutionary movement acquired something of a mass base, principally in the Pacific Northwest of the United States and Canada, where there were settled some 15,000 Indians, most of them Sikhs. The *Ghadr* ('Revolution') Movement, founded in San Francisco in 1913, was, however, soon crushed by the British.

In the more recent past terrorism has become extensive in India, as in much of the contemporary world, and reports of terrorist action, generally against civilians, and mostly intended to force a government to bring about some kind of political change, are a staple of the daily news. India has become known for terrorism perpetrated both from the outside, most commonly by Islamic groups that have—or are believed to have—bases in Pakistan, and from within. The Naxalites/Maoists, carrying on the insurgency that has been described by the prime minister as constituting the gravest internal security threat the country has ever faced, are only the most notorious of very many groups associated by government with terrorism. The South Asia Terrorism Portal, a project set up in Delhi by a prominent former police officer, lists as many as thirty-nine 'Terrorist, Insurgent and Extremist Groups' in the north-eastern state of Manipur, thirty-six in Assam, thirty-two in Jammu and Kashmir, and thirty in Tripura, with smaller numbers in several other states, as well as six 'Left-Wing Extremist' groups, and nine other 'Extremist' organizations, including the Students Islamic Movement of India, which has been associated with a number of attacks. The attack carried out by Islamists from Pakistan in Mumbai in November 2008, however, which went on over three days and was covered in television reports throughout the world, is perhaps the most dramatic of very many terrorist incidents that have occurred on Indian soil.

The use of terrorist tactics has undoubtedly become a major problem in India, as it has very widely. But the charge of 'terrorism' can quite easily be twisted and turned to frame opponents. 'Terrorist' is how you brand your enemies if you can't call them 'Naxalite'. This has probably been happening in India with increasing frequency, both on the parts of irresponsible journalists and of politicians—as in the justification of some killings by security forces of innocent people, for instance in Kashmir and in Gujarat. The Hindi word for terrorism, 'atankwaada', is also used by powerful institutions in a cynical manner to denigrate specific populations. For example, after the murder of two Hindus by a group of Muslims in western Uttar Pradesh on 27 August 2013, a regional newspaper was quick to refer to a wave of 'Muslim terrorism' in the region. Hindu nationalists exerted heavy influence over the newspaper's reports, which in turn served to stoke religious communal tension. 'Atankwaada' or the English word 'terrorism' have been used as 'word weapons' in many similar communal or caste-based conflicts in India.

Counter-terrorist measures, too, can be manipulated and used for political advantage. In the wake of a series of attacks, including that by Islamic terrorists on parliament in December 2001, the BJP-led National Democratic Alliance, then in government, passed into law the Prevention of Terrorism Act in 2002 (known as 'POTA'), giving the security forces a range of special powers. The Act quickly came to be perceived as being misused, for example to crack down on political opponents, and it was repealed by the incoming United Progressive Alliance in 2004—though then replaced with similar measures through amendment of the Unlawful Activities (Prevention) Act of 1967. The use of force in actions to counter 'terrorism' can lead to spiralling violence, as has happened in some of the areas of India in which Naxalite/Maoist insurgents are active.

• See also **Naxalite, violence**

Time

In the *Oxford English Dictionary* the noun 'time' has two main meanings: first, 'the continuous progress of existence and events in the past, present, and future'; and second, 'a specific point in time'. It is the first definition of time—the constant flow of events—that is most important in India, where the abstraction of time into hours and the passage of days and years—clock time and calendar time—is a relatively recent phenomenon. The spread of colonialism was bound up with the dissemination of new ideas about how the passage of life and events should be ordered and understood. Clocks, calendars, and such like became part of the 'civilizing mission' in Africa and Asia and also integral to the opening up of distant lands for capitalist exploitation. These new visions of time typically came into contact with older ways of dividing up the passage of days and seasons, many of which were tied to religion and agriculture. The spread of colonialism also resulted in the proliferation of new ideas about how the human life cycle should be mapped onto the passage of time. Colonialism superimposed notions of childhood, youth, adulthood, and old age on other countries, where they sometimes meshed with older models of 'life stages', such as the Hindu notion of *ashramas*—the four phases of life: *brahmacharya* (student life), *grihastha* (household life), *vanaprastha* (retired life), *sannyasa* (renounced life).

Colonialists tended to imagine India as a society in which culture was fixed, and therefore a place lacking history. Such a view also colours accounts of contemporary India, where various practices—such as caste—are wrongly imagined to have existed unchanged 'for time immemorial' or 'for centuries'. During the postcolonial period, another temporal trope has come to dominate foreign imagination of India: India is depicted as in a stage of transition or development towards a more evolved (Western-style) society and economy.

One of the popular stereotypes of contemporary India—which is also repeated within the country—is that people lack an understanding of time. 'Time has no value in India' is the type of statement that one hears quite often in conversations with people in India. The notion of Indians' aversion to 'time' as a disciplining device is a trope of several Bollywood movies, too: scenes in which an Indian tourist is befuddled by European train timetables and traffic lights, for example. In some cases, people refer to 'Indian time' as a parallel system in which deadlines, punctuality, and timekeeping are unimportant. But concern over the passage of time features prominently in public and private discussion in India. People complain about having to expend time either in repetitive work or in meaningless activity, such as waiting on public transport or queuing in government offices, and for some marginalized people time may become an almost overwhelming topic of concern, as for example among those forced to migrate away from their families in search of work. In many agrarian societies, too, time—when to plant crops, when to harvest, the timing of weather events—is a pressing everyday concern. The division of each day into auspicious and inauspicious times or phases, shown in popular almanacs, is also a common matter of concern. A journey, for example, should not be started in one of the inauspicious periods.

Poor education, rising unemployment, and an absence of effective state welfare mean that time is often a particular worry of youth in contemporary India. They are unable to obtain the social goods, such as a secure white-collar job, that connote 'development'; they cannot move into gendered age-based categories, especially male adulthood; and they are incapable of conforming to dominant visions of how people should comport themselves with respect to linear time—they 'miss years' or have 'gaps' on their résumés, for example. In the face of such temporal suffering, unemployed young people in urban North India sometimes refer to their lives as simply exercises in 'timepass', a word that suggests a sense of endless surplus time, detachment from the world, and a feeling of being trapped in a life phase of chronic youth.

Conversely, the rich in India have been able to use their control over time to bolster their position. The upper middle classes are often able to avail themselves of time-saving devices, such as the washing machine, and technologies that allow them to communicate or travel more efficiently. At a more everyday level, upper middle classes can often use money to conquer time, as for example when they bribe school principals to allow their children to miss out a year of school, or where businesspeople pay off the state with a view to jumping the queue for planning permission. At the same moment, even among the middle classes, issues of waiting and boredom may be becoming more important, sometimes reflecting a broader dissatisfaction with contemporary urban life. It is small wonder, then, that the English word 'time' is now widely used in the Indian subcontinent.

• See also **development, education, history, modern, youth**

Tradition

The *Oxford English Dictionary* defines 'tradition' as a long-established custom or belief. Alternatively, it can refer to a method or style established by an artist subsequently taken up by their followers. For something to qualify as 'long-established' it is typically imagined that it should have been transmitted from at least one generation to the next.

India is currently moving from a period in which social, economic, and cultural beliefs and practices were *relatively* stable and 'long-established' to a period in which such beliefs and practices are being eroded. Joint families are sometimes becoming nuclear in form. People are abandoning hereditary occupations. Well-established norms around gender, caste, and authority are being questioned in new ways. Moreover, new forms of individualism and a greater degree of reflexivity about one's 'life' and 'career' are becoming more evident in contemporary India.

But we must nevertheless resist the idea that India is moving straightforwardly from an era of tradition to one of modernity, if for no other reason than that what counts as tradition is often not, when subject to scrutiny, in fact very long-established. In their seminal work *The Invention of Tradition*, the historians Eric Hobsbawm and Terence Ranger point out that tradition is a myth, something conjured up for politically motivated reasons to persuade other people to do certain things or think certain ways. For example, Bernard Cohn has described the process through which the British in India in the mid-nineteenth century tried to establish consent for rule through inventing a range of public ceremonies (called '*durbars*') at which loyal Indian subjects were showered with titles and gifts, a reinvention of a Mughal practice of patronage that was given the imprimatur of being a tradition.

Many of India's so-called traditional features emerge on close analysis to be fairly recent phenomena. For example, the types of caste system analysed by anthropologists in the mid-twentieth century were not a taken-for-granted cultural form that had existed unchanging through time, but rather reflected the particular social and economic conditions prevailing in different parts of India at that time. Similarly, the practice for the parents of a bride to give a dowry to the groom's family at the point of marriage has waxed and waned in different parts of India at different times—it is nothing like a static tradition.

Reflecting on these points, anthropologists and others have tended to recoil from trying to analyse transitions from tradition to modernity, in favour of studying how people and organizations use the idea of tradition to advance their own political goals. As Edward Said famously argued, colonialism was founded in part on an ideology that pitted a positive modern, rational, flexible 'West' against a negative traditional, heathen, leaden-footed 'East'. The British frequently depicted India as a place of relative disorder in which aberrant traditional practices—such as caste, and the burning of widows on their husbands' funeral pyres—were rife. Early development theorists of the so-called 'Modernization School' made somewhat similar moral judgements about India. Tradition was what India needed to abandon in order to enjoy the fruits of modernity. The political scientists Lloyd and Susanne Rudolph, however, in a seminal book with the felicitous title *The Modernity of Tradition*, showed how in many different ways traditional institutions served modern ends.

Reactionary sections of society in postcolonial India have often invoked tradition to justify their political campaigns: Hindutva activists have promulgated the notion that traditional India is unequivocally Hindu; higher-caste men in pockets of North India have used appeals to tradition as a means of justifying the meting out of harsh punishments on young people who marry out of caste; men have also commonly explained their control over paid employment and family decision-making in the name of tradition or with reference to an equivalent word in an Indian language such as '*parampaara*' in Hindi. Tradition is also a marketing device. The Government of India has deployed images of traditional India to attract tourists, and Indian corporations often make great play of tradition in their attempts to market consumer goods—the *sadhu* (holy man) driving a motorcycle or 'traditional' rural woman talking on a mobile phone is a stock in trade of advertisements in the country.

• See also **caste, culture, Hindutva, modern**

Unemployment

Unemployment is a social category referring to those above a specified age (often 18) who are not in paid employment or self-employment and are available for work. 'Unemployment' ('*berozgaar*' or '*bekam*' in Hindi) is also a perceptual category, a means through which people may define their relationship not only to the labour market but also to other people, the state, and their own previous and anticipated future activity.

In 2012 the Indian Government announced with some fanfare a reduction in unemployment in the country from 8.3 per cent in 2004/2005 to 6.6 per cent in 2009/2010, drawing on data supplied by the National Sample Survey Office (NSSO). But there are some notable problems with the NSSO figures on unemployment. The survey tends to record as 'employed' even those who have only temporary work. In practice, very few people in India are wholly unemployed, for the simple reason that there is nothing like an unemployment benefit in India, and usually no logic to remaining jobless. People have to work either on an unpaid basis in the household, in the case of many women, or in low-paid, temporary insecure work in the informal economy. The apparent decline in the unemployment rate is likely to reflect the withdrawal of many people, especially women, from the labour market. It may also reflect a move among those formerly waiting for 'good jobs' to enter fallback employment in the informal economy.

Large sections of the Indian workforce are therefore underemployed, often in the informal economy. They work in temporary, part-time jobs that offer little long-term security and are burdensome, even dangerous. They do not receive state support, such as pensions or sick leave, and they are not protected by employment legislation, for example regarding harassment in the workplace or unfair dismissal. In addition, they rarely obtain training or opportunities for skills development. Where people in this sector are also in education, their qualifications bear little relation to the work they are doing.

Widespread unemployment and underemployment reflect the failure of the Indian economy to create jobs outside agriculture. Economic liberalization since the early 1990s has not created large numbers of jobs in manufacturing and services, and has often led to a decline in the rate of growth in positions in government employment. India, it has been said by many commentators, has been characterized by 'jobless growth'. According to data presented by the National Commission on Enterprises in the Unorganized Sector, the numbers of protected 'formal sector' jobs actually declined slightly, from 33.7 million to 33.4 million, between 1999/2000 and 2004/2005. The much-discussed growth of the software industry and data processing does little to ameliorate this problem. It has been calculated that the IT sector creates roughly 1 million jobs a year, but India has a working population of more than 350 million, with at least 12 million entering the labour force every year. There has been little growth in small businesses either, reflecting the problem of an education sector out of kilter with the needs of the economy, poor infrastructure, low availability of cheap institutional credit, and corruption. Vocational and technical training in India is inadequate and most institutions are poorly provisioned and poorly run.

Unemployment affects people of different ages, as the Dutch sociologist Jan Breman's work on deindustrialization and the experience of unemployment among older workers in western India has shown. But people in their late teens and twenties are disproportionately affected by India's employment problem. Many young people have acquired high-school certificates and a small proportion have obtained degree qualifications, but very few can make the next step into secure work. While this problem is old, it has become much more intense during the past two decades, especially in North India. Some young people, especially those with parental financial support, spend long periods self-consciously 'unemployed'—advertising, as it were, their status as people 'on the road to something else'. While engaging in such cultural activity, they also often accumulate degrees and try to find fallback, status-saving work in the informal economy. Demoralization and suicide are major problems. Actual or perceived 'unemployment'—especially among young people—is a common theme of recent ethnographies of provincial India, of novels such as Chetan Bhagat's *Revolution 20:20*, and of Bollywood films.

In its recent Development Report, the World Bank uses a selection of surveys to argue that youth unemployment is the biggest single cause of political violence in the global South. Several scholars have likewise emphasized the reactionary, self-serving nature of educated unemployed young people's mobilization. Other research, however, has identified the positive role that educated unemployed young people may play in society; they often have the time, motivation, and energy to engage in community leadership.

Unemployment is a crucial electoral issue too. Political parties have tried to establish small funds for those who are unemployed. More important, however, has been the establishment of multiple government programmes in India aimed at creating employment opportunities, either indirectly through the provision of cheap loans and microfinance or directly through offering jobs to the unemployed and underemployed. The most significant of these has been the National Rural Employment Guarantee Scheme, recently renamed the Mahatma Gandhi National Rural Employment Guarantee Scheme (MGNREGS), which in principle provides 100 days of paid work to every household in rural India, mainly in local infrastructural projects. The effectiveness of this scheme varies widely across India, however. For example, the Comptroller Auditor General's reports from Uttar Pradesh show that intermediaries embezzle a proportion of the funds meant for the MGNREGS and labourers often have difficulty getting paid. And MGNREGS cannot solve the problem of unemployment in India because it can only ever provide temporary work.

• See also *development, informal, labour*

Village

The common understanding in English of a village is of 'a collection of dwelling-houses or other buildings, larger than a hamlet and smaller than a town, or having a simpler organization and administration than the latter' (*OED*). The word has its equivalents in Indian languages. In colonial India, however, the word acquired a particular meaning because of the significance of the village in administration, and especially in regard to the collection of land revenue (land tax). As the colonial civil servant B. H. Baden-Powell wrote in his *Short Account of the Land Revenue and its Administration in British India* (1894), 'needless to say that the term is used in a special sense different from that which it bears with reference to modern English agricultural life'. He went on: 'The village is an aggregate of cultivated holdings with, or without some waste area belonging to it, or attached to it, and usually it has a central site for the dwelling-houses congregated together... The village moreover often boasts a grove, or at least a tree under which the local assemblies will take place [suggesting the existence of local self-government]; there is also some kind of public office where the village patwari [accountant or record keeper, responsible to the ruler] keeps his books.'

Colonial administrators saw the village, therefore, as an economic and political unit with a good deal of social integrity and political autonomy: 'The village communities are little republics', one said, famously. There was disagreement amongst them, however, as to whether the existence in India of village communities should be welcomed, as the foundation of social order, or whether they should be seen rather as obstacles to economic growth and progress. Growth and progress would be advanced by the strengthening of individual property rights, but this would be at the expense of what were thought of as 'ancient village institutions' that were supposed to emphasize collective ownership and common property. The idea of 'the village' thus played an important part in the colonial imaginary.

It did, as well, in that of the Indian nationalists, and for none more so than for Gandhi who saw in the village the social foundations of the morality that he believed distinguished India from Western civilization. For him, independent India should be made up essentially of reconstructed villages, where people would use simple technologies, producing largely for their own use and not for profit, and govern themselves to a great extent through their panchayats (local councils). Independent India did not take this road, of course, but the influence of Gandhi's ideas is reflected in the protection still given by the state to 'cottage' (handicraft) industries—such as handloom weaving—and in the system of local government known as panchayati raj.

Successive governments have continued to devise projects around the idea of the 'village community', as in the Community Development Programme of the 1950s, or in more recent efforts in 'participatory development'. Throughout, in both the colonial and postcolonial periods, there has run a tension between the idea of the village as a fairly autonomous community of people, presupposing a fair degree of equality among them, and the empirical reality of village societies that are often characterized by high levels of inequality, notably in land ownership, and by hierarchical social relations given by caste. Studies of villages, as more or less discrete social arenas, were the stock-in-trade of anthropologists of India in the later twentieth century. They showed that members of one particular caste community usually dominated village societies; they owned much of the land, controlled most of the labour, and often exercised political power. These 'dominant castes', as they are called, have been able to manipulate development schemes to their own advantage, though they are also quite commonly divided by rivalries between particular individuals who have formed factions within the village. Village-level collective action and community development are constrained by these fissiparous tendencies.

Latterly, however, it appears that the village is no longer so important as a unit in Indian society, as both members of the locally dominant castes—the principal landowners—and labourers have come increasingly to take up opportunities, or have been forced to find alternative means of livelihood, outside their villages and often outside the rural economy altogether.

The 'village' remains a significant unit as far as administration is concerned, even though land revenue no longer makes up more than a tiny share of all government taxation. What is understood to be 'the village' may be a 'revenue village' in which there are several quite distinct 'collections of dwelling-houses', and revenue villages differ significantly in size. The units that are taken for village panchayats may differ in a similar way. 'The village' may also be divided spatially between the habitations of upper castes, and those of lower castes and untouchables—and there are different words in some Indian languages that denote these differences.

• See also *community, Gandhi, panchayat, peasant*

Violence

The *OED* defines violence as 'behaviour involving physical force intended to hurt, damage, or kill someone or something'. One of the most important forms of violence, in this broad sense, is the destruction of natural habitats, pollution, and the release of damaging gases into the atmosphere in India. Cruelty to animals is another area where violence is very common indeed but which—with the possible exception of controversies sparked by efforts to eliminate urban stray dogs—has not garnered much public attention.

Violence in contemporary India could be crudely divided into forms that are more 'private' in nature—hidden and individualized—and 'public', in the sense of being collectively practised and experienced. Much of the private violence that occurs is directed against girls and women. It is notoriously difficult to obtain accurate data on gender violence, but the National Crimes Record Bureau's statistics suggest a marked increase between the 1980s and 2000s in the murder of young women over dowry, the harassment of young brides around the issue of dowry, and so-called 'honour killings', where a young woman is punished for contravening social norms. Everyday violence against women is common, including psychological torture, beatings, and rape, and the harassment of women in public settings—sometimes euphemistically labelled 'eve-teasing'—is endemic. Violence against women and girls begins before birth. According to UNICEF, sex-selective abortion is responsible for the death of almost 7,000 female foetuses in India every day, and the sex ratio at birth in India declined from 972 in 1901 to 933 in 2001.

Children and youth in India, especially girls, are often subjected to sexual violence, and children are regularly beaten in the home. One poorly documented aspect of everyday life in India is the frequency with which corporal punishment is employed in schools, colleges, and tutorials. Violence witnessed by children or visited upon children often has long-term psychological effects, leading to further violent practices in the future, including suicide.

Of the types of public violence occurring in India, religious communal conflict is perhaps the most obvious. The partition of India was associated with huge loss of life, and religious communal violence has periodically flared up in independent India, for example in Bombay in the early 1990s. Urban communal riots have raised questions about cultures of masculine violence and everyday 'symbolic violence', for example where a government school principal decorates classrooms with Hindu gods.

Politically motivated violence is common in India. This includes well-publicized acts of violence against members of the public in major cities, such as the bomb blasts in Mumbai in 2008, the violent activities of some Naxalite organizations in central India, and much smaller-scale killings carried out by powerful political figures. The state is often involved in defining such violence as 'terrorism'.

Caste violence sits somewhere between the 'private' and 'public'. The caste hierarchy was underpinned by the tacit threat of higher-caste violence. In recent years, and buoyed sometimes by the emergence of low-caste political organizations, low castes have often fought back. This, in turn, has led to reactive higher-caste violence, including aggressive efforts to 'teach low castes a lesson'.

The ubiquity of private and public violence in India raises thorny questions about the state, which has been complicit in urban violence, for example in the anti-Sikh riots in Delhi in 1984 and the pogrom of Muslims in Ahmedabad in 2002. The police in India have been involved in more routine violence, sometimes through extra-judicial 'encounter' killings in which officers assassinate alleged criminals. Another set of questions concern the role of the state in promoting a bellicose culture, for example through its decision to test nuclear weapons in 1998 and its aggressive posture with respect to Pakistan. And some commentators, among them Akhil Gupta, argue that the state's failure to address problems of poverty in India constitutes, in itself, a 'violent' act.

Violence, precisely because of its shocking character, can sometimes be a spur to positive change, and it is often the conversion of private acts of violence to ones that are more public in nature that brings such change about. One of the notable features of contemporary Dalit politics in India is how activists use particular individual incidents of violence—which are often presented as 'atrocities'—as an occasion for exposing routine forms of everyday oppression. An 'atrocity' such as the rape of a Dalit woman or beating up of a Dalit man becomes, in some cases, the moment for testing and developing networks that link Dalits to sympathetic agencies within the state, human rights organizations, and other marginalized communities; a range of specialist 'atrocity activists' exists in local areas in India. There is a parallel here in the manner in which women's organizations and students used the rape of a young Delhi woman late in 2012 to launch campaigns for gender justice. Violence, in this view, is not only an occasion of intense private suffering but also an opportunity for civil society groups to problematize aspects of oppression and define what it means to be a citizen of India. There is a further parallel in the work of activists in the sphere of environmental protection, where specific acts of violence perpetrated on the natural environment become the context for campaigns whose goals and remit go well beyond the original source of anger.

• See also *caste, community, gender, state*

Water

Water is central to the reproduction of life and livelihoods and, as such, it has featured prominently in social science and popular discussion of Indian development. Large sections of the Indian population—mostly, but not only, those living in rural areas—either have to walk a long distance for water or can obtain only polluted or poor-quality water. In many urban areas, the poor are compelled to pay very high prices for this basic resource. Reflecting these difficulties, water is a crucial topic of everyday discussion and a major focus of development and government (political) concern—the Indian Government has made the provision of safe potable water a key development goal.

Water has long been a prominent public policy issue, but the deteriorating state of the environment in India has lent a new urgency to discussions of water access. Environmental concerns include the polluting of watercourses as a result of unregulated or poorly regulated business and urban expansion; the lowering of the water table following the excessive sinking of boreholes; the negative effects of increased use of chemical inputs in farming; the adverse implications of the introduction of highly 'thirsty' crops; and the environmental destruction associated with damming rivers and other major infrastructural projects. In addition, environmental catastrophes related to water are seemingly becoming more common in India, flooding in Andhra Pradesh and Assam in 2012 and drought in Maharashtra in the same year being recent examples.

In large cities, the rich have often been able to steal water through sinking their own boreholes, and they typically pay much less proportionally for water than do the poor. Many recent reports from the slums of Delhi and Mumbai point to the extreme burden placed on poor households by the need to purchase water, and the increasing criminalization of the poor as they are compelled to steal water to survive. One study of pavement dwellers in Mumbai pointed to how these communities are often compelled to scavenge for water, illegally tapping fire hydrants in the face of being excluded from community standpipes and individual taps. Much of this everyday discussion of water occurs among women and children, who are primarily responsible for collecting water and water-related tasks in rural and small town households.

Water is important for Indian religions and in terms of cultural practice. Bathing is a central component of Hindu and Muslim religious practice, at the everyday level and—especially among Hindus—at large festivals like the *kumbh mela* held every eleven or twelve years (according to an astrological clock, not the Gregorian calendar) at Allahabad in North India. Culturally, the monsoon in India has long held a place in the Indian social and cultural imagination, and water has a rich and complex symbolic significance in Bollywood films.

At the village and town neighbourhood levels, caste continues to play a role in who has access to public water facilities—especially handpumps—at different times of the day. Likewise, there are histories of intense conflicts between villages at different points on river systems over the use of water for irrigation, and battles within individual villages between different caste and class groups. At a much broader level, changes in the governance of water provision are heightening the prominence of water issues in the public consciousness. The state in India is retreating from subsidizing cheap water for the poor and placing more stress on recovering costs and ensuring profitability. One notable dimension of this trend is the government's move to divest responsibility for water provision to community-managed institutions. Such initiatives appear to have had mixed results. Several studies suggest that elites and government officials have subverted community water initiatives. India's major anti-dam construction movements and demands for water as part of a suite of human rights also highlight the significance of water in the national political imagination. At the international level, there is intense dispute between India and its neighbours, Bangladesh and Pakistan, over control of rivers that straddle national borders, and likewise conflict within India over access to water from rivers that cross state boundaries. Water emerges as the grounds upon which power conflicts are played out at different scales.

• See also *environment, politics, state*

Youth

According to the *OED*, 'youth' refers to a stage of life between childhood and adulthood and to those people who are at this stage in their lives. Youth is a sociological category not a biological one (the term 'adolescent' refers to puberty) and it can therefore be applied to people in varied age ranges. Many of the early writers on youth included people within fifteen years of adolescence. In many parts of the West, the age range of 'youth' is often narrower—for example 16 to 24. Ultimately, youth is a relational category: a 70-year-old is young relative to a 90-year-old.

In the West in the nineteenth and early twentieth centuries, influential commentators institutionalized the idea of various 'life stages', which of course is a much older idea. 'Youth' was typically conceptualized as a period of relative uncertainty and danger, or 'storm and stress'. This general idea of youth as a danger took hold in the mid-twentieth century, such that by the last two decades of the twentieth century 'youth' was loaded with strongly negative associations—as in 'a gang of youths'. Yet 'youth' also enjoyed a different career, being increasingly present in government reports and NGO documents, where it typically had connotations of promise, vitality, energy, and hope.

The Government of India, in line with many international institutions, now defines youth as those aged 16 to 30, and most 'youth' NGOs in India operate with a somewhat similar age bracket. But youth is a hazy category in popular speech, sometimes seemingly detached altogether from age. Some 'youth politicians' are in their fifties. Bollywood stars likewise often style themselves as 'youth' long after the onset of middle age.

Youth is a crucial public issue in India. In 2011, 63 per cent of the Indian population was under the age of 30, and roughly a quarter of the population falls between the ages of 16 and 30. Like governments in other parts of the world, the Indian state veers between positive and negative interpretations of this vast demographic. Youth, on the one hand, are a 'demographic dividend' that might drive economic growth through their productive work and savings, and on the other hand a 'demographic time bomb', capable of undermining the social fabric and good governance.

There are vast inequalities within the youth population in India. There is a thin upper stratum of late teenagers and twenty-somethings that has acquired education and moved into good jobs, often in IT. Members of this elite are part of India's upper middle class. They are often highly mobile, and commentators have identified this generation as a source of hope for India—part of 'India Shining'. At the same time, the vast majority of young people have failed to acquire good educational qualifications, most work in poorly paid and insecure, sometimes also dangerous, sections of the informal economy or engage in gruelling household work in the home. Youth poverty is rife in India.

Youth is also a site of contradictions. Increasing numbers of young people have been drawn into formal education and have, as a consequence, set their sights on service employment and an urban, middle-class life. But economic reforms have failed to generate large numbers of skilled jobs for graduates. This has led to frustration and disorientation, even to suicide—nearly half of the suicides that occurred in India in 2009 were among those aged 16 to 30. The figure of the 'demoralized youth' now haunts the Indian social imagination. This problem is often imagined to be one primarily affecting men, but young women, too, are often suffering in the context of a rise of aspirations and precious few opportunities.

The Indian Government published a draft National Youth Policy in 2012 which identifies a wide range of areas for potential improvement in young people's lives, including investigation of why children drop out of school, greater opportunities for political participation, the introduction of better vocational training, and the development of more job-relevant school and college curricula. At the same time, politicians are becoming more active in politicizing young people. Politicians such as Rahul Gandhi (Congress) and Akhilesh Yadav (Samajwadi Party) make great play of their own 'youth'.

But 'youth' is not as important as a political category in India as it is in most parts of Africa. And youth have not been as visible in politics in India as they were, say, in South Africa during the anti-apartheid era or in Tunisia and Egypt in 2010–11. The 1974 anti-corruption movement led by the social reformer (and co-founder of the Congress Socialist Party in 1934) Jayaprakash ('JP') Narayan (1902–79) is probably the only large-scale 'youth' social movement to have emerged in postcolonial India. And it is organizations of the extreme right (the forces of Hindutva) and the extreme left (such as the Naxalites) that have been most effective in politicizing youth on the ground. But this may be beginning to change. For example, in December 2012 very large numbers of young people came out onto the streets in India's largest cities to demonstrate on the issue of the gang rape of a young woman in Delhi. There is also considerable evidence of young people's involvement in everyday political action, for instance acting as intermediaries between poor people and the state, or participating in small-scale demonstrations, for example around issues of education.

Youth have been influential in the realms of culture, through their consumption, attitudes towards sexuality, and language. Youth have developed novel forms of cultural expression through their participation in urban college cultures, involvement in social networking, and close association with the film industry. Young people are often conduits for the emergence of new cultural forms in small towns and villages, and they are predictably among the most global of India's citizens in terms of what they consume and where they want to travel in the future. Young people are also changing everyday language, for example through their use of English words in Indian languages—what is sometimes called 'Hinglish'—and adoption of phrases and ideas circulating in the media. 'Youth' is a crucial market in India.

• See also *culture, education, politics, unemployment*

REFERENCES AND FURTHER READING

Note: Full bibliographic details are found in the Bibliography

Adivasi: Corbridge (1988); Ghurye (1943); Guha (1999); Shah (2010)
Ambedkar: Jaffrelot (2005); Jaoul (2006); Zelliot (1992)
Bollywood: Baskaran (1981); Bose (2006); Prasad (2008)
Bourgeois: Damodaran (2008); Kosambi (1946); Stein (1991)
Bureaucracy: Corbridge, Harriss, and Jeffrey (2013), chapter 8
Capitalism: Chandavarkar (2003); Corbridge, Harriss, and Jeffrey (2013); Marx (1975 [1853]); Marx and Engels (2004 [1848])
Caste: Dumont (1970); Kothari (2011); Shah et al. (2006); Srinivas (1996)
Charity: Haynes (1987); Parry (1986); Watt (2011)
Citizenship: Chatterjee (2004); Jayal (2013); Turner (2005)
City: Chattopadhyay (1969); Gooptu (2011); Irving (1981); Khilnani (1997)
Civil Society: Appadurai (2002); Chatterjee (2004); Kaviraj (2001)
Class: Bayly (2012); Harriss (2010); Herring and Agarwala (2006)
Colonialism: Dirks (2001); Stokes (1973); Washbrook (1998)
Commons: Jodha (1986); Whitehead (2012)
Communism: Sengupta (1972); Westad (2005)
Community: Chatterjee (1998); Sinha (2008)
Congress: Corbridge and Harriss (2000)
Constitution: Austin (1966); Austin (1999); Corbridge and Harriss (2000); Khilnani (1997)
Consumerism: Das (2000); Fernandes (2006); Mazzarella (2003)
Corruption: Gupta (2012); Myrdal (1968); Tarlo (2003)
Cricket: Guha (2002); Majumdar (2008); Nandy (1989)
Criminal: Berenschot (2011); Pandian (2009); Yang (1985)
Culture: Bourdieu (1984); Said (1978); Uberoi (2006)
Dalit: Chandra (2004); Ciotti (2010); Lerche (2008)
Democracy: Corbridge, Harriss, and Jeffrey (2013); Khilnani (1997); Mehta (2003)
Development: Corbridge and Harriss (2000); Corbridge, Harriss, and Jeffrey (2013)
Diaspora: Clifford (1994); Ghosh (1989); Qureshi (forthcoming)
Education: Jeffrey et al. (2008); Krishna (2010); Sen (1999)
Empowerment: Agarwala (2013); Sen (1994); World Bank 2002
Enterprise: Das (2000); Jeffrey (2010); Rose (1993)
Environment: Agrawal and Sivaramakrishnan (2000); Guha (1989); Shiva (1988)
Equality: Breman (2007); Dumont (1970)
Faction: Dumont (1970); Hardiman (1982)
Family: Patel (2005); Shah (1974); Shah (1998); Uberoi (1998)
Federalism: Austin (1966); Corbridge (2011); Mitra and Pehl (2010)

Feminism: Forbes (1990); Jeffery and Basu (1998); Roy (2013)

Forests: Agarwal (2010); Guha (1989); Kumar (2002); Rangan (2000)

Fundamentalism: Fuller (2004); Madan (1997)

Gandhi: Parekh (1997); Rudolph and Rudolph (2006); Sengupta (2012)

Gender: Agarwal (1994); Jeffery and Basu (1998); Osella and Osella (2006)

Generation: Jeffrey (2010); Rushdie (1981); Uberoi (2006)

Globalization: Bardhan (2010); Corbridge, Harriss, and Jeffrey (2013); Mazzarella (2003)

GMO: Harriss and Stewart (2014); Herring (2007)

Green Revolution: Harriss and Stewart (2014); Lipton and Longhurst (1989)

Hindu (Hindustan, Hindustani): Bayly (1998); King (1994)

Hinduism: Frykenberg (1989); Fuller (2004); Scheifinger (2009); Sen (2010); von Stietencron (1989); Zavos (2000)

Hindutva (Hindu Nationalism): Hansen (1999); Jaffrelot (1996); Reddy (2011); Savarkar (2009 [1923])

History: Lal (2003); van der Veer (1994)

Identity: Corbridge and Harriss (2000); Khilnani (1997); Mines and Lamb (2010)

Individual: Dumont (1965); Marriott (1955); Mines (1988)

Informal: Agarwala (2013); De Soto (1989); Harriss-White (2003); Hart (1973)

Justice: Kaur (2010); Mehta (2007); Sen (2009)

Labour: Breman (1997); Chari (2004); Corbridge, Harriss, and Jeffrey (2013), chapter 4

Land: Borras et al. (2011); Neale (1969); Thorner (1976 [1956])

Language: King (1994); Ramaswamy (1997)

Law: Galanter (1968); Mehta (2005); Rudolph and Rudolph (1967a)

Liberal, Liberalism: Bayly (2012); Parekh (2005)

Marriage: Clark-Decès (2011); Donner (2002); Oldenburg (2004)

Masculinity: Alter (2012); Chopra (2006); Osella and Osella (2006)

Media: Doron and Jeffrey (2012); Jeffrey (2000); Manuel (1993); Rajagopal (2001); Sundaram (2010)

Microfinance: Holvoet (2005); Rai and Ravi (2011); Young (2010)

Middle Class: Baviskar and Ray (2011); Fernandes (2006); Harriss (2006)

Modern, Modernity: Mazzarella (2003), Sivaramakrishnan and Agrawal (2003)

Muslim: Banerjee (2010); Basant and Shariff (2010); Sachar (2006)

Nation, Nationalism: Bayly (1998); Khilnani (1997)

Naxalite: Banerjee (2002); Kennedy and Purushotham (2012)

Nehru: Ali (2005); Inden (1995); Nehru (2005 [1946]); Tharoor (2013); Zachariah (2004)

Neo-liberal, Neo-liberalism: Corbridge, Harriss, and Jeffrey (2013); Harvey (2005)

NGO: Edwards and Hulme (1996); Watt (2011)

Panchayat: Ananthapur and Moore (2010); Dumont (1970)

Patronage: Brass (1965); Breman (1993); Harriss-White (2003); Price and Ruud (2010)

Peasant: Beteille (1974); Ludden (1999); Marriott (1955); Thorner (1976 [1956])

Police: Bayley (1969); Jauregui (2011)

Politics: Brass (2010); Corbridge and Harriss (2000); Corbridge, Harriss, and Jeffrey (2013)

Population: Dyson (2013); Hodges (2004); Jeffery and Jeffery (2006)

Populism, Populist: Harriss (2000); Laclau (1977); Thachil (2013)

Poverty: Corbridge, Harriss, and Jeffrey (2013)

Rape: Das (1996); Teltumbde (2013)

Reservations: Beteille (1992); Dirks (2001); Jaffrelot (2003); Youth for Equality website
Rights: Chatterjee (2004); Jayal (2013); Sen (2010)
Roads: Arnold (2012); Kipling (1994)
Secularism: Bhargava (1998); Madan (1997); Sen (2010)
Slum: Bhan (2009); Björkman (forthcoming); Ghertner (2008); Gooptu (1996); Inden (2010)
Socialism, Socialist: Corbridge and Harriss (2000); Jaffrelot (2003)
Society: Chatterjee (2004); Kaviraj (1990); Marriott (1955)
(The) State: Corbridge, Harriss, and Jeffrey (2013); Gupta (2012); Khilnani (1997); Pritchett (2009)
Subaltern: Amin (1984); Chaturvedi (2012); Chibber (2013); Spivak (1988)
Terrorism: Allen (2006); Sarkar (1983); South Asia Terrorism Portal website
Time: Jeffrey (2010); Parry (1999); Thompson (1967)
Tradition: Cohn (1983); Rudolph and Rudolph (1967b); Said (1978); Uberoi (2006)
Unemployment: Corbridge, Harriss, and Jeffrey (2013); Jeffrey (2010); Joshi (2009)
Village: Baden-Powell (1894); Dumont (1970); Marriott (1955)
Violence: Bhattacharya (2004); Bloch and Rao (2002); Gupta (2012); Hansen (2005)
Water: Baviskar (2007); Sharma (2010); Wade (1988)
Youth: Dyson (2008); Jeffrey (2010); Lukose (2009)

BIBLIOGRAPHY

Agarwal, B. (1994). *A Field of One's Own: Gender and Land Rights in South Asia*. Cambridge: Cambridge University Press.

Agarwal, B. (2010). *Gender and Green Governance: The Political Economy of Women's Presence within and beyond Community Forestry*. Oxford: Oxford University Press.

Agarwala, R. (2013). *Informal Labor, Formal Politics and Dignified Discontent in India*. New York: Cambridge University Press.

Agrawal, A. and Sivaramakrishnan, K. (2000). *Agrarian Environments: Resources, Representations, and Rule in India*. Durham, NC: Duke University Press.

Ali, T. (2005). *The Nehrus and the Gandhis: An Indian Dynasty* (2nd edition). London: Picador.

Allen, C. (2006). *God's Terrorists: The Wahhabi Cult and the Hidden Roots of Modern Jihad*. London: Little, Brown.

Alter, J. (2012). *Moral Materialism: Sex and Masculinity in Modern India*. London: Penguin.

Amin, S. (1984). 'Gandhi as Mahatma: Gorakhpur district, Eastern UP, 1921–2', *Subaltern Studies*, 3: 1–61.

Ananthapur, K. and Moore, M. (2010). 'Ambiguous Institutions: Traditional Governance and Local Democracy in South India', *Journal of Development Studies*, 46, 4: 603–23.

Appadurai, A. (2002). 'Deep Democracy: Urban Governmentality and the Horizon of Politics', *Public Culture*, 14, 1: 21–47

Arnold, D. (2012). 'The Problem of Traffic: The Street-life of Modernity in Late-colonial India', *Modern Asian Studies*, 46, 1: 119–41.

Austin, G. (1966). *The Indian Constitution: Cornerstone of a Nation*. Oxford: Clarendon Press.

Austin, G. (1999). *Working a Democratic Constitution: The Indian Experience*. New Delhi: Oxford University Press.

Baden-Powell, B. H. (1894). *A Short Account of the Land Revenue and its Administration in British India: With a Sketch of the Land Tenures*. Oxford: Clarendon Press.

Banerjee, S. (2002). 'Naxalbari: Between Past and Future', *Economic and Political Weekly*, 37, 22: 2115–16.

Banerjee, M. (ed.) (2010). *Muslim Portraits: Everyday Lives in India*. Bloomington, IN: Indiana University Press.

Bardhan, P. (2010). *Awakening Giants, Feet of Clay: Assessing the Economic Rise of China and India*. Princeton: Princeton University Press.

Basant, R. and Shariff, A. (eds) (2010). *Handbook of Muslims in India: Empirical and Policy Perspectives*. New Delhi: Oxford University Press.

Baskaran, S. T. (1981). *The Message Bearers: The Nationalist Politics and the Entertainment Media in South India, 1880–1945*. Madras: Cre-A.

Baviskar, A. (2007). *Waterscapes: The Cultural Politics of a Natural Resource*. New Delhi: Permanent Black.

Baviskar, A. and Ray, R. (eds) (2011). *Elite and Everyman: The Cultural Politics of the Indian Middle Classes*. New Delhi: Routledge.

Bayley, D. H. (1969). *The Police and Political Development in India*. Princeton, NJ: Princeton University Press.

Bayly, C. A. (1998). *Origins of Nationality in South Asia: Patriotism and Ethical Government in the Making of Modern India*. Oxford: Oxford University Press.

Bayly, C. A. (2012). Recovering Liberties: Indian Thought in the Age of Liberalism and Empire (The Wiles Lectures Given at the Queen's University of Belfast 2007). Cambridge.

Bennett, T., Grossberg, L., and Morris, M. (2005). *New Keywords: A Revised Vocabulary of Culture and Society*. Oxford: Blackwell.

Berenschot, W. (2011). 'On the Usefulness of Goondas in Indian Politics: "Moneypower" and "Musclepower" in a Gujarati Locality', *South Asia: Journal of South Asian Studies*, 34, 2: 255–75.

Béteille, A. (1974). *Studies in Agrarian Social Structure*. Delhi: Oxford University Press.

Béteille, A. (1992). *The Backward Classes in Contemporary India*. Delhi: Oxford University Press.

Bhan, G. (2009). '"This is No Longer the City I Once Knew": Evictions, the Urban Poor and the Right to the City in Millennial Delhi', *Environment and Urbanization*, 21, 1: 127–42.

Bhargava, R. (ed.) (1998). *Secularism and its Critics*. New Delhi: Oxford University Press.

Bhattacharya, R. (2004). *Behind Closed Doors: Domestic Violence in India*. New Delhi: Sage.

Björkman, L. (forthcoming). 'Making of a Slum: Criminalizing Infrastructure in Liberalization-era Mumbai', *International Journal of Urban and Regional Research*.

Bloch, F. and Rao, V. (2002). 'Terror as a Bargaining Instrument: A Case Study of Dowry Violence in Rural India', *American Economic Review*, 92, 4: 1029–43.

Borras, S., Hall, R., Scoones, I., White, B., and Wolford, W. (2011). 'Towards a Better Understanding of Global Land Grabbing: An Editorial Introduction', *Journal of Peasant Studies*, 38, 2: 209–16.

Bose, M. (2006). *Bollywood: A History*. Stroud, Gloucestershire: Tempus.

Bourdieu, P. (1984). *Distinction: A Social Critique of the Judgment of Taste*. Cambridge, MA: Harvard University Press.

Brass, P. R. (1965). *Factional Politics in an Indian State: The Congress Party in Uttar Pradesh*. Berkeley and Los Angeles: University of California Press.

Brass, P. R. (ed.) (2010). *Routledge Handbook of South Asian Politics: India, Pakistan, Bangladesh, Sri Lanka, and Nepal*. New York: Routledge.

Breman, J. (1993). *Beyond Patronage and Exploitation: Changing Agrarian Relations in South Gujarat*. New Delhi. Oxford University Press.

Breman, J. (1997). *Footloose Labour: Working in India's Informal Economy*. Cambridge: Cambridge University Press.

Breman, J. (2007). *The Poverty Regime in Village India: Half a Century of Work and Life at the Bottom of the Rural Economy in South Gujarat*. Delhi: Oxford University Press.

Burgett, B. and Hendler, G. (2007). *Keywords for American Cultural Studies*. New York: New York University Press.

Chandavarkar, R. (2003). *The Origins of Industrial Capitalism in India: Business Strategies and the Working Classes in Bombay, 1900–1940*. Cambridge: Cambridge University Press.

Chandra, K. (2004). *Why Ethnic Parties Succeed: Patronage and Ethnic Head Counts in India*. Cambridge: Cambridge University Press.

Chari, S. (2004). *Fraternal Capital: Peasant-workers, Self-made Men and Globalization in Provincial India*. Stanford, CA: Stanford University Press.

Chatterjee, P. (1998). 'Community in the East', *Economic and Political Weekly*, 33, 6: 277–82.

Chatterjee, P. (2004). *The Politics of the Governed: Reflections on Popular Politics in Most of the World*. New York: Columbia University Press.

Chattopadhyay, B. (1969). 'Marx and India's Crisis', in P. C. Joshi (ed.), *Homage to Karl Marx*. Delhi: People's Publishing House.

Chaturvedi, V. (ed.) (2012). *Mapping Subaltern Studies and the Postcolonial* (2nd edition). London: Verso Books.

Chibber, V. (2013). *Postcolonial Theory and the Specter of Capital*. London and Brooklyn, NY: Verso.

Chopra, R. (2006). *Reframing Masculinities: Narrating the Supportive Practices of Men*. New Delhi: Orient Longman.

Ciotti, M. (2010). 'Futurity in Words: Low-caste Women Political Activists' Self-representation and Post-Dalit Scenarios in North India', *Contemporary South Asia*, 18, 1: 43–56.

Clark-Decès, I. (2011). 'The Decline of Dravidian Kinship in Local Perspectives', in I. Clark-Decès (ed.), *A Companion to the Anthropology of India*. Oxford: Blackwell, 517–35.

Clifford, J. (1994). 'Diasporas', *Cultural Anthropology*, 9, 3: 302–38.

Cohn, B. (1983). 'Representing Authority in Victorian India', in E. Hobsbawm and T. Ranger (eds), *The Invention of Tradition*. Cambridge: Cambridge University Press, 165–210.

Corbridge, S. (1988). 'The Ideology of Tribal Economy and Society: Politics in the Jharkhand, 1950–1980', *Modern Asian Studies*, 22, 1: 1–42.

Corbridge, S. (2011). 'The Contested Geographies of Federalism in Post-Reform India', in S. Ruparelia, S. Reddy, J. Harriss, and S. Corbridge (eds), *Understanding India's New Political Economy: A Great Transformation?* London and New York: Routledge, 66–80.

Corbridge, S. and Harriss, J. (2000). *Reinventing India: Liberalization, Hindu Nationalism and Popular Democracy*. Cambridge: Polity Press.

Corbridge, S., Harriss, J., and Jeffrey, C. (2013). *India Today: Economy, Politics and Society*. Cambridge: Polity Press.

Damodaran, H. (2008). *India's New Capitalists: Caste, Business and Industry in a Modern Nation*. Ranikhet: Permanent Black.

Das, G. (2000). *India Unbound*. London: Penguin.

Das, V. (1996). 'Sexual Violence, Discursive Formations and the State', *Economic and Political Weekly*, 31, 35–7: 2411–23.

De Soto, H. (1989). *The Other Path: The Informal Revolution*. New York: Harper & Row.

Dirks, N. B. (2001). *Castes of Mind: Colonialism and the Making of Modern India*. Princeton: Princeton University Press.

Donner, H. (2002). 'One's Own Marriage: Love Marriages in a Calcutta Neighborhood', *South Asia Research*, 22, 1: 79–94.

Doron, A. and Jeffrey, R. (2012). *The Great Indian Phonebook*. Cambridge, MA: Harvard University Press.

Dumont, L. (1965). 'The Modern Conception of the Individual: Notes on its Genesis and that of Concomitant Institutions', *Contributions to Indian Sociology*, 8: 13–61.

Dumont, L. (1970). *Homo Hierarchicus: The Caste System and its Implications*. Chicago: University of Chicago Press.

Dyson, J. (2008). 'Harvesting Identities: Youth, Work, and Gender in the Indian Himalayas', *Annals of the Association of American Geographers*, 98, 1: 160–79.

Dyson, T. (2013). 'On Democratic and Demographic Transition', *Population and Development Review*, 38, 1: 83–102.

Edwards, M. and Hulme, D. (eds) (1996). *Beyond the Magic Bullet: NGO Performance and Accountability in the Post-Cold War World*. W. Hartford, CT: Kumarian Press.

Fernandes, L. (2006). *India's New Middle Class: Democratic Politics in an Era of Economic Reform*. Minneapolis: University of Minnesota Press.

Forbes, G. (1990). 'Caged Tigers: "First wave" Feminists in India', *Women Studies International Forum*, 5: 525–36.

Frykenberg, R. E. (1989). 'The Emergence of Modern "Hinduism" as a Concept and as an Institution: A Reappraisal with Special Reference to South India', in H. von Stietencron, G. D. Sontheimer, and H. Kulke (eds), *Hinduism Reconsidered*. Delhi: Manohar: 29–49.

Fuller, C. J. (2004). *The Camphor Flame: Popular Hinduism and Society in India* (2nd edition). Princeton: Princeton University Press.

Galanter, M. (1968). 'The Displacement of Traditional Law in Modern India', *Journal of Social Issues*, 24, 4: 65–91.

Ghertner, A. (2008). 'An Analysis of the New Legal Discourse behind Delhi's Slum Demolition', *Economic and Political Weekly*, 43, 20: 57–66.

Ghosh, A. (1989). 'The Diaspora in Indian Culture', *Public Culture*, 2, 1: 73–8.

Ghurye, G. S. (1943). *The Aborigines—So-Called, and Their Future*. New Delhi: Oxford University Press.

Gooptu, N. (1996). 'The "Problem" of the Urban Poor Policy and Discourse of Local Administration: A Study in Uttar Pradesh in the Interwar Period', *Economic and Political Weekly*, 31, 50: 3245–54.

Gooptu, N. (2011). 'Economic Liberalization, Urban Politics and the Poor', in S. Ruparelia, S. Reddy, J. Harriss, and S. Corbridge (eds), *Understanding India's New Political Economy: A Great Transformation?* London and New York: Routledge.

Gordon, George (Lord Byron), *Child Harold's Pilgrimage*, Canto III <http://www.poetryatlas.com/poetry/poem/960/> (Last retrieved 13 July 2013).

Guha, R. (1989). *Unquiet Woods: Ecological Change and Peasant Resistance in the Himalaya*. New Delhi: Oxford University Press.

Guha, R. (1999). *Savaging the Civilised: Verrier Elwin, His Tribals, and India*. Chicago: University of Chicago Press.

Guha, R. (2002). *A Corner of a Foreign Field*. London: Picador.

Gupta, A. (2012). *Red Tape: Bureaucracy, Structural Violence, and Poverty in India*. Durham and London: Duke University Press.

Hansen, T. B. (1999). *The Saffron Wave: Democracy and Hindu Nationalism in Modern India*. Princeton: Princeton University Press.

Hansen, T. B. (2005). *Violence in Urban India: Identity Politics, 'Mumbai', and the Postcolonial City*. Delhi: Orient Blackman.

Hardiman, D. (1982). 'The Indian "Faction": A Political Theory Examined', in R. Guha (ed.), *Subaltern Studies 1*. Delhi: Oxford University Press, 215–25.

Harriss, J. (2000). 'Populism, Tamil Style: Is it Really a Success?', *Review of Development and Change*, 5, 2: 332–46.

Harriss, J. (2002). *Depoliticizing Development: The World Bank and Social Capital*. London: Anthem.

Harriss, J. (2006). 'Middle-class Activism and the Politics of the Informal Working Class: A Perspective on Class Relations and Civil Society in Indian Cities', *Critical Asian Studies*, 38, 4: 445–65.

Harriss, J. (2010). 'Class and Politics', in N. G. Jayal and P. B. Mehta (eds), *The Oxford Companion to Politics in India*. Delhi: Oxford University Press, 139–53.

Harriss, J. and Stewart, D. (2014). 'Science, Politics and the Framing of Modern Agricultural Technologies', in R. J. Herring (ed.), *The Oxford Handbook of Food Politics*. New York: Oxford University Press.

Harriss-White, B. (2003). *India Working: Essays on Economy and Society*. Cambridge: Cambridge University Press.

Hart, K. (1973). 'Informal Income Opportunities and Urban Employment in Ghana', *Journal of Modern African Studies*, 11, 1: 61–89.

Harvey, D. (2005). *A Brief History of Neoliberalism*. Oxford: Oxford University Press.

Haynes, D. E. (1987). 'From Tribute to Philanthropy: The Politics of Gift Giving in a Western Indian City', *Journal of Asian Studies*, 46, 2: 339–60.

Herring, R. (ed.) (2007). *Transgenics and the Poor: Biotechnology in Development Studies*. London and New York: Routledge.

Herring, R. and Agarwala, R. (2006). 'Introduction: Restoring Agency to Class: Puzzles from the Subcontinent', *Critical Asian Studies*, 38, 4: 323–56.

Hodges, S. (2004). 'Governmentality, Population and Reproductive Family in Modern India', *Economic and Political Weekly*, 39, 11: 1157–63.

Holvoet, N. (2005). 'The Impact of Microfinance on Decision-making Agency: Evidence from South India', *Development and Change*, 36, 1: 75–102.

Inden, R. (1995). 'Embodying God: From Imperial Progresses to National Progress in India', *Economy and Society*, 24, 2: 245–78.

Inden, R. (2010). 'From Village to Shantytown: Poverty and Mobility in the Popular Films of the New India', in D. P. Mines and N. Yazgi (eds), *Village Matters: Relocating Villages in the Contemporary Anthropology of India*. Delhi: Oxford University Press, 241–55.

Irving, R. (1981). *Indian Summer: Lutyens, Baker, and Imperial Delhi*. New Haven: Yale University Press.

Jaffrelot, C. (1996). *The Hindu Nationalist Movement and Indian Politics: 1925 to the 1990s*. London: Hurst & Co.

Jaffrelot, C. (2003). *India's Silent Revolution: The Rise of the Low Castes in North Indian Politics*. New Delhi: Permanent Black.

Jaffrelot, C. (2005). *Dr Ambedkar and Untouchability: Analysing and Fighting Caste*. New Delhi: Orient Blackswan.

Jaoul, N. (2006). 'Learning the use of Symbolic Means: Dalits, Ambedkar Statues and the State in Uttar Pradesh', *Contributions to Indian Sociology*, 40, 2: 175–207.

Jauregui, B. (2011). 'Law and Order: Police Encounter Killings and Routinized Political Violence', in I. Clark-Decès (ed.), *A Companion to the Anthropology of India*. Chichester: Wiley-Blackwell, 371–88.

Jayal, N. G. (2013). *Citizenship and its Discontents: An Indian History*. Cambridge, MA: Harvard University Press.

Jeffery, P. and Basu, A. (1998). *Appropriating Gender: Women's Activism in South Asia*. London: Routledge.

Jeffery, P. and Jeffery, R. (2006). *Confronting Saffron Demography: Religion, Fertility and Women's Status in India*. Delhi: Three Essay's Collective.

Jeffrey, C. (2010). *Timepass: Youth, Class, and the Politics of Waiting in India*. Stanford, CA: Stanford University Press.

Jeffrey, C., Jeffery, P., and Jeffery, R. (2008). *Degrees without Freedom? Education, Masculinities, and Unemployment in North India*. Stanford, CA: Stanford University Press.

Jeffrey, R. (2000). *India's Newspaper Revolution: Capitalism, Technology and the Indian-Language Press 1977–1999*. London: Palgrave Macmillan.

Jodha, N. S. (1986). 'Common Property Resources and Rural Poor in Dry Regions of India', *Economic and Political Weekly*, 21, 27: 1169–81.

Joshi, V. (2009). 'Economic Resurgence, Lop-sided Performance, Jobless Growth', in A. Heath and R. Jeffery (eds), *Continuity and Change in Contemporary India: Politics, Economics, and Society*, New Delhi: Oxford University Press, 73–106.

Kaur, R. (2010). 'Khap Panchayats, Sex Ratios, and Female Agency', *Economic and Political Weekly*, 45, 23: 14–16.

Kaviraj, S. (1990). 'On State, Society and Discourse in India', *IDS Bulletin*, 21, 4: 10–15.

Kaviraj, S. (2001). 'In Search of Civil Society', in S. Kaviraj and S. Khilnani (eds), *Civil Society: History and Possibilities*. Cambridge: Cambridge University Press, 287–323.

Kennedy, J. and Purushotham, S. (2012). 'Beyond Naxalbari: A Comparative Analysis of Maoist Insurgency and Counterinsurgency in Independent India', *Comparative Studies in Society and History*, 54, 4: 832–62.

Keywords for American Cultural Studies <http://keywords.fordhamitac.org> (Last retrieved 15 July 2013).

Khilnani, S. (1997). *The Idea of India*. London: Hamish Hamilton.

King, C. R. (1994). *One Language, Two Scripts: The Hindi Movement in Nineteenth Century India*. Delhi: Oxford University Press.

Kipling, R. (1994). *Kim*. London: Wordsworth.

Kosambi, D. D. (1946). 'The Bourgeoisie Comes of Age in India', *Science & Society*, 10, 4: 392–8.

Kothari, R. (2011). *Caste in Indian Politics*. New Delhi: Oxford University Press.

Krishna, A. (2010). *One Illness Away: Why People become Poor and how They Escape Poverty*. Oxford: Oxford University Press.

Kumar, S. (2002). 'Does "Participation" in Common Pool Resource Management Help the Poor? A Social Cost–benefit Analysis of Joint Forest Management in Jharkhand, India', *World Development*, 30, 5: 763–82.

Laclau, E. (1977). *Politics and Ideology in Marxist Theory: Capitalism, Fascism and Populism*. London: New Left Books.

Lal, V. (2003). *The History of History: Politics and Scholarship in Modern India*. Delhi: Oxford University Press.

Lerche, J. (2008). 'Transnational Advocacy Networks and Affirmative Action for Dalits in India', *Development and Change*, 39, 2: 239–61.

Lipton, M. and Longhurst, R. (1989). *New Seeds and Poor People*. London and Boston: Unwin Hyman.

Ludden, D. (1999). *An Agrarian History of South Asia*. Cambridge: Cambridge University Press.

Lukose, R. (2009). *Liberalization's Children: Gender, Youth, and Consumer Citizenship in Globalizing India*. Durham: Duke University Press.

Madan, T. N. (1997). *Modern Myths, Locked Minds: Secularism and Fundamentalism in India*. New Delhi: Oxford University Press.

Majumdar, B. (2008). *Cricket in Colonial India, 1780–1947*. London and New York: Routledge.

Manuel, P. (1993). *Cassette Culture: Popular Music and Technology in India*. Chicago: University of Chicago Press.

Marriott, M. (ed.) (1955). *Village India: Studies in the Little Community*. Chicago and London: University of Chicago Press.

Marx, K. (1975 [1853]). 'Future results of the British Rule in India', in K. Marx and F. Engels, *Collected Works*, 12, Moscow: Progress.

Marx, K. and Engels, F. (2004 [1848]). *The Communist Manifesto*. Harmondsworth: Penguin.

Mazzarella, W. (2003). *Shoveling Smoke: Advertising and Globalization in Contemporary India*. Durham, NC: Duke University Press Books.

Mehta, P. B. (2003). *The Burden of Democracy*. Delhi: Penguin Books.

Mehta, P. B. (2005). 'India's Judiciary', in D. Kapur and P. B. Mehta (eds), *Public Institutions in India*. Delhi: Oxford University Press, 158–93.

Mehta, P. B. (2007). 'The Rise of Judicial Sovereignty', *Journal of Democracy*, 18, 2: 70–83.

Mines, D. P. and Lamb, S. (eds) (2010). *Everyday Life in South Asia* (2nd edition). Bloomington, IN: Indiana University Press.

Mines, M. (1988). 'Conceptualizing the Person: Hierarchical Society and Individual Autonomy in India', *American Anthropologist*, 90, 3: 568–79.

Mitra, S. K. and Pehl, M. (2010). 'Federalism', in N. G. Jayal and P. B. Mehta (eds), *The Oxford Companion to the Politics of India*. New Delhi: Oxford University Press, 43–60.

Myrdal, G. (1968). *Asian Drama, an Inquiry into the Poverty of Nations*. New York: Pantheon.

Nandy, A. (1989). *The Tao of Cricket: On Games of Destiny and the Destiny of Games*. New York: Viking.

Neale, W. C. (1969). 'Land Is To Rule', in R. E. Frykenberg (ed.), *Land Control and Social Structure in Indian History*. Madison, WI: University of Wisconsin Press.

Nehru, J. (2005 [1946]). *The Discovery of India*. New Delhi: Penguin.

Oldenburg, C. (2004). *Dowry Murder: The Imperial Origins of a Cultural Crime*. New York: Oxford University Press.

Osella, C. and Osella, F. (2006). *Men and Masculinities in South India*. New York: Anthem Press.

Oxford English Dictionary <http://www.oed.com/> (Last retrieved 15 July 2013).

Pandian, A. (2009). *Crooked Stalks: Cultivating Virtue in South India*. Durham, NC: Duke University Press Books.

Parekh, B. (1997). *Gandhi: A Very Short Introduction*. Oxford and New York: Oxford University Press.

Parekh, B. (2005). 'Liberalism', in T. Bennett, L. Grossberg, and M. Morris (eds), *New Keywords: A Revised Vocabulary of Culture and Society*. Malden, MA and Oxford: Blackwell Publishing, 198–200.

Parry, J. (1986). 'The Gift, the Indian Gift and the "Indian Gift"', *Man*, New Series, 21, 3: 453–73.

Parry, J. (1999). 'Lords of Labour: Working and Shirking in Bhilai', *Contributions to Indian Sociology*, 33, 1–2: 107–40.

Patel, T. (2005). *The Family in India: Structure and Practice*. New Delhi: Sage.

Prasad, M. M. (2008). 'Surviving Bollywood', in A. P. Kavoori and A. Punathambekar (eds), *Global Bollywood*. New York: New York University, 41–51.

Price, P., and Ruud, A. E. (eds) (2010). *Power and Influence in India: Bosses, Lords and Captains*. New Delhi: Routledge India.

Pritchett, L. (2009). 'Is India a Flailing State? Detours on the Four Lane Highway to Modernization', HKS Faculty Research Working Paper Series RWP09-013. Cambridge, MA: John F. Kennedy School of Government, Harvard University.

Putnam, R., with Leonardi, R. and Nanetti, R. Y. (1993). *Making Democracy Work: Civic Traditions in Modern Italy*. Princeton: Princeton University Press.

Qureshi, K. A. (forthcoming). 'Culture Shock on Southall Broadway: Re-thinking "Second Generation" Return Through "Geographies of Punjabiness"', *South Asian Diaspora*.

Rai, A. and Ravi, S. (2011). 'Do Spouses Make Claims? Empowerment and Microfinance in India', *World Development*, 39, 6: 913–21.

Rajagopal, A. (2001). *Politics after Television: Hindu Nationalism and the Reshaping of the Public in India*. Cambridge: Cambridge University Press.

Ramaswamy, S. (1997). *Passions of the Tongue: Language Devotion in Tamil India, 1891–1970*. Berkeley: University of California Press.

Rangan, H. (2000). *Of Myths and Movements: Rewriting Chipko into Himalayan History*. London: Verso.

Reddy, D. S. (2011). 'Hindutva: Formative Assertions', *Religion Compass*, 5, 8: 439–51.

Rose, K. (1993). *Where Women are Leaders: The SEWA Movement in India*. London: Zed Books.

Roy, S. (2013). *New South Asian Feminisms: Paradoxes and Possibilities*. Delhi: Zed Press.

Rudolph, L. I. and Rudolph, S. H. (1967a). 'Legal Cultures and Social Change: Panchayats, Pandits and Professionals', in *The Modernity of Tradition*. Chicago: University of Chicago Press, 251–93.

Rudolph, L. I. and Rudolph, S. H. (1967b). *The Modernity of Tradition: Political Development in India*. Chicago: University of Chicago Press.

Rudolph, L. I. and Rudolph, S. H. (2006). *Postmodern Gandhi and other Essays: Gandhi in the World and at Home*. Chicago: University of Chicago Press.

Rushdie, S. (1981). *Midnight's Children*. London: Jonathan Cape.

Sachar, R. (2006). *Social, Economic and Educational Status of the Muslim Community in India*. Delhi: Cabinet Secretariat, Government of India.

Said, E. (1978). *Orientalism*. London: Vintage.

Sailaja, P. (2009). *Indian English*. Edinburgh: Edinburgh University Press.

Sarkar, S. (1983). *Modern India 1885–1947*. Delhi etc. Macmillan India.

Savarkar, V. D. (2009 [1923]). *Hindutva: Who is a Hindu?* Bombay: Veer Savarkar Prakashan.

Scheifinger, H. (2009). *Conceptualising Hinduism*. Singapore: Asia Research Institute, National University of Singapore.

Sen, A. (1999). *Development as Freedom*. New Delhi: Oxford University Press.

Sen, A. (2009). *The Idea of Justice*. Cambridge, MA: Belknap Press/Harvard University Press.

Sen, G. (1994). 'Women's Empowerment and Human Rights: The Challenge to Policy', in F. Graham-Smith (ed.), *Population—the Complex Reality*. London: The Royal Society, 363–72.

Sen, R. (2010). *Articles of Faith: Religion, Secularism, and the Indian Supreme Court*. New Delhi: Oxford University Press.

Sengupta, B. (1972). *Communism in India*. New York: Columbia University Press.

Sengupta, M. (2012). 'Anna Hazare and the Idea of Gandhi', *The Journal of Asian Studies*, 1, 1: 1–9.

Shah, A. (2010). *In the Shadows of the State: Indigenous Politics, Environmentalism, and Insurgency in Jharkhand, India*. Durham, NC: Duke University Press.

Shah, A. M. (1974). *The Household Dimension of the Family in India: A Field Study in a Gujarat Village and a Review of other Studies*. Berkeley and Los Angeles: University of California Press.

Shah, A. M. (1998). *The Family in India: Critical Essays*. New Delhi: Orient Blackswan.

Shah, G., Mander, H., Thorat, S., Deshpande, S., and Baviskar, A. (eds) (2006). *Untouchability in Rural India*. New Delhi: Sage.

Sharma, K. (2010). *Waiting for Water: The Experience of Poor Communities in Mumbai*. Mumbai: SPARC.

Shiva, V. (1988). *Staying Alive: Women, Ecology, and Development*. New Delhi: Kali for Women.

Sinha, S. (2008). 'Lineages of the Developmentalist State: Transnationality and Village India, 1900–1965', *Comparative Studies in Society and History*, 50, 1: 57–90.

Sivaramakrishnan, K. and Agrawal, A. (eds) (2003). *Regional Modernities: The Cultural Politics of Development in India*. Stanford, CA: Stanford University Press.

South Asia Terrorism Portal <http://www.satp.org> (Last retrieved 28 February 2014).

Spivak, G. C. (1988). 'Can the Subaltern Speak?', in C. Nelson and L. Grossberg (eds), *Marxism and the Interpretation of Culture*. Urbana: University of Illinois, 271–313.

Srinivas, M. N. (ed.) (1996). *Caste: Its Twentieth Century Avatar*. New Delhi: Viking.

Stein, B. (1991). 'Towards an Indian Petty Bourgeoisie: Outline of an Approach', *Economic and Political Weekly*, 26, 4: PE9–PE20.

Stokes, E. T. (1973). 'The First Century of British Colonial Rule in India: Social Revolution or Social Stagnation?', *Past and Present*, 58: 136–60.

Sundaram, R. (2010). *Pirate Modernity: Delhi's Media Urbanism*. London: Routledge.

Tarlo, E. (2003). *Unsettling Memories: Narratives of The Emergency in Delhi*. Berkeley and Los Angeles: University of California Press.

Teltumbde, A. (2013). 'Delhi Gang Rape Case: Some Uncomfortable Questions', *Economic and Political Weekly*, 48, 6: 10–11.

Thachil, T. (2013). 'Is Indian Politics Populist?', *The Indian Express*, 4 September 2013.

Tharoor, S. (2013). *Nehru: The Invention of India*. New York: Arcade.

Thompson, E. P. (1967). 'Time, Work-discipline, and Industrial Capitalism', *Past & Present*, 38: 56–97.

Thorner, D. (1976 [1956]). *The Agrarian Prospect in India*. Bombay: Allied Publishers.

Turner, B. (2005). 'Citizenship', in T. Bennet, L. Grossberg, and M. Morris (eds), *New Keywords: A Revised Vocabulary of Culture and Society*. Malden, MA and Oxford: Blackwell Publishing, 29–32.

Uberoi, P. (1998). 'The Diaspora Comes Home: Disciplining Desire in DDLJ', *Contributions to Indian Sociology*, 32, 2: 305–36.

Uberoi, P. (2006). *Freedom and Destiny: Gender, Family, and Popular Culture in India*. New Delhi: Oxford University Press.

University of Pittsburgh Keywords Project <http://keywords.pitt.edu/contact_us.html> (Last retrieved 15 July 2013).

Veer, P. van der (1994). *Religious Nationalism: Hindus and Muslims in India*. Berkeley: University of California Press.

von Stietencron, H. (1989). 'Hinduism: On the Proper Use of a Deceptive Term', in H. von Stietencron, G. D. Sontheimer, and H. Kulke (eds), *Hinduism Reconsidered*. New Delhi: Manohar, 11–27.

Wade, R. (1988). *Village Republics: Economic Conditions for Collective Action in South India*. Cambridge: Cambridge University Press.

Washbrook, D. A. (1998). 'Progress and Problems: South Asian Economic and Social History c.1720–1960', *Modern Asian Studies*, 22, 1: 57–96.

Watt, C. A. (2011). 'Philanthropy and Civilizing Missions in India 1820–1960: States, NGOs and Development', in C. A. Watt and M. Mann (eds), *Civilizing Missions in Colonial and Postcolonial South Asia: From Improvement to Development*. New York: Anthem Press, 271–316.

Westad, O. A. (2005). *The Global Cold War: Third World Interventions and the Making of Our Times*. Cambridge and New York: Cambridge University Press.

Whitehead, J. (2012). 'John Locke, Accumulation by Dispossession and the Governance of Colonial India', *Journal of Contemporary Asia*, 42, 1: 1–21.

Williams, R. (1985 [1976]). *Keywords: A Vocabulary of Culture and Society*. Oxford: Oxford University Press.

World Bank (2002). *Empowerment and Poverty Reduction Sourcebook*. Washington, DC: World Bank.

Yang, A. (ed.) (1985). *Crime and Criminality in British India*. Tuscon: University of Arizona Press.

Young, S. (2010). 'The 'Moral Hazards' of Microfinance: Restructuring Rural Credit in India', *Antipode*, 42, 1: 201–23.

Youth for Equality <http://www.youthforequality.com> (Last retrieved 24 September 2012).

Zachariah, B. (2004). *Nehru*. London: Routledge.

Zavos, J. (2000). *The Emergence of Hindu Nationalism in India*. New Delhi: Oxford University Press.

Zelliot, E. (1992). *From Untouchable to Dalit: Essays on the Ambedkar Movement*. Delhi: Manohar.